The New York Times
Book of Antiques

MARVIN D. SCHWARTZ
and
BETSY WADE

BOOKS BY
MARVIN D. SCHWARTZ

Collector's Guide to Antique American Glass

Collector's Guide to Antique
American Ceramics

American Interiors 1675-1885; A Guide to
the American Period Rooms in the
Brooklyn Museum

Catalogue of the Emily Winthrop Miles
Collection, Brooklyn Museum

History of American Porcelain
(with Richard Wolfe)

BOOKS BY
BETSY WADE

The Encyclopedia of Clothes Care

Eugene, Why Don't You Paint?

The New York Times
Book of Antiques

by
MARVIN D. SCHWARTZ
and
BETSY WADE

Designed by Ben Kann

QUADRANGLE BOOKS **NYT** A New York Times Company

Library of Congress Card Number: 72-77672

CONTENTS

Ceramics

Pictures

Metals

Glass

Collecting Bargains

Introduction

THE JOYS OF COLLECTING

Antiques have been collected seriously for only about seventy years, but interest has intensified so rapidly since then that some objects now hardly get dusty in a shop before they are snapped up. Prices have moved up rapidly too. A chest nearly junked in 1900 fetched a nice price by 1920, passed out of the range of the middle class in 1950 and is probably now in a museum. A sociologist could gather material for a creditable doctoral thesis on the whys of this dizzying growth. The closing of the frontier would certainly be one traceable cause; Americans are shut in and largely urbanized with little place to roam but in the past. Another factor would be the planned obsolesence of objects made today. Large sums of money are now spent on furniture and bedding that will be taken to the dump in ten years. Thus, things that were made lovingly, to endure and to give many kinds of satisfaction, are precious to many today.

The pleasure that arises from owning one of a kind and showing expertise in its choice is surely a factor. An under-the-surface cause may be the wish of some of the newly rich to look oldly rich. Some of the interest must originate in the collecting instinct common to most of us. Certainly, wistfulness for a day of less rush and confusion—even a day, like the Golden Age, that may never have been—affects us all.

As a professional in the field of decorative arts, I still cannot make a judgment as to which factors are strongest, or why. But they all seem to operate—I see them every day.

In writing this book, I endeavor to show what is available in what fields, to give brief historical background on the evolution of styles and to offer some help through murky waters. I do not discuss all collectable objects by any means. To some dealers, "antique" means anything not in current production, including Shirley Temple cereal bowls and fancy whisky bottles. I do not take these up, not out of snobbishness, but because they involve little aesthetic judgment: they are there and you buy them if you like them. I interpret the word "antique" to mean decorative objects usually created for a practical purpose, probably in the home, that are representative of the fashion of the period in which they were made. My cutoff dates are flexible.

If you want to bring an antique into the United States, customs regulations exempting an object from duty require your documentation to show it to be at least one hundred years old. If, for some reason, this definition were to be legislated on domestic sales, most antique dealers in this country would soon be out of business. And if I followed it, I would miss talking about many things that are esthetically worthwhile and a number of things that are in the lower price range. To me, the purpose of collecting is both to enliven the home and to evoke the spirit of a period that is past. It is perhaps this spirit of objects, more than a dictionary definition, that has guided me in the kinds of things I discuss in this book.

Serious collecting does not have to cost a lot, although it is much more fascinating if it does. Chests that bring $100,000 are a joy, no mistake, and there are no adequate $100 substitutes. But there are relatively inexpensive good objects in every field for the collector who knows how to sort out his priorities. Prices are based on supply and demand. The collector on a budget must seek out what is being ignored.

The financial aspect of collecting is a delicate subject. Rises in prices of antiques in the last twenty years make them appear a shrewd investment; the supply is limited and the demand growing; thus appreciation in value is inevitable. The problem is that demand is based on fashion and it is difficult to predict how long any particular style will retain its popularity. Statisticians analyzing the antique market a few years ago discovered that the biggest increases in value occurred at the two extremes: the great rarities and the junk. If investment is your game, be so advised. This fact would also indicate that a collector concerned with esthetics as well as with protecting his investment should find a field generally ignored and collect only the greatest examples from it.

Right now prices are highest for elegant objects from the 1700's. At the top of the list are the finest examples of Louis XV furniture. Several of these have brought over $400,000 at public auctions. The most extraordinary English, American and Continental pieces in the equivalent of the Louis XV style bear price tags of $100,000 to $300,000. Silver and porcelain in contemporary styles are also very expensive. Nonetheless, not all eighteenth-century work is that expensive. Modest interpretations were made for country merchants—and these are sometimes still under $1,000. The eighteenth-century rococo style has tremendous appeal today because it seems to fit into the way of life of the affluent.

The massive proportions of Renaissance and baroque designs of the 1500's and 1600's have less appeal and prices for such objects are lower. It is hard to say just why members of the jet set feel more comfortable surrounded by remnants of the Bourbons than the Medici. Medici furniture is a little large for the cozy arrangements popular with many interior designers today, but it can be used in fresh juxtapositions, as the more adventuresome are finding. Interest in Renaissance and baroque has been increasing steadily so that many great examples are costly, but the representative examples are more reasonably priced than eighteenth-century work of equal quality. The monumental scale of the design of the period is exciting to those who take the time to study it with care.

Oddly enough, when Gothic pieces of the 1400's come up they are often bargains because many collectors hesitate to acquire them. The pieces are so rare that it is difficult to recognize some fine, authentic examples. If you can study and compare good work in museum collections, there are possible discoveries.

The real bargains are in fields that have not been explored, and that means a good part of the nineteenth century. Many aspects of the 1800's have yet to be understood. There has been a continuing interest in the obvious innovations, but much traditional has been passed over as mere reproduction. On the American scene pressed glass and Belter furniture have already attracted collectors. In England anything that shows the influence of reformer and designer William Morris is regarded seriously. Everywhere the bentwood furniture developed by Thonet has become fashionable. Prices for examples of these popular styles are much lower than for earlier work, but the real bottom of the price scale is often the decorative work of the late 1800's, which may strike one initially as overelaborate. Some of this neglected work reflects the designers' discovery of the Near and Far East in their effort to escape the endless cycle of revivals of the first half of the

6 century. Other pieces are a part of an academic effort to re-create early style. Good enough to have passed for reproductions a few years ago, the decorative objects made for the great houses of the turn of the century appear now to have their own originality and should be investigated further.

Art Nouveau, the experimental design of the same period, and those of the 1920's and 1930's—Art Deco and Bauhaus—have been a focus of interest. The best of these styles can now command prices above those for simple eighteenth-century pieces.

Some collectors will prefer periods where the objects seem familiar. Others are eager to find new material or at least to get into a field that offers a fresh approach. Whatever the direction, any decision is a bit on the mystical side. Part of the magnetism is a certain awe for work of the past. But this awe, in my view, should be honed and sharpened so that you can discern the differences between the originals of the past and the reproductions of the past, which some people insist they prefer. The most elegantly worked reproduction chair is usually sterile and clumsy when compared intelligently with even the most modest original version of the same style. There is a reason for this. The craftsman making a reproduction concentrates on the details and places them where he has seen them on the original. He is generally careful about dimensions, but somehow he can rarely achieve the same balance as in the original. The early craftsman did not have to concentrate on detail because the whole design came more naturally to him.

Although furniture craftsmen making reproductions often use the same methods as those used for the originals, in other media the differences between old and new are greater because the materials and techniques have changed. For instance, the clays used for ceramics today are generally purer than they were a hundred years ago. This automatically eliminates some of the texture that was a part of the early work. Delft reproductions, for example, look a little pale because they are just too smooth. Of course one advantage of the delftware reproduction is that the ceramic body is harder and the reproduction does not sweat on the tabletop as the original did.

The faker presents still another problem. The craftsman making a reproduction is gen-

erally interested in repeating a design without suggesting that the result is old; the faker wants you to think the object he has just made is an authentic antique. The faker is less concerned with design than appearance, so he will work very hard on the simulation of age and possibly not as hard on details. One of the most famous furniture fakers, a provincial French antiquarian and craftsman named André Mailfert, confessed all the tricks of the trade in an autobiography. He always presented his work as that of a previously unknown school of eighteenth-century cabinetmakers. Any differences that the connoisseur might have detected were explained as characteristic of this unusual group of craftsmen. The lesson is there, but so far as I know there are collectors who pride themselves still on owning examples of the work of this mythic school.

Detecting a fake is obviously easier when the object can be compared with documented, authentic pieces. The crucial differences are seen in the way the object has aged and in the way details are rendered. Careful examination will reveal the age of a piece without the benefit of any gadgets or tests. The "tools" a collector needs most are his own senses, used intelligently.

I am asked frequently about having objects appraised or authenticated. It is perfectly possible to have both done, but the results are often subject to error. The best person to get, if he'll do it (and I won't), is a museum curator, because he will be disinterested, even to the point of embarrassing you

about something you really like. He charges a certain fee for this kind of work. It's probably easier to find a local dealer to do it, but, while I have found dealers to be excellent in discerning value in their fields of speciality, outside it they can miss completely. One dealer who assessed a houseful of furniture for my brother pegged the Empire examples flawlessly but passed over four Chippendale chairs and an eighteenth-century mirror with the history of its ownership glued on the back. Curiously, when a dealer appraises a large collection, although he may miss on individual pieces, his errors average out. His appraisal may thus be ideal for insurance purposes, less good for allocating objects of value in a will. Listen carefully to what the dealer does *not* say if you're getting an appraisal. A tactful dealer I know, besought by a friend of mine to examine a houseful of junk, said: "It's out of my field, but it's interesting." My friend, alas, thought he heard "great" in the word "interesting."

Where to buy is the next obvious question. Antiques are bought more often in shops than at auctions at shows or from owners. There are really three sorts of shops. The first caters to a large clientele that likes to spend small amounts—the kind you may find on one of the older routes like U.S. 1. It will be stocked with decorative curiosities that catch the eye, but which may be of ordinary quality and not very old. Often, what is offered are old reproductions. Shops geared to

more serious collectors begin with the small dealer who serves his area as a source of interesting but not expensive old decorative objects. He offers representative but not rare examples of many styles and may include a mixture of recent reproductions and some original work to offer maximum variety at minimum prices. As expertise increases, collectors and their dealers get more and more discerning about their narrowing interests. The most serious dealers and collectors restrict their holdings to work from a single period, a single country, or even a single material. Collector and dealer know their field well, and theirs is the conversation of experts.

If you love to acquire but do not really care about the quality of what you buy, you should be satisfied with the many shops of the first type, chock full of relatively inexpensive nineteenth-century objects that are elaborately detailed but of no particular importance. You may be happiest with designs that look good in contemporary interiors and prefer your antiques to serve as a kind of pop art. It is difficult to get serious about 1910 barber poles and 1880 tea cans, but they can be entertaining. Tables and chairs from ice cream parlors can accent an interior, but you will find there is not much point in investigating the field extensively.

The local professional dealer, you will learn, has often been in business for a relatively long time. He will usually tell you if an object is a reproduction, or it is cracked, or give you other useful information if neither of you rushes the other. A good education is to be had at such a shop, and it will grow in value as your relationship unfolds. This seems a good place to warn you that the dealers I have found to be the best have seemed unpleasant at first; it must be an occupational hazard. I seldom pursue discussions with someone who insults me off the bat, but I do find that the grumpier dealers will warm when they encounter seriousness. The gruffness may be a way of driving off those who aren't really interested.

The collector who becomes interested in objects that document the evolution of style finds that he must consult ever more serious dealers. If you are concentrating on the highest quality rarities of the seventeenth, eighteenth and early nineteenth centuries, you soon discover that you have drastically narrowed the list of dealers you frequent. But there is a range to the specialists, too. Some handle objects only of museum quality. Others understand top quality but cannot afford to invest in the best, so they offer good, interesting material that is authentic but less exciting. As a general rule the serious dealers are most interested in work that was done before 1850. The exceptions are Art Nouveau and Art Deco objects; a special market in these has been developed by a keen group of dealers.

Despite the possibilities of error there are no greater pitfalls shopping for antiques than for anything else. I am more comfortable with antique dealers than automobile salesmen, for instance, because I know the average antique dealer is not intentionally deceptive. I was taken by our local car dealer. The heater on our $5,000 station wagon never did what it was supposed to and the glove compartment door never closed properly. The dealer did lots of talking but no real fixing. But when you buy a $200 antique chest, you can try it out, and the dealer will take it back willingly for any reason. Try that with the next appliance you buy.

Most problems between collectors and dealers arise because one is trying to outwit the other. The collector after a bargain may think he can fool a dealer, and the dealer out to make a quick sale may forget to say as much as he should about the object. In any field of endeavor haste can cause trouble; it just seems more painful in antique collecting. Regardless of who the dealer is, he will hold frank discussions on condition and price with the serious collector who asks the proper questions.

Buying antiques requires the same kind of precise dealing as any field where confusion is possible. When you spend a lot of money you should get a guarantee that eliminates some of the risk. The guarantee should consist of a detailed description of the object you are buying, including the seller's opinion of where and when it was made. Omissions in guarantees are significant. The first dining room chairs my wife and I bought were early eighteenth-century ladderbacks that looked a little like New England examples I had seen. They also resembled chairs made in Yorkshire. The dealer had discussed the chairs in a way that implied New England, but when the bill arrived the description called them eighteenth-century without saying where they might have been made. Obviously the dealer was not prepared to defend an American attribution. Since the chairs were inexpensive, it was not a tragic matter, but the difference between what I was hearing in my optimism and what I read is worth noting.

The omission of country of origin is one way of avoiding saying something that the buyer may not want to hear. We were shopping for more chairs recently and found a set of early nineteenth-century neoclassical examples. The shape was unusual and we wondered if they could be English. The bill that accompanied them omitted the country of origin, but when I asked the dealer what he knew about them, he told me they had been found in Sweden and he thought they were probably Swedish. He clearly did not think we looked sufficiently pro-Swedish to put that on the bill.

The world of antiquarians is small, and there's lots of gossip, but you should not accept as fact all terrible tales. Through the years I have found the people who say the worst things about each other become, after a time, close associates. All dealers and collectors have some favorite objects restored, despite what they may say, and there is a line between the restored piece and the fake, even though sometimes wavery. Some of the terrible tales have their roots in prejudice. A dealer is not more or less honest because he is unschooled and rough; fashionable dealers and doughty women in tweeds are subject to as many vagaries as the rest. Try to set aside your own prejudices and meet the dealer in terms of your mutual interest, rather than attempting to fence with credentials.

Many collectors take a lot of stock in the location of an antique shop. They say you should deal only with the biggest city shops, or only country shops, or small merchants who keep their shops in bad neighborhoods. As a man who has been to them all, I find you can't make rules based on geography. Of course, there are likely to be a greater number of first-quality objects at shops where prices are highest, but when you are looking for something specific, you can't predict where you will find it.

Often the smaller dealer believes he can do better selling an unusual treasure to a bigger dealer rather than to a collector. He

may thus set his price close to what his most fashionable competitor would ask. But often enough, the fashionable fellow won't buy the object—it really isn't that good—and the little dealer is left sitting with his overpriced item, awaiting the arrival of the pot of gold. The small dealer is really best on objects of medium quality and price. These are what he knows thoroughly and can sell at the fairest prices. Country dealers are no longer simple rustics who ferret out local treasures; they, too, travel the world hunting. Most of them will no longer see the casual visitor but expect to receive a telephone call for an appointment.

Collectors are inevitably gleeful when they find a bargain. One way the collector can increase his chances is learning each dealer's specialty, then looking in a shop for what should not be there. The porcelain specialist might want to dispose of pottery quickly. The English-furniture specialist is eager to get rid of Italian examples that he had to buy to get some really extraordinary piece. Observe how often you hear a collector say: "... and it was the only thing of that sort he had!"

One of the best ways to find dealers with whom you will enjoy doing business is by going to antique shows. Dealers at shows are looking for new clients; they have brought their most salable items and generally put on their company manners. The level of shows varies. Some are for the person who wants to be amused while others are for the more serious. A few outstanding shows attract the most important dealers and collectors. Antique shows are ideal for comparison shopping and buying, because prices are generally fairly visible and the dealers tend to be competitive. Another advantage of the antique show is policing of the dealers; each is keen on protecting the reputation of the show, and no one will tolerate mistakes in attribution. If a fake is unwittingly brought onto the floor of the show by a dealer, he is soon told of his error in judgment.

I first learned about bargaining with antique dealers at an antique show. An overly anxious dealer thought my hesitation was based on the price and volunteered to reduce it. Ever since I have asked for discounts. Some dealers are offended; others are delighted to discuss price. Usually if one decides quickly and expects to pay promptly there is justification in testing for softness in price. I like the English way of phrasing the discount-giving: English dealers will consent to "assist you on the price" should you feel it is too high. When you do business regularly with dealers and things go pleasantly, there is very often no need to ask; the dealer will volunteer when he feels it fair.

No matter where you shop or how you find your dealers it is important to have a clear idea about what you want to buy. You have to be your own expert most of the time, but be prepared to be stymied once in a while. There are areas where research is not complete and the expert may be as baffled as you. Also, even the best dealers have examples in their stock that are meant as decorator's pieces rather than as collector's specimens. Recently one of the top London dealers had a Regency cabinet in his window that looked just right for a London parlor I was trying to furnish. He sent it around for me to try and I was shocked to discover, in daylight, that the surface and the brasses on the cabinet were new. The dealer was irritated because I had not said that I cared about condition as well as appearance and thought I should have known that $5,000 would never buy what I wanted.

If you ever feel there is no rhyme or reason to antique prices, going to an auction will restore your confidence. Collectors and dealers bid vigorously against each other but the prices they pay have a standard relationship to prices at the shops. Unless an unusual clash breaks out to push the prices up, an ordinary object—for example, a pitcher like any number on shop shelves—will sell at wholesale price, which is a half to two-thirds of the retail price. A rarity, such as a documented and signed French dressing table from Versailles, will bring a high price, possibly more than most dealers would dare ask.

Auctions get some of the blame for driving up the prices of American furniture from the 1700's. I remember a dealer who was astonished to find a customer at an auction paying $27,000 for an armchair similar to one he was offering at $18,000. After the auction he rushed back to raise his price and got there just before a few collectors who remembered the bargain they had seen.

Auction houses vary from the posh establishments on both sides of the Atlantic to very simple places that mix antiques with second-hand goods. The stylish galleries publish catalogues describing their offerings in some detail while the simple places have lists of objects that say "chair," "table," and little more.

Reading the fuller descriptions, like reading real estate ads, takes a little education. The less said, the worse the piece. The more that is said, the more positive the auction house is of the origin and quality of an object. Thus, when a chair is described at length with date and place of origin, the chances are that it is a fine example, or at least that it should be inspected with care. If it is listed as Renaissance-style chair, you should wonder if it is a reproduction or simply undistinguished. Inspecting is crucial at auction houses because the catalogues are written quickly and mistakes creep in.

The smaller auction houses and the country auctioneers make no pretense of knowing what they are handling. They mix good and bad, with the emphasis on the latter. When something good does turn up, it may have slipped by the notice of collectors and dealers and be sold at a bargain price. But more and more often, everybody seems to know somehow when a great chest comes up for sale in a little field outside of a small Vermont village. A couple of years ago an American chest selling at a Danish auction brought at least as much as it would have brought in New York.

Serious buying at auctions is for the experienced because there is much possibility for error. What looks great at first glance may have all kinds of troubles that are not revealed until one takes time for close, slow inspection. A grimy, scratched piece covered with a dark varnish on casual inspection will look just like a nineteenth-century reproduction until it is properly cleaned, and it takes an astute eye to spot it before then. Poorly restored porcelains look like nothing until properly fixed, and they come up at auction looking their worst.

Another danger of the auction is the fun. Even the most experienced succumb to the thrill of bidding against the world for something much desired. Sitting and waiting and then fighting will give even the coolest of us sweaty palms. You never know how high to go, and in the thick of battle it is very difficult to stop waving your arm. I was once delegated by the museum for which I was curator to bid on a very important silver bowl. I had suggested to the trustees that the top price ought to be $20,000. Before I knew it, my $20,000 limit had been passed and I just could not stop. When I had my hand up at $24,000 I glanced at the woman who was my only adversary and realized from her calm manner that she was prepared to go on indefinitely. I bowed out, rather relieved that I did not have to convince the museum that it was glad to have spent $4,000 extra. It turned out my instinct was right; the woman was bidding for a very determined man who had set no limit. (All auction anecdotes demonstrate how astute the teller was; mine is no exception.) Generally speaking all sales at auction are final so one should be very sure about what is on the block before bidding. For the auctioneer, the object on the block is whatever you see and he is not concerned about its quality or origin.

The most avid collectors shop at the big and little dealers in the city and the country and try not to miss an auction. The wisest use every means at their command to learn all they can about what they are buying. They make friends with all the dealers and fellow collectors, and often frequent museums just to see what they can. Viewing the finest quality selections can lead to a better understanding of the simpler objects you value.

When you can't see what you want in a museum, you may find books with pictures that can be helpful. The literature on antiques is growing steadily, and building a library is a good idea. There is a list of appropriate books at the end of this volume that might serve as a guide.

As the father of four and husband of a remarkably busy woman, I consider it part of my expertise to be casual about living with antiques. The six of us live surrounded by antiques without any more tribulation than families in completely modern surroundings. The only accident of the year was the splintering of a piece of plastic dinnerware marked unbreakable. A cut glass punch bowl has survived ten years at the foot of a stairway where balls occasionally bounce down.

Any kind of furniture needs to be protected from an excess of central heating. Dry rooms are not good for any kind of wood, so it is a good idea to keep up humidity, if only by having water near the heat source. Furniture—old or new—should be protected by wax polish. The old formulas for oiling furni-

14

ture are now scorned because they tend to darken the color of the wood. Gentle washing once in a while with a mild detergent is helpful. If the surfaces are too grimy and bubbly, a vinegar or alcohol rub can help remove the muck. Furniture should be protected from electric appliances that bang them up. There are cosmetics for scratches and bumps. In getting repairs done, one should find a craftsman who understands how to do as little as possible to hide damage. Big repairs can be very expensive, so it is wise to avoid buying pieces that require them.

Unless the finish on furniture is in deplorable condition, or has been badly restored, the finish should be left alone. Refinishing should be done only by an experienced professional or by an amateur who understands the process.

One should avoid jarring repaired pieces of ceramic and glass, and it might be wiser to resist buying repaired pieces. One of my favorite pitchers had a repaired spout that looked fine until it got tapped with the end of a broom. If it had been a perfect piece the break would never have occurred. Cleaning should be done sparingly. Even if a piece has a repair, soap and water work fine, but don't soak it.

Conservators are concerned about the metal removed in polishing, but it is very hard to keep silver and brass looking decent if you don't polish them. Most of the lacquer coatings I have seen looked splendid to start but soon wore off in spots, and the coating had to be removed entirely. I wonder how much of the metal is lost after you rub extra hard.

To conclude, I welcome, as do the dealers, the new collectors. We wish them pleasure, excitement and satisfaction with their avocation. The whole world of the past is open: step in.

Furniture

*Writing table by Charles Cressent, Paris,
about 1735*

THE BIG LURE

When most people hear the word "antiques," they think of furniture, even though the average collector purchases far fewer pieces of furniture during his lifetime than, say, ceramics or glass. Perhaps it is the durability of furniture or its tendency to dominate a room that prompts the association. Whatever it may be, when one hears "they have a house full of antiques," the mind furnishes it with chairs, tables and chests, rather than with dishes, ewers, prints and brass.

For the average collector, buying furniture is more nerve-racking than buying other objects. Because of its size, an unfortunate furniture purchase is hard to hide; because of its price, it may be difficult to dispose of and replace without crippling the budget. The first necessary decision is something no book can advise upon. As a collector you must know in what area your basic impulses lie, whether in plain or fancy, delicate or massive, sophisticated or primitive pieces. Plunging into the marketplace without knowing what pleases inevitably leads to confusion. Next come corollary decisions: Will you want good but unimportant examples, or must you have pieces of museum quality? Is appearance from a distance sufficient, or must the piece be wholly intact? Must the objects be currently in vogue with other collectors, or can they be from a period on one side or the other of the peak period?

Were our purses all bottomless, these questions could be answered on an entirely emotional basis, but reality dictates that they also be framed in monetary terms: What do you like that you can afford? As a guide for those still pondering this pivotal question, a word about the current market is in order.

Again, bear in mind that the furniture from the 1700's is the top of the market in popularity and consequently in price. The scale, the comfort and the elegance of this furniture work well in today's houses. The rococo —called Louis XV and Chippendale—is the prime design of this prime period. Furniture from slightly earlier and slightly later is on the slopes of the peak. Later neoclassical examples—Louis XVI, Adam, Hepplewhite and Sheraton—are in the same livable scale but are more severe and thus somewhat less popular. The earlier Louis XIV, or William and Mary, trails because it tends to be heavy and monumental.

For those to whom it's the vogue or nothing, it is important to know some of the variations. French and English rococo are in demand everywhere, but in any country local examples can bring a premium. The best eighteenth-century rococo French pieces go for hundreds of thousands of dollars in major auction houses on both sides of the Atlantic, while comparable American work would be ignored in Paris—but will still bring a hundred thousand in New York or Philadelphia.

Clearly, for those intent on collecting rococo, it's probably wise to begin by looking at early reproductions. French rococo has been reproduced for over a century, and good examples from the 1880's are still available, although even these can cost more than

18

French Louis XV period work table made about 1765 by Bernard van Risen Burgh. It is painted in an adaptation of oriental lacquer that is called Vernis Martin and has Sèvres porcelain plaques on the top and shelf and gilt bronze mounts. Elaborate, elegant and in the style most in demand, this is not a piece that could be found easily today.

simpler provincial—but authentic—rococo. English Chippendale reproductions are also in demand. There are many well-made nineteenth- and early twentieth-century reproductions around. Close inspection will reveal the proportions to be a little off, the carving too fussy or too rough, but they can look fine from a distance.

In fact, the quality of some 50- to 75-year-old reproductions is amazing. A few years ago, two well-known dealers in the American field fought over the authenticity of an American Chippendale chair that one had sold to the other. The construction was correct for an eighteenth-century example, the color of the wood looked right, and even the carving was about as good as it should

be. Nonetheless, after owning the chair for a few weeks, the buyer was convinced that its thin proportions and over-all appearance were signs that it was a reproduction. The seller was equally sure that only an eighteenth-century craftsman could have made it. The dispute was settled when the man who had made it came forward to claim authorship. He was a cabinetmaker trained in Russia at the turn of the century, who had started working in the Chippendale style when he settled in Connecticut in the early 1900's. His chair was one of many made as quality reproductions between 1900 and 1930. This type is worth $300 to $500 now—more than many authentic but plain eighteenth-century chairs.

If all these caveats sound like a gentle effort to guide you away from the most competitive part of the market, so be it. More adventuresome collectors are beginning to discover pleasure in earlier or later styles. To them, representative work from any period, if it has the quality to withstand minute inspection, is more satisfying than most of what remains from the peak period. Some move out of the eighteenth century entirely. Gothic, Renaissance and baroque furniture from the fifteenth to the seventeenth century is more massive than anything of eighteenth-century vintage, and using it in contemporary homes involves developing some new concepts in interior design. Although this furniture is rare, prices on what can be found are not out of reach if one skips the pieces destined for museums. At the other end of the

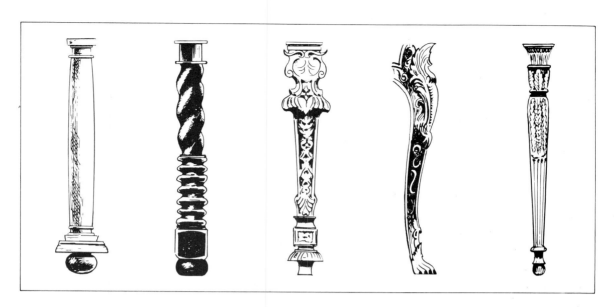

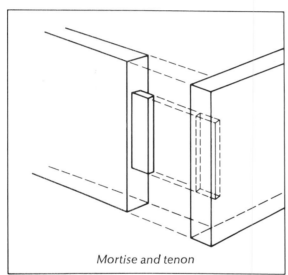

Mortise and tenon

The basic element of each of the important styles between 1600 and 1800 is classical, but there are changes in how the ornament is used and in the proportions and scale of the furniture. Early designs are more architectural; a typical design for a leg is a column. Animal-form legs were popular in the eighteenth century until a delicate version of the column came into fashion with the advent of neoclassicism. Oriental influence was also felt in seventeenth- and eighteenth-century design but is seen in decoration more than in forms.

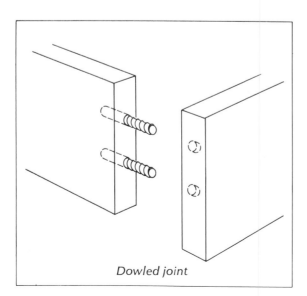

Dowled joint

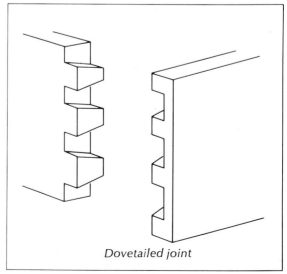

Dovetailed joint

spectrum, nineteenth-century styles are beginning to be taken a little more seriously, although many collectors will shy away from the more typically Victorian examples. Interest has focused instead on turn-of-the-century Art Nouveau, which has become more expensive than pieces from the mid-century rococo revival, and on Art Deco of the 1920's. The Empire style, fashionable at the start of the nineteenth century, is also attracting more attention these days.

The question of furniture as an investment inevitably comes up; though it is basically outside the purview of this book, a word or two seems appropriate. Simply stated, the values of objects of highest quality will appreciate the most on a percentage basis, regardless of period. A seventeenth-century chest with magnificent carving but new feet will bear a reasonable price tag, but it may never go up much in value. A rare Sheraton work table may not be hopelessly out of reach now, but if you buy it you can reasonably expect it to be worth a fortune when the demand for Sheraton increases. But the main issue is collecting, not making money, and I would consider it silly to live with a Sheraton table that means nothing to you in hopes of dying rich, when the seventeenth-century carving gives you pleasure and pride.

Knowledge of authenticity, or lack of it, is important in buying. There's nothing wrong with buying the seventeenth-century chest with new feet, so long as you know they're new feet. Similarly, a reproduction that you know is a reproduction causes no harm. It's being duped that hurts. In most cases, a thorough inspection with the eye sharpened by a number of authenticated examples in the desired style is all that's needed. The object should be looked at from every angle, inside as well as out. There may be a reason it's stuck in the corner of the shop or backed up against a wall.

Auctions are fine sources when there's time to examine the object, but catalogues are not definitive; even those with lengthy entries are not always as accurate as you would like them to be. As a rule of thumb, auctions are where objects of average quality tend to go for bargain prices while rarities fetch thousands. In general, buying at auctions is for advanced collectors who have learned how to examine objects carefully.

Many dealers, fair and foul, will discuss the possibility of guaranteeing an object, but one should make sure that any guarantee is worded precisely. Date, country of origin and condition should all be mentioned in writing to avoid confusion.

Pieces completely out of style that are ignored by the antique dealers and the auction rooms are the biggest bargains today. These are conservatively styled pieces made between the 1880's and the 1920's and they are generally found in plain used or second-hand furniture shops. Remarkably rarely, they can be picked up in thrift shops. The challenge is to find, amongst the dust and piles of used books, furniture of high quality and designs that will prove as enjoyable in a year as at first glance.

Those hamstrung by the budget can safely select a seventy-year-old copy of rococo, or they can branch out into something more adventuresome that may prove more fun in the long run. If you are a budget-bound collector you can hew to a simple guideline: Decide what you would pay for a modern table or chest of good quality, and let that price guide you in selecting your second-hand or antique table or chest. You may be pleasantly surprised, and you'll never be worse off.

For all collectors, a broader guide: Decide whether quality or fashion is more important to you, if you cannot afford both.

GOTHIC AND RENAISSANCE

Before the 1400's, with few exceptions, European furniture was basic and functional, even crude. In medieval palaces, the wealth of the lords was displayed in textiles and metals, and the only furnishings were plain box-like chests, simple tables and a few chairs reserved for the most important people. By the 1400's, furniture began to be considered another way of demonstrating wealth and status. The two styles of the 1400's and 1500's, Gothic and Renaissance, vary in detail, but they are both relatively massive and simple. The grander European castles were still sparsely furnished, and not everyone sat on chairs. Furniture built for strength was usually of oak, but as carving gradually came into favor, walnut was also chosen.

In northern Europe, designs were based on a decorative phase of the Gothic, a style that had flourished for centuries. The creators of this type of ornamentation adapted tracery —the thin framework of the pointed-arch openings typical of Gothic—and embellished their work with naturalistic leaf designs. The other favored decoration was a carved pattern based on the outline made by textile wall hangings. This design, called linen-fold, was used extensively on panels of wood that formed the sides of chairs and cupboards and the backs of large, high-backed chairs. Originals in the Gothic style are rare, but ordinary representative pieces cost less than fine eighteenth-century furniture.

Gothic furniture from the 1800's is encountered more often. It had its origins in a "back-to-purity" movement of the sort that

French Gothic stool made of oak in the fifteenth century. Decorative details on the skirt of this stool are integral parts of the form; the pierced pattern seems functional. Notice how the bracing for the seat and the sides of the legs have decorative details.

Desk and bookcase, Gothic revival style, American, by J. & J. W. Meeks, New York, about 1840, made of rosewood and satinwood. The Gothic ornament is used as surface decoration without any attempt to suggest a furniture form of the Gothic era. The style of this piece could easily be changed by taking the traceries off the door. Other craftsmen, particularly in England, made pieces that were closer to the fifteenth-century models.

often erupts during periods of reform. A group of theorists and reformers headed by the English designer A. W. Pugin saw Gothic as an ideal vehicle to express their belief that form should follow function. Pugin published books of fifteenth-century Gothic furniture designs that were correct in every detail. These were copied extensively but, alas for Pugin, they were also interpreted. Nineteenth-century Gothic revival furniture is thus generally a free variation on the theme and is more decorative than functional.

As the Gothic notion spread, it became a principal source of inspiration for both American and European designers of the nineteenth century. Gothic revival furniture made between about 1820 and 1850 has

Table, Renaissance style, Italian, sixteenth century, made of walnut. The combination lion's paw, leaf and scroll is based on an ancient Roman model, but the carving has the same monumental quality characteristic of sixteenth-century work as the bench. The table is easily disassembled by taking off the top and removing the stretcher. Tops were often replaced. Reproductions of the turn of the century have more realistic details.

become of special concern to a number of collectors who are interested more in the variations than in faithful copies of fifteenth-century styles. These revival pieces, in walnut and mahogany more often than in oak, take ornament as an integral part of the design. The pointed arch or rose window of the thirteenth-century cathedral is adapted to serve as the back of a chair or as the motif for a secretary door. The originals had plain utilitarian legs; the revivals have handsomely carved columnar legs. Even the most elaborate fifteenth-century examples are stark compared with their nineteenth-century echoes, which have a distinction of their own because of the intricacy of their patterns.

For those who like sparse interiors, Gothic

—both the accurate reproductions and the originals—will be appealing. The 1820–50 revival designs attract those who search for unusual and challenging examples. These have a market that has been fairly constant in the last few years; chairs range from $50 to a few hundred dollars, and the best pieces, elaborate secretaries, get up to a little over $1,000.

The Renaissance can be traced to Italy at the start of the 1400's, but its influence on furniture design was slight before the 1500's. The Renaissance style is characterized by a revival of classical canons of beauty, which are markedly different from the Gothic. Renaissance designers took the repertory of architectural motifs and used it for every

Cassone, or chest, Renaissance style, Florentine, about 1475, made of polychrome and gilt fruitwood. The painted panels often showed idealized or mythological scenes, here the Conquest of Trebizond. The carved motifs suggest the variety that Renaissance craftsmen employed. Gold was applied in leaf over a gesso, or plaster, ground.

kind of object: Any support was conceived as a column, the tops of chests often looked like roofs, and a panel on the side of a cabinet was often cut in patterns like those of marble panels employed on ancient structures. The only elaborately decorated Italian pieces of the 1400's are handsomely painted chests called cassone. The earliest cassone are shaped like trunks, but by the end of the fifteenth century there are examples that resemble ancient Roman sarcophagi. Panels painted with any number of mythological scenes are often a main decoration on the more ornate examples.

Italian Renaissance furniture became more elaborate and elegant during the 1500's. The emphasis was on classical motifs, in designs covering the spectrum from repetition of ancient classical styles to ideas that were completely new. Table pedestals were often copies of the ancient so faithful that an unusual marble table in the Metropolitan Museum was mistaken at first for a Roman example. Desks and cupboards, on the other hand, were devised to meet sixteenth-century needs and the designs can be fairly ornate. Chests were frequently carved with imaginative mythological scenes rather than painted.

The chair appeared in three special versions. First, there is an X-shaped folding chair derived from Roman magistrates' chairs. This style is called the Savonarola when it consists of a series of crossed members placed close

a

a
Folding armchair called Savonarola, Renaissance style, Italian, 1490–1520, made of walnut. The back of the Savonarola lifts up and off making it possible to close the chair. Gouged-work decoration is rather schematic; other examples have either relief carving or shell inlays.

b
Sgabello, a wooden stool, Renaissance style, Italian, sixteenth century, made of walnut. Rich carving is generally used on the small Renaissance chairs. The form was popular all over Italy in the sixteenth century. In the seventeenth, eighteenth and nineteenth centuries a simpler version was adapted as a peasant chair in many parts of northern Europe. Reproductions of the early 1900's are more delicately carved.

together, and the Dantesca when there are just two crossed members making the frame. Second is the wooden stool, often made with a back that becomes the vehicle for handsome carving. This is known as a sgabello. Its supports are sometimes a pair of panels, at other times just three plain legs. The third type, one that was continued into the 1600's, is a plain rectangular form, with seat and back of leather, fabric or wood.

Italian Renaissance furniture is rare, but one occasionally finds an authentic sixteenth-century wooden chair or chest that can be recognized by its simple construction. Sixteenth-century carving was stylized but consistent; nineteenth-century reproductions are schematic in an inconsistent way, with some

b

26

Cupboard, Renaissance style, French, sixteenth century, made of walnut with marble insets. The two-part cupboard is a typical French Renaissance design. Carving is used as a device to create a surface texture that differs from the Italian accentuation of individual motifs. Here the decoration is in low relief, but it has a similar effect when cut deeper.

opposite
Page from Plusieurs Menuiseries by Paul Vredeman de Vriese, probably published in Amsterdam, 1658. Designs of the sixteenth century were repeated in a number of the seventeenth-century publications. While contemporary furniture makers carved details thicker than they appeared in the engravings, the nineteenth-century workmen copied more closely with disastrous results, because the fussy details are not consistent with the heavy proportions of actual furniture.

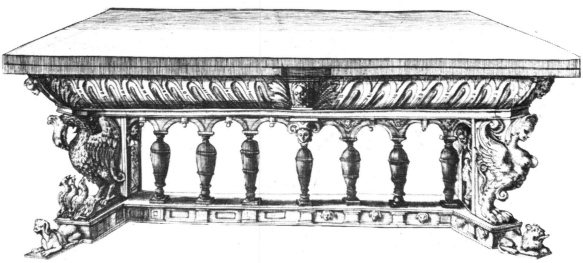

parts realistic and others rough. At the turn of the nineteenth century, some Renaissance-style rooms were furnished with combinations of genuine and reproduction furniture. Both types come onto the market these days, as the old houses are demolished.

During the 1500's the Renaissance spread north. In France, the classical designs have more surface ornament and appear more elaborate than in Italy. A distinctive chair with arms, called the caqueteuse, or gossip, was made of oak or walnut by French cabinetmakers. It has straight columnar legs, and a tall narrow back carved with classical ornament or profile portrait medallion. The rich carving and strong interest in the classical sometimes make French furniture hard to distinguish from Italian. French and Italian Renaissance tables, in particular, are similar.

But typically French cupboards are carved more elaborately than anything Italian; the carving is relatively flat but rich in detail.

In the 1600's and 1700's, a few books of furniture designs were published and these have had a sharp effect on collecting. These books made life easier for nineteenth-century copyists, but make judging authenticity tougher for the collector. Craftsmen, following the illustrations, were able to create truly sophisticated revivals, reproductions and copies. The later copies, however, often give themselves away by crudeness of construction. They tend to be like objects made for the stage—to be seen only from a certain angle and only from a distance. The prospective buyer who looks underneath will often find thinly disguised new lumber.

ENGLISH AND AMERICAN OAK

After the Renaissance, in places where high fashion was not important, oak continued to be the most common wood for furniture. This was the case, for example, in Tudor England during the 1500's and in America in the 1600's. The best Tudor furniture was of oak, stained dark to resemble finer woods. The designs continued the simplicity and utility dominant during the medieval era, but classical decoration was added. Because oak is very hard, the carved patterns tend to be flat and shallowly cut. Such typical ornaments as the tree of life, an urn of flowers or a vine with leaves emerged so flattened that they even look a bit abstract.

English craftsmen also used bold and plain patterns of inlay. Designs are in the Renaissance style, but plainer. A characteristic item is the court cupboard. It has three shelves, one or two of them covered by doors; the middle enclosure is recessed. One variation, the press cupboard, has a lower section enclosed for storage. The simple rectangular chest, better known as the blanket chest, was made in a variety of designs. An arcade with carved floral patterns centered under each arch was popular as decoration. Chests with inlaid patterns on architectural themes became known as Nonesuch chests, after a palace, now long gone, built by Henry VIII. The characteristic table was rectangular with heavy vase-shaped carved legs. One important English chair of the 1500's was made with a solid paneled back and seat. Another had elaborately turned posts, with a seat of solid wood or rush.

Finding an original Tudor item is not out of the question because Tudor-style houses were popular in the 1920's, when affluence inspired collecting and the owners of large Tudorish houses in the suburbs often elected to furnish them with the appropriate furniture. But reproductions of Tudor have been common since the turn of the century, so it is wise to be skeptical. A possible giveaway is inconsistent carving or an inept abstract pattern.

The American parallel to Tudor furniture is usually called Pilgrim, and its documented samples in the main date from the end of the 1600's. Although the kinship with English Tudor is clear, American craftsmen developed their own distinctive style. A Pilgrim piece in good condition is generally stained a reddish color to look like walnut. A second wood is used for details such as dentils (teeth-like devices) on lintels or columns, which are often painted black to look like ebony.

American Pilgrim decoration is more limited than Tudor. There is flat carving and, very rarely, painted decoration, but none of the more elaborate Tudor carving. Turned parts—legs or pillars—are vase-shaped and plain, rather than carved. Few tables of the period have survived. American cupboards, both the court and the press, combine the textures of the 1500's with contrasting colors that are more typical of the 1600's. The small chest-on-stand is a form whose original function has been forgotten; it may have been a washstand or a place to store books. The

a
Bed, Tudor style, English, late sixteenth century, made of oak. Rich stylized carving and stark inlays are the two kinds of ornament on this huge bed. English craftsmen used heavier hands than their colleagues on the Continent. Results have a distinctive gusto. Here the design is rendered with a certain amount of sophistication, but often the carving is more schematic.

b
Armchair, Tudor style, English, sixteenth or seventeenth century, made of oak. Turned posts were used for chairs in the Middle Ages and were popular in Tudor England and seventeenth-century New England. They have also been reproduced in quantity since the mid nineteenth century. Early English examples have heavy turning and details such as the rows of punched stars. They should be as complex as this one. If the design is like this but simple and has initials and a date as specifically early as 1568, beware.

a

a
*Chest on frame, Pilgrim style, Massachusetts,
late seventeenth century, made of oak, pine and
maple. Before the end of the seventeenth
century Americans made a variety of small
furniture forms. This could have been used as a
book chest or it might have served
as a wash stand.*

b
*Chest, Hadley type, Massachusetts, 1715, made
of oak and pine. This is one of a group of dower
chests traced to the area of Hadley, Mass. The
flat designs on each example are similarly
abstracted in a combination of low relief and
incised line. Originally this was painted red,
green and possibly black.*

slant-topped book or Bible box is a more
familiar form. American blanket chests of the
period occasionally have one or two drawers
below the main storage area, and when
turned spindles are applied as a kind of
architectural framing, the central panels become a vehicle for almost abstract tulips and
sunflowers. Another version, called the Hadley chest after an area in Massachusetts
where most were found, is characterized by
flat, abstract leaf patterns.

b

CAROLINGIAN, WILLIAM AND MARY

The Carolingian and the William and Mary periods of design, the first English and the second American, reflect the baroque style of the 1600's. The English version dates from about 1660 to the end of the century, while the American work was done between about 1690 and 1730. Classical designs became more vibrant in this period, with the woods carefully selected for contrasting grains and often embellished with inlays. To get a fine, showy graining, furniture makers often applied veneers, which are thin layers of wood, over the surface. Earlier column-like supports lost some of their heaviness, while bulbous vase shapes were transformed into more delicate trumpet-shaped or twisted spiral columns. And the chest of drawers, relatively rare before, became more important. When placed on a stand that sometimes has a row or two of drawers, the chest becomes what Americans call a highboy. English provincial cabinetmakers made chests of drawers with drawer fronts of heavy oak panels, like the early blanket chests; but more typically, handsome veneers and inlays cover relatively simple forms. Occasionally, English craftsmen used marquetry, a technique of inlaying elaborate over-all floral patterns. Americans used plainer designs.

Chairs often had elaborately carved frames enclosing tall, thin backs. Cane was introduced for seats and backs, but you can find them upholstered in leather as well. Elegant leaf and scroll patterns often framed the backs even when the piece was otherwise relatively simple; backs were often simply a

Highchair, Charles II style, English, about 1670, made of walnut with some gilding. The spiral-turned back stiles and arm supports are a good foil for the flowers, crowns and cupids; each of the motifs is in the baroque spirit of the time. Notice the economy of detail in flowers and leaves. The 1890 version would be fussier and the turnings thinner.

Cabinet, William and Mary period, English, late seventeenth century, made of walnut and exotic woods. The scroll legs and bun feet are baroque-style elements. The over-all pictorial pattern inlaid into the upper part is a type of marquetry that was particularly fashionable when the piece was new. The bold cornice molding conceals a drawer.

Gateleg table, English, seventeenth century, made of walnut. Turnings on table legs in the seventeenth century are thick; the English examples often have complex rings separating the oval or sausage shapes. Later tables are lighter in proportion.

High chest, William and Mary style, American, about 1700, made of walnut with burl walnut veneer. Trumpet-shaped turned legs are another design in the baroque spirit. Surface decoration on the American scene was more often achieved with patterns of graining instead of the more elaborate marquetry.

row of half-balusters that look as if they had been borrowed from a stairway. English and American chairs can generally be distinguished: The American is simpler and more straightforward, with ornament secondary to function.

The source of inspiration for most baroque design of the late 1600's was the furniture of the court of Louis XIV. Although it is just about impossible to find these pieces now, knowing a little about them helps one's understanding of contemporary styles. French cabinetmakers working for the circle around Louis XIV offered flamboyant designs executed with the greatest elaboration. For carved ornament, they called on almost the entire repertory of Greco-Roman motifs. Their interest in richly ornamented surfaces led to the development of what is called Boulle, or Buhl, work. Named for a fine cabinetmaker, André Charles Boulle, this work is characterized by patterns of inlay in brass, tortoiseshell and fine wood veneers. The tapering columnar leg, shaped like a Roman pedestal, was used, along with scroll and animal-form legs, by Parisian cabinetmakers at the end of the 1600's when the style of Louis XIV was at its prime. Console tables, stands, desks, and cabinets show this style at its most elaborate. But it is easier to trace the Louis XIV style in Continental than in English and American work.

COUNTRY
AND PROVINCIAL

It is called country furniture when it comes from England or America, provincial when it comes from the Continent. It is a bold style, simple and relatively heavy. The scale, the proportion and the feeling of country pieces are closer to their predecessors than to the pieces of the later 1700's, even though most country-provincial furniture was made relatively late.

When a collector speaks of country or provincial furniture, he means furniture from the 1700's and 1800's, made presumably by rural craftsmen. Sometimes the designs are lighter versions of something that was popular in the 1600's; sometimes they are simplified versions of what city craftsmen were making at the same time. The city crafts-

Slat-back armchair, American, 1725–50, made of ash and maple. The slat-back is a country form on both sides of the Atlantic. Basically a design of the 1600's, it was popular into the 1800's. This early American example shows the type at its simplest. French examples have more complex turnings and proportions are squatter.

High chest, English, late seventeenth century, made of oak. The paneled drawers of the upper section are a holdover from Tudor design, and the chest is provincial in its conservatism. English country craftsmen used some seventeenth-century design well into the eighteenth century.

men's woods were fine walnut and mahogany, but country and provincial workmen chose pine, fruitwood, maple and oak—woods that grew locally. Country workmen often painted their product, because the available woods required protection and because it was simpler to decorate with paint than with inlays or carving. Complex ornamentation was simplified to make it easier and more economical to manufacture; thus an intricate shell carving on a city piece might be reduced to a geometric motif—a series of flutes in a fan-like arrangement, for example.

Good English country furniture might be typified by a slat-back chair with turned legs. If compared with an earlier chair, it shows fairly thin parts and somewhat small dimensions. Another typical form is the kitchen dresser with tall, narrow, turned legs, a lower section of doors and drawers, and an upper section of shallow shelves for displaying plates. Shops featuring English country pieces often show oak or fruitwood tables with gatelegs of turned balusters; these can be small enough to serve as occasional tables, or large enough to seat eight comfortably. The turnings on the legs are fairly nondescript on mediocre examples, but the tables themselves are serviceable and inexpensive.

Plain English adaptations of fashionable designs of the 1700's, often of oak but sometimes of hickory, chestnut or fruitwood, are common. City designs—Chippendale and Hepplewhite—are simplified radically. Although it is attractive, this furniture is hard to date and much of it may be of late nineteenth-century workmanship. Because of this, premium prices should not be paid for such furniture. A good guide for pricing the more ordinary country pieces is to compare them with the going rate for decent furniture made today. Thus a plain pedestal table of oak, in an eighteenth-century English style with proper moldings and patina, might reasonably go for $200. It is wise, with other antique furniture as well as with these English imports, to avoid buying anything so crude and rough that it is impossible to find clues to the date of manufacture.

Provincial French furniture runs a close parallel to the English, with fruitwoods the favored medium. Carved decorations are often primitive adaptations of fashionable motifs, such as the rococo shell. The French provincial kitchen doubled as a parlor so that useful objects—such as the trough for dough and the cabinet for storing bread—were often made in charmingly fashionable designs. Large armoires—storage pieces for china or linens and such—and cupboards in two sections were popular. Chair designs ranged from simple adaptations of early slat-back chairs to more up-to-date but simplified designs. Sometimes the wooden backs were cut out and carved in rococo or neoclassical designs. Curved-front low chests of drawers with boldly carved skirts were another popular provincial form. In the country versions, rococo curves were sometimes dropped in favor of the straight lines of the neoclassical Louis XVI style. Rococo designs are particularly confusing now, because some of them were made fairly recently in shops probably much like those of the original provincial craftsmen. Most French forms are fairly large in scale, and most often the rural examples are bigger than those of Paris. Provincial Canadian designs are also well worth looking into, since persistence of the seventeenth-century influence into the eighteenth century is more noticeable in Canadian work than elsewhere.

American country style includes some of the most delightful furniture of the New World. It can be a sure, knowing simplification of an urban design or a seemingly timeless, utilitarian form. The emphasis in American work is on the functional, so that it has less ornamentation than European provincial pieces.

Two approaches to design were taken in the American countryside. In one, the forms of the 1600's were updated. In this group are found a small number of forms—chests and chests of drawers, frequently of pine, usually painted; tables with elongated, turned legs, and chairs that are slat-backs or variants of European designs.

The other approach is more fashionable, and is one of the most exciting aspects of American furniture design. The most desirable of these pieces have the typical simplified country carving—shells, rosettes and flowers worked into geometric patterns. Sometimes the curving legs of an eighteenth-century high-style design were straightened by country craftsmen so they could make the piece more quickly. Not surprisingly, eighteenth- and early nineteenth-century exam-

Desk, American, 1770–1800, made of maple. Plain designs in maple are typical of country manufacture. Here the molding around the drawers and the cut of the feet are telltale signs of its date. English provincial examples are even plainer, particularly because they are made of a less decorative wood.

Chest, Pennsylvania German, American, early nineteenth century, made of painted yellow pine and poplar. This is one of the finest types of chests and well enough known to have been reproduced. The painted design should be flat and schematic. Details of the moldings on the base around the drawers and the top should be generously curved on early painted pieces, even when the surface is just marbleized.

ples of this work command stunning prices. A good Connecticut highboy with a flattened shell on the top and bottom center drawers, for example, can cost over $20,000. The expensive and most desirable examples have a curious primitive charm that is obvious in the most elaborate decorative elements. There are also stripped-down models without an inch of carving to be found. These are easy to fake, so care and caution are required. When one finds an authentic plain piece in the right proportions and with all the right moldings, and it's not expensive, this is something of a miracle.

These country pieces originated in the smaller centers of New England, the more remote parts of Pennsylvania, and the South.

Recent research has shown that simple country was also made in Newport, Philadelphia and other large centers. Among German settlers in Pennsylvania, a distinctive style developed, based on Tyrolean peasant designs. This painted furniture is erroneously called Pennsylvania Dutch. The known examples are sharply limited in form and design, almost always of pine, cut in simple forms with elaborate but limited decoration. The dower chest is one important item. Following their traditions on the Continent, the Pennsylvania Germans gave chests to their daughters to hold their dowry linen; they were painted in colorful floral or figure patterns evoking German, Swiss and Central European peasant models. Many European

Windsor chair, by I. Always, New York, made about 1760 of maple, hickory and ash. The Windsor is a design made in England and the United States, from the early eighteenth century to today. The good early examples have relatively thick turnings. Rare examples are marked with a brand on the bottom of the seat.

variations are passed off as Pennsylvania German and it is wise to be skeptical. Pennsylvania examples are distinguished by the moldings, brasses and outline of the plain bracket feet, all of which look close to details on very different English-influenced chests of drawers.

In the 1820's and later, the painted decoration, modified now into simple cut bird patterns, was applied to desks and other case pieces in designs influenced by Hepplewhite and Sheraton. Imports are generally heavier in details like moldings. Since most European examples that turn up date from the middle to late nineteenth century, the colors are pastel shades, more varied than the typical American dark blues, greens and reds.

Many people collect nineteenth-century country furniture but prefer to think they own creations of eighteenth-century craftsmen. The confusion develops because good, simple eighteenth-century designs such as Windsor chairs, slat-back and country Queen Anne were mass-produced in furniture factories during the early nineteenth century. Shaker chairs, both the slat-back and variations with seats and backs of canvas webbing, are dated by some as early as 1790. But these chairs are best known in their post-Civil War versions, as made in Shaker community factories. Advertisements from the 1870's and 80's call Shaker chairs the best of their kind, which suggests that originally there were also competitive items that dis-

Side chair, Pennsylvania, about 1825, made of maple and other woods. Painted chairs with stenciled decoration were popular in the early nineteenth century on both sides of the Atlantic. American examples tend to be simpler.

appeared and re-emerged as "original Shaker" items. Chests, cupboards and tables made by the Shakers, usually for their own homes, prove how the tradition of simple rural design persisted through the 1800's.

Furniture factories of the nineteenth century also produced modified versions of fashionable designs that appealed to rural tastes. Painted chairs following either Sheraton or Empire styles were made in quantity all over the country from about 1820 to 1850. Several of these manufacturers also put out sets of bedroom furniture decorated with colored paints. While the chairs, popularly called Hitchcock, after the best-known maker, now turn up fairly often, painted bedroom sets have become rather hard to find. Quaint and squat pieces, with heavy turnings on the feet in a design that inspired the name "spool," are another product of factories active before the Civil War. Spool-turned beds, dressers, chairs and tables, generally stripped of their paint, were very common and collectable a decade or so ago, but they proved so popular that they are now hard to track down. The next cycle may drive them back onto the market again.

Customarily, nineteenth-century factory furniture is not expensive, and just a few hundred dollars will buy several matching pieces. Unfortunately, the term "country furniture" has become a catch-all for primitive pieces that are only partly old or much remodeled. Pine furniture that was mass-produced between 1840 and 1890 is often stripped down and the telltale Victorian hardware removed. The resulting plain and primitive-looking object is then sold as something else. Such a chest, at $45, would be a good substitute for a badly made modern chest, but it should not be confused with a real antique in the collector's sense.

There is a further gloomy aspect to the elasticity that the term "country" is developing. Every cobbler's bench of thirty years ago has been made into a coffee table; bellows, drums, crates and almost anything else of suitable height has been hauled into the living room to hold magazines and coffee cups. Stripping these objects, removing their veneers, hardware and paints, makes them of no value to the collectors of bellows, drums and crates. Stripping may make them into furniture, but not into good country furniture.

ROCOCO OR LOUIS XV

The most coveted and expensive furniture collected today dates from the mid-1700's. Curved legs on forms decorated with shell, leaf, scroll and garland motifs—sometimes almost unrecognizable—are earmarks of this era. The scale is perfect for the grand modern interior, though it is a bit oversized for more modest homes.

Rococo is the most suitable name for this style; it probably derives from the French word rocaille—a certain kind of shell—and the name was first used derisively. The most innovative work in the rococo mode was done in France, beginning about 1720, during the interim reign of the Regent; it continued well into the reign of Louis XV, when the style flourished. The best work is from Paris. Frequently, in the finest examples, the name of the cabinetmaker will be found stamped on a hidden part of the frame, but a number of fine examples that must have been the work of the ablest craftsmen were never marked. Because faking marks is easy, it must be borne in mind that marks are not so significant as style and quality. This period is not for the collector with a thin wallet: a very fine commode, or chest of drawers, will command $20,000 to $100,000. Several pieces have brought over $400,000 at auction. Even nineteenth- or twentieth-century reproductions of fine work have gone into the thousand-dollar bracket because of demand, since many people are content to compromise with nicely made old copies. Parisian work, more elegant than anything made elsewhere, is the most desirable. The rococo style did

Commode, by Bernard van Risen Burgh, Paris, about 1760, made of tulipwood and kingwood. Elaborate gilt bronze, also called ormolu, is an embellishment on the finest rococo furniture. Used in combination with elegant marquetry, the bronze emphasized the curves of the form. The best examples have bronze and marquetry in clearly related designs. When the two do not connect, the bronze may have been added as a later improvement.

42

spread all over Europe, however, and some German and Italian examples vie with Parisian models for interest. Although in Munich the German model is apt to be very expensive, in New York it may be a bargain.

The rococo was at its prime in the Court of Louis XV and it spread extensively from there. As the style of elegance it inspired a broad range of forms: small tables of every sort, large chests for storing just about anything, and a host of other pieces for specific purposes. Rococo-style chairs have handsomely carved frames that were originally painted or gilded. The seats and backs are almost invariably upholstered, and the proportions are relatively large. These chairs were much imitated in later eras, and distinguishing between early and later is a bit tricky.

The carving provides one clue to date. In the 1700's, the leaf, flower or shell was conceived as a whole design so that details were generalized; the motif may be unrecognizable at first glance. Nonetheless the carving is crisp and fine. In later imitations, however, either the details pop out realistically or the generalization is clumsy.

The same sort of stylistic generalizing affects early inlay and ormolu—or gilt bronze —work. A human head done in ormolu during the rococo period is a perfect mask, not intended to resemble anybody or to convey emotion. Later imitations have a disarming way of smiling or looking over-wise. Perhaps this conveys the amusement of the artist at his imposture.

Armchair, by Jean-Jacques Pathier, Louis XV style, Paris, about 1760, made of gilded wood. The curving carved frame is typical of the rococo style. Leaf and flower motifs should dominate, but occasionally unusual classical motifs like the Greek key border on the skirt appear. Rococo period carving is crisp and the reproductions of the early 1900's are rather flat.

opposite
Desk by J. F. Hache, Grenoble, France, mid eighteenth century

Candlestand, rococo style, south German, 1725–50, made of gilt and carved wood. The flamboyance of the rococo seems a little more emphatic in German examples. The idea of using a combination of scrolls to form a stand is international. The crisp carving and relative thickness are typical of eighteenth-century examples.

One aspect of rococo furniture is full of pitfalls: not that made for the very rich, but examples made for the affluent middle class. These designs are less elaborate, but they are not so simple as the provincial. Even the experts dispute the authenticity of much of this work, so hard is it to distinguish originals from later copies. If you decide you want an example of simple French rococo, don't pay more for it than you would for something you know to be a nineteenth-century variation.

GEORGIAN

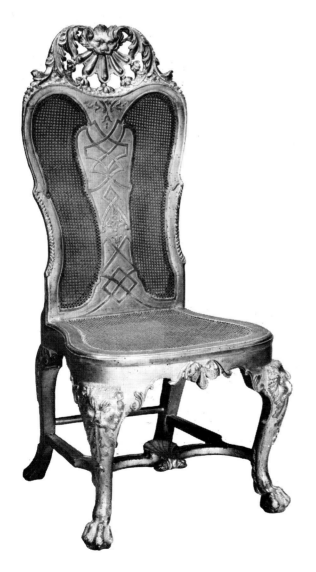

Georgian is a catch-all term covering English decorative work from most of the 1700's; the Georges began their reigns in 1714 and continued into the nineteenth century. Many collectors are infuriated when eighteenth-century English furniture contemporary with Louis XV is termed rococo, but the basic approach is nonetheless the same. Forms are unified and organic rather than built up part by part, as they would have been in the seventeenth century, and the scale is as small as that of most French rococo. However, until the French influence became very strong, about 1750, English designs were simpler and, instead of using the whimsical decorative devices of rococo, English furniture-makers closely followed classical models.

Side chair, Georgian style, English, about 1730, made of gilt wood. English furniture makers tended to make all wooden chairs with a minimum of upholstery. The curving back with its solid splat and the caning are elements inspired by the Orient. The masks, lion's-paw feet and other carved details reflect classical interest. Gilding is rarely intact on pieces offered for sale and can cover up all kinds of changes, so gold surfaces should suggest an extra-careful examination.

English furniture of the eighteenth century, particularly from about 1740 to 1780, has great appeal because it represents a combination of elegance and utility. Cabinetmakers used fine woods such as walnut and mahogany in rich but restrained designs. As a result, collectors from Rome to Los Angeles seize upon English furniture as perfect for their chic but quiet interiors, often uprooting it from brokerage offices where it had been bespeaking prosperous solidity for years. The proportions, the obvious quality and the over-all simplicity are easier to like than the more extravagant expressions of the Continental craftsmen during the same period. Esthetic considerations apart, the quantity of English furniture available until recently was greater than that from any other country. But bargains are now rare, and most often you will have to go to the finer antique shops to find good examples. Brokerage offices have gone in for Knoll; if one could still find the sort of office Marquand wrote about, however. . . .

Early in the eighteenth century, the English concentrated on rediscovering the classical while the French more inventively played variations on classical themes. English architects went to the sixteenth-century Renaissance for inspiration and developed a style that is basically a reinterpretation of North Italian Mannerism. This is called the Palladian style, after the architect Palladio, who was responsible for important work in Vicenza, Verona and Venice in the 1500's. This architecture affected the design of large storage and display pieces. Pediments and surface embellishments were copied out of architectural handbooks that suggested Palladian details to builders. Langley's *Builders Treasury,* one of a number of design sources published before 1750, offered ideas for furniture along with ideas for fireplaces and doorways.

The classical was not the only source of eighteenth-century inspiration; the oriental was also important. Oriental lacquer had been copied and interpreted in late seventeenth-century decoration, but actual furniture was the basis for some of the lighter designs of the early eighteenth century. A new solid-backed chair that appeared before 1716 was an adaptation of the Chinese chairs

Console table, Georgian style, English, 1730–40, made of gilded wood. This is an example of the extravagant efforts by classical designers supplying furniture for the large Palladian houses of the period. Scrolls and garlands of heavy proportions were favored by the group of designers that included William Kent and Batty Langley.

Medal cabinet, by William Vile, English, about 1760, made of mahogany. The classical approach continued past 1750 in designs that can just barely be called rococo. The collector is more apt to find the straight pedimented form in a simple desk and bookcase, but this extraordinary example made for George III suggests the quality of carving possible in outstanding pieces.

then becoming known in the West. The typical chair is one that Americans call Queen Anne. It has half-round stiles and a top rail framing a center splat that is often vase-shaped and sometimes pierced. The curving legs, called cabriole, are in animal form. They terminate in simple pads, hoofs or claw-and-ball feet.

Whether the over-all design is based on oriental or classical models, or, often, a combination of the two, the details tend to be crisp and classical. Moldings at the edges of supports or panels on authentic work are neatly executed. Even at its simplest, a good eighteenth-century piece will show signs of the cabinetmaker's ability. Rough execution is more likely to be the mark of nineteenth- or twentieth-century work.

CHIPPENDALE

The closest English equivalent of full-blown rococo is the furniture that Americans call Chippendale, but that the English consider a subordinate aspect of Georgian design. Designs and the elaborate decorations typical of this style reflect a strong French influence. The carved leaves, scrolls and flowers meandered far from their classical beginnings and began to look distinctly eighteenth-century. Gilt console tables are often in the most flamboyant rococo form and English examples look less whimsical than the French models, in that they have more solid parts and less openwork. Inlays and ormolu mounts are used more sparingly on chests and cabinets.

There is an irony in the use of the term Chippendale. Thomas Chippendale, who was born about 1718 and died in 1779, operated a London cabinet shop and many examples of later neoclassical furniture can surely be traced to his shop. But not one single object of what is popularly considered "Chippendale furniture" can securely be attributed to the workshop of Chippendale. The association of his name with a whole mode of work stems from a book of designs published by him in 1754. Called *The Gentleman and Cabinet-Maker's Director*, it offered designs in the "Gothic, Chinese and modern taste." This book, reprinted several times in the next nine years, compiled some of his own high-fashion designs and some that he bought from other designers. The book documented rather than innovated, but its influence was such that Chippendale became the American term for the most stylish furniture of the period.

The Chippendale style sharply marks the merging of classical and exotic tendencies. It features rococo whimsy in asymmetric patterns on forms that curve generously. Following the French lead, variations of leaf, shell, ribbon and scroll designs were introduced. The typical chair makes a perfect illustration: The back has a yoke-shaped top rail, inspired by the Chinese but transformed to the rococo; it is probably carved all over, and the back has an intricately pierced splat. Curved legs are also elaborately carved, with the feet either scrolled or in essence classical.

However, furniture showing the rococo influence accounts for only one aspect of design between 1740 and 1780. In the same period as the curving forms of full-blown rococo are equally richly carved classical designs. Bookcases, desks and clothes presses are often straight-sided and topped by richly detailed angular pediments. These designs are in keeping with the dominant architectural settings, which were similarly lavish but classical in tone rather than rococo. The smaller rococo pieces seem to have been a foil to relieve formality, while case pieces reinforced the basic design of the room.

The most distinctive designs in Chippendale's book are Chinese in tone. They could combine restraint and whimsy in a way that was particularly appealing to the English. Light, intricate takeoffs on Chinese furniture work very well in polished mahogany: Fretwork in patterns inspired by Chinese openwork designs was cut as openwork or applied to solid wooden backing. The straight leg of typical eighteenth-century Chinese forms was adapted, and wherever possible the suggestion of Chinese taste was emphasized by a pagoda on top.

The Georgian era was affluent and the demand for luxuries kept increasing. More varied forms of furniture were made in response. But the increasing number of ambitious, upwardly mobile people was reflected, unfortunately, by larger numbers of pieces that were not as good as they might have been. These were created for strivers who were willing to compromise and be half-right, or who didn't know the difference. Flamboyant examples that are badly put together should be avoided. Some are indeed period pieces, but they only show the worst side of this fascinating age. Others are later copies that look as if they had been made for a single evening, to be thrown away afterward with the empty bottles.

The simpler, stripped-down models occasionally have all the quality of the most elegant work, and these are worth waiting for. It is important to remember, however, that simplified variations were often made in the nineteenth century as well. A serious examination will reveal overly thin moldings and sloppy construction that will eventually make the piece annoying.

The styles of the 1700's were revived rather soon after they first went out of fashion. Chippendale's book was republished before 1830, and cabinetmakers went to work making over-literal interpretations of his engravings. In the 1700's, draftsmen understood the necessity of transforming these engravings into thicker patterns that made more sense in wood. Later craftsmen, however, took the engravings literally and produced flimsy, inept renditions that finally are just too fussy.

Fine English furniture of the eighteenth century commands a broad range of prices. The best desk, with a flat top and richly carved and paneled sides, may bring over $100,000 where a simpler but equally great piece may cost $5,000 and an ordinary, really basic, stripped-down model perhaps $500. A spectacular chest of drawers resembling French work will command $40,000, while a good-looking but small paneled-door wardrobe or press, on a nicely carved stand, may

Side chair, Chippendale style, English, about 1750, made of mahogany. Rococo design in England is associated with Thomas Chippendale. Examples like this show how the ribbon, scroll and leaf motifs emerged thicker in furniture than in engravings. Flimsy ornament is often late nineteenth century.

50   *Desk and cabinet, Chippendale style, English, about 1760, made of mahogany. Chinese influence was an important element of the English rococo. The pagoda top and the latticework doors are in the Chinese taste recommended by Chippendale.*

bring only $2,000. Rarity and demand have their effect on all prices, and English furniture is no exception. Small tables sell fast, and the best-made flamboyant examples are expensive. Storage pieces and oddball items such as pianos go begging at relatively low prices.

Alas, some imitations are very good. Sometimes they sell for high prices because they are practical. A 1920 sideboard scaled down for a modern house is more desirable to many than the fine old side table with simple pad feet and a marble top, and it may accordingly cost more in shops that cater to people who are furnishing rather than collecting. If you are interested in collecting, examine with care and take the time to spot troubling inconsistencies. Overly realistic or flat, clumsy carving is a sign of recent workmanship. Inspecting the interior may help in making a determination: Eighteenth-century cabinetmakers were generally interested in doing a good job even where it would not show. Primitive construction is more likely to result from fast, recent production than from naïve early hands.

AMERICAN PRE-REVOLUTIONARY CITY FURNITURE

The two most important styles in America in the 1700's were Queen Anne and Chippendale. The first term, which refers to the English monarch who reigned from 1702 to 1714, is applied to American work created between 1730 and 1760. Chippendale furniture, named for the English cabinetmaker, was high fashion from about 1750 to 1780. The styles are closely related: Both are conservative, and both depend upon English Georgian models. But they can be differentiated. Queen Anne is simple, with a minimum of carved decoration, while Chippendale is more elaborate, with much carved ornamentation. Mahogany was popular with cabinetmakers working in both styles, but walnut is found more often in Queen Anne

High chest, Chippendale style, Philadelphia, about 1765, made of mahogany. Although this form was out of style in England before 1750, the carving was in London fashion. The carving of birds on the center drawer illustrates an Aesop fable and follows an idea suggested by Chippendale.

opposite
Blockfront secretary, cherry, Connecticut, about 1770

examples than in Chippendale. The curving cabriole leg is popular in both styles, and both styles combine oriental and classical influences.

The chair best points up the divergences of style. The Queen Anne chair is designed in a series of curves that flow together. There is an emphasis on simplicity and richness in the wood color and in the execution of detail. The only extra embellishments are shells occasionally applied to the top rail and to the knees of the cabriole legs. The Chippendale chair is a more complex design combining curves with straight lines. The back is topped by a yoke-shaped rail that projects at both ends. The splat on the back is generally pierced. Designers sometimes used straight legs based on Chinese models rather than cabriole legs. Carving covers the surfaces of the most elaborate examples, but equally fine Chippendale chairs are relatively plain.

American Queen Anne furniture tends to be simple but elegant, with the total effect arising from over-all design rather than from elaborate detail. Because of this simplicity, fine construction is doubly important. Just about every form made in the Queen Anne style was also popular in the Chippendale style. Tea tables, game tables, and side tables are found plain—in the Queen Anne style—and elaborately carved—in Chippendale—as well as in variations hard to categorize. One factor to keep in mind is that the simpler things are easier to copy and there are thus a certain number of Queen Anne fakes

Mahogany side chair, Chippendale style, Philadelphia, about 1770

Side chair, Queen Anne style, Newport or New York, about 1745. The curving back of the early Georgian chair was more stylized and regular in fine American examples. The carefully carved plain shells are used on Queen Anne pieces. The claw and ball should be generously proportioned because on reproductions they are frequently flat and indistinct.

56 on the market. When construction is sloppy, caution is advisable. Dark stains on the undersides of chests or tables often cover up new wood. Although details are sometimes very nicely repeated by the faker, he often misses on the over-all proportions. Turn-of-the-century reproductions tend to be elongated while recent fakes are frequently too squat.

American design tends to be simpler and more direct than English design. Even the most elaborate pieces are trim, and the emphasis is on the outline rather than on the ornament. Among examples of American work one begins to discern differences reflecting local practices or local taste. In the eighteenth century, Philadelphia was a center of elegant work; New Yorkers favored heavier proportions; Boston and Newport craftsmen favored delicacy of detail. American Chippendale tends to appear inconsistent, since conservative forms were being used along with the latest known London fashions. Forms fitting the English classification of early Georgian were made right up to the American Revolution, but at the same time one finds examples comparable to what was being made in London in the 1770's. The highboy was out of fashion in England well before 1750, but it was still the vehicle for the best Philadelphia carving on the eve of the Revolution. In contrast, the chest of drawers on low bracket feet was fashionable on both sides of the Atlantic during the 1760's and 1770's. American examples are often very plain, but some have elaborately

carved front corners or engaged quarter columns, as well as feet that may also be embellished with some kind of decoration.

The blockfront chest is a variation much coveted by American collectors. Its name is inspired by projecting and recessed blocks on the front of its drawers, topped by shells carved boldly and well. The blocking is often cut extravagantly from a single thick board. This design was encountered at the beginning of the eighteenth century in English and French work, but it must have been considered unusual when taken up by the Newport cabinetmakers, who originated the best American examples. Blockfront pieces were made in Newport and other parts of New England until about 1800. Most were made

Slant-top desk, Queen Anne style, Connecticut, about 1750. The plain pad is one characteristic of the Queen Anne style. Simplicity is a positive factor in the subtle curves of the drawers inside the desk. Feeling under the skirt, one should find an uneven molded quality, not sharp corners, to confirm the age of a piece.

while the Chippendale style flourished, but the design was probably introduced some time before. The extraordinarily fine but subtle craftsmanship of blockfront pieces has been sought by collectors since the late nineteenth century, so there are a number of rather old reproductions. In the basement of an antique shop in Maine, I once found one that looked very good in the dark. I tried to be cagey and ask about it without showing that I thought it was a steal at $900. The dealer was way ahead of me. He said he was sending it out to be refinished the very next day so I had to decide immediately. In a quick inspection, the carving looked good, but the scale was wrong and then, opening the drawers, I found that it was constructed fast and without any of the loving care typical of the eighteenth century. I passed. Not every time a dealer puts on pressure is there something wrong with the piece, but pressure should indicate a need for caution.

Countless reproductions of eighteenth-century Chippendale forms have been made with no thought of fooling anybody. But fifty years is long enough to give wood the proper color and logical signs of wear. Fine, simple pieces ought to be very well made if one is going to pay the price asked for eighteenth-century work.

The slant-top desk is another very popular form. This is often mysteriously known as the Governor Winthrop desk, although it was first made after the Governors Winthrop departed this life. There is a broad range, with many examples large in scale and with the writing surface high. If the piece is intended for regular use, it is a good idea to sit down and try it out to see if you can write comfortably. The most elegant desks have elaborately fitted interiors with delicately curving pigeonholes and a center box with flanking columns concealing narrow drawers. The center section should come out, and there ought to be a few secret drawers. The better examples generally are supported on claw-and-ball feet, while plain bracket feet are standard for routine pieces. The most elaborate variation is topped by a cupboard for books. This is popularly known today as a secretary, although in the early records it was referred to as a desk and bookcase. The most elegant examples have a serpentine lower front, kettle-shaped sides and carved hairy-paw feet. Often doors on the upper part are glazed or mirrored and are flanked by pilasters.

Elegantly made American furniture has become very expensive. A richly carved Chippendale-style table may bear a price tag of $100,000, but the range is broad; simple but good examples begin at about $500. There are chests of drawers of exquisite workmanship that have brought over $200,000, half the peak price for rare French examples but still much more than most people are prepared to spend. Armchairs for more than $30,000 and highboys at $75,000 make it clear why faking and repairing may be profitable. If an example is simple but finely made, it can cost a lot less and still be authentic. Nonetheless, it is getting more and more important to take the time to examine a piece at length before making a purchase. Careful inspection with the naked eye and an inquiring mind is as good as using any special machine. Fakers can rarely get proportions right if they concentrate on the carving; or the proportions may be excellent but the carving peculiar. If the carving is blurred to make it look older, beware. Aging that appears to have a pattern, and wear spots in places not likely to be subjected to wear should be cause for caution. Bottoms darkened with paint are often recent wood never colored with age. The smell of new wood or fresh varnish might suggest that a piece is not as pristine as it might be.

NEOCLASSICAL DESIGNS: LOUIS XVI, ADAM, SHERATON, HEPPLEWHITE, FEDERAL

The budget-minded collector is still likely to recoil in surprise at the work of this period, although prices are much lower than for the best rococo. Average examples of rococo and neoclassical are much closer to each other in price than superb examples will be. A brief summary of the work of the period may serve as a guide in avoiding spurious pieces and might alert the collector to something more than worthwhile in Aunt Sophie's parlor. Not so very long ago, neoclassical furniture was selling at prices low enough for Aunt Sophie to have purchased something as a substitute for something new, or to have acquired it as leftover furniture when she bought the house.

Neoclassicism was an international phe-nomenon. Its roots can be traced to a group of artists and architects of many nationalities who were in Rome in the early eighteenth century. The earliest successful neoclassical designs appeared in England and France, and there is some disagreement about which came first. The initial efforts date from the 1750's, but it was close to 1770 before neoclassical furniture was made in any quantity. By then it was made on both sides of the Channel. Whatever its specific form, the neoclassical vogue implies designs based on simple geometrical elements: circles, ovals, rectangles and squares. Straight, tapering legs, either round or square in cross section, were characteristic. Neoclassicism in a fundamental sense was a rebellion against the rococo, and as such it reached back toward the classical. Its first outcropping was in architecture, and it arrived under the leadership of the English architect Robert Adam (1728–92) and a group of French intellectuals, of which another architect, Jacques Germaine Soufflot (1713–80), was a member.

The new style put an end to the liberties that had been taken with classical design since the start of the seventeenth century. The small scale of the rococo was saved, and most of the same forms were used, but this new furniture was decorated with delicate ornaments based on Roman models. Curving legs and scalloped tops were forgotten; straight legs with straight, round or oval tops came into style.

English and French neoclassical furniture designs differ in about the same way that the two rococo designs differ: The French approach was more flamboyant and involved more virtuoso craftsmanship; the English was more practical and restrained and sought high style without extravagance.

In Paris, neoclassical furniture was introduced before the coronation of Louis XVI in 1774, even though the style usually bears his name. Inlays and gilt bronze, or ormolu, mounts were important vehicles for decoration as they had been earlier, but crisp Roman patterns became the motifs. The new taste for delicate ornamentation inspired use of porcelain and lacquer plaques for surface decoration. Designs from the beginning of the century—Louis XIV styles—were revived,

Secretary, Louis XVI style, Paris, about 1790, made of thuya, purple wood, mahogany, satinwood, ebony veneers on oak with porcelain and marble. Consistency in the design and the crispness of detail differentiate the masterpieces of neoclassicism from later reproductions made in Paris between 1860 and 1880.

Armchair, by George Jacob, Louis XVI style, Paris, about 1780, made of carved and gilded wood. The straight lines and intricate details are typical of the neoclassical. The embroidered silk upholstery repeats the classical themes on a larger scale and is in the style of Philippe de Lasalle, the best-known French silk designer of the neoclassical style.

62   since they also were classical in tone. The turned trumpet-shaped foot reappeared and cabinets close in style to those of the Louis XIV period were made again during the years of Louis XVI. Top-quality work from this period is very expensive, and $100,000 price tags are hardly deemed newsworthy since they are so much lower than those for the Louis XV rarities. Even nineteenth-century reproductions now cost in the thousands, since they are remarkably well made. It should go without saying that the chances of finding bargains in French court furniture are very slight. The only reason for optimism lies in the fact that a lot was sold and shipped out of France during the early nineteenth century, and some of it has since disappeared.

Side table, Adam style, English, about 1780, made of mahogany. Carving is more delicate in neoclassical furniture than in the earlier rococo and the effect is more linear. The rams' heads are encountered on fine examples.

opposite
Painted walnut secretary, French, about 1780

Conceivably there are pieces cached in attics in Colorado or Vladivostok. A few years ago at an auction of the furnishings of a splendid Brooklyn movie palace, several fine marked examples of French eighteenth-century furniture turned up. Evidently they had been in the movie lobby for decades without anyone's suspecting that they were the real thing. But more often, mediocre reproductions are displayed prominently in the grand parlors of movie moguls who think they have the true palace treasure.

Neoclassicism continued in vogue through and after the French Revolution. But the new government inspired simpler ornament and designs, reflecting increased interest in archeology. Between the Revolution and Napoleon the government of France went through several phases, and one of them gave its name, Directoire, to the furniture that was then popular.

In England, the approach of neoclassical designers was close to that of their French colleagues, but, since the tradition was different, so were the results. There is, however, a small amount of English furniture made in the French way. Handsomely inlaid commodes with gilt bronze mounts were made by some of the finer London cabinetmakers. Painted decoration was more popular in England than in France, and restrained designs seem more common than flamboyant ones.

The architect Adam designed the first English neoclassical furniture for use in rooms he conceived. Much of this was of mahogany and it largely followed in the English tradition, although the motifs were new. He also produced some furniture painted in patterns inspired by the frescoes of Herculaneum and Pompeii. Adam's sideboard was quickly taken up by other English designers.

To the novice, two names—Hepplewhite and Sheraton—loom large in English neoclassical, and their fame represents an anomalous situation. George Hepplewhite (?–1786) was a London cabinetmaker and designer, and Thomas Sheraton (1751–1806) was a designer who never even had a shop of his own. Their fame stems from two books, rather than from anything they built. Their books (Hepplewhite's appeared in 1788, Sheraton's in 1791), like Chippendale's, recorded and documented the designs of their times. These days Hepplewhite is credited with the shieldback chair and Sheraton with the rectangular-back neoclassical chair. Hepplewhite is associated with complex forms used with inlays, and Sheraton with simpler designs that were frequently relieved by delicate carving. Nonetheless, these two men were basically documenters, and for this reason their books overlap to a considerable degree.

In the late 1700's, hundreds of London shops were producing fashionable furniture. Unfortunately, most of what has survived bears no maker's mark, so attribution is all but impossible. Thus it is a convenience for dealers to be able to refer to "Hepplewhite," "Sheraton" and "Adam" as differentiated versions of the neoclassical, with the silent understanding that the manufacture is English.

Mahogany continued to be the wood English craftsmen used for fine furniture through the neoclassical period, although light-colored woods such as satinwood and maple were often used when painted decoration was to be added. Inlaid ornamentation increased, some of it simple and almost geometric abstractions of classical subjects. Veneers were introduced in contrasting colors, and wood grains became the highlights of simple pieces. There were few new forms in this period, but familiar forms underwent a number of variations. Small tables were made in greater numbers and embellished forms like the lady's desk and the work table became common in many neoclassical rooms. The cellarette for storing bottles and the

opposite
Painted side chair, Hepplewhite style,
Philadelphia, 1796

Side chair, Hepplewhite style, English, about 1785, made of mahogany and painted. Drapery swags, ribbons, feathers and a variety of architectural motifs were used as decoration on shield-back chairs. Paint is less usual than plain carving, or carving and inlays. Tapering fluted legs ending in plain feet are customary.

sideboard for storing silver and other small precious objects appear to have been inventions of this time.

Hepplewhite and Sheraton designs were used by several large furniture manufacturers in England in the 1880's and later. Since these late pieces were mass-produced, they tend to be constructed poorly with decoration not so detailed as on the originals. Simplified English designs made when neoclassical was first fashionable are finely put together. It is important to inspect these construction details because a ninety-year-old reproduction will show signs of age that can be deceiving.

Federal furniture, made by American craftsmen after the Revolution, was much closer to English models than to the French forms. The Americans however tended to be less elaborate in their use of classical motifs, though there exist some examples as handsomely inlaid or carved as their English prototypes. Americans did avoid the more elaborate painted decoration, though they occasionally used paint on Adam designs. On the one hand there are American examples right out of the design books, and on the other, familiar old forms are combined by cabinetmakers with the latest taste in carved decoration. Samuel McIntyre, a woodcarver from Salem, Mass., active in the early 1800's, was responsible for sofas having the camelback forms of Chippendale style framed with the latest neoclassical carving. Work by McIntyre, or even his poorest contemporary imitators, is not often encountered. Card tables and a variety of small tables with the characteristic American simplicity do turn up, however, and prices from $250 to $1,000 will buy respectable though probably not great pieces.

The desk with an upper section for books was created as an updated version of the Chippendale design, but it was more elaborate, with side sections added so that it looks more like what we call a breakfront today. Either type is generally handsomely veneered and may be embellished with inlays. New England, particularly Salem and Boston, was a center of their production.

The most famous American cabinetmaker, Duncan Phyfe, began his career in New York in 1790 and worked until about 1840. Typical Phyfe designs were neoclassical in style, and many resemble Sheraton's suggestions. Phyfe

a

a
Side chair, Sheraton style, English, about 1795, made of West Indian satinwood, beech and birch. Painted polychrome decoration was fashionable on late eighteenth-century furniture in lightwoods. The rectangular back with swags, the drum seat and tapering round legs are characteristic Sheraton elements; these are generally thinner in proportion in the reproductions made as early as the 1880's.

b
Sideboard, Sheraton style, made of mahogany with light wood inlays, probably by John and Thomas Seymour, Boston, about 1810. The neoclassical emphasis on surface ornament led the Seymours and many other American craftsmen to use veneers and inlays on their furniture. The band of half-moons just under the top, the pilasters on the center section and the ivory urns around the four main keyholes are all details characteristic of the style, as is the low relief carving on the legs.

b

Window seat, Sheraton style, possibly by Duncan Phyfe, New York, about 1815, made of mahogany with caned seat and sides. Reeded frames were popular on New York furniture of the early 1800's and on the English Regency models that were being followed.

preferred delicate carving to inlays. The Phyfe chair, with curving back based on the Greek klismos design, comes from a Sheraton book of 1803. The chair was related to a phase of neoclassicism first seen in France in designs associated with the Directoire style.

Phyfe was distinguished by his use of adventuresome designs that recall those of London and Paris cabinetmakers more clearly than those of his American contemporaries in Boston or Baltimore. This English-Continental approach has come to be called the New York style. Since Phyfe furniture was extremely popular at the turn of the century, a number of later reproductions have survived, but a museum is now the most likely place to see real Phyfe work.

EMPIRE, REGENCY, BIEDERMEIER AND OTHERS

A second phase of neoclassicism began on the Continent about 1780. Designers began producing furniture that recalled Greek and Roman prototypes, rather than simply echoing Greco-Roman ornaments on whatever they happened to be making. A steady interest in ancient art underlay this new phase of neoclassicism, and cabinetmakers hastened to display their fresh historical awareness. Faint glimmerings of the new approach can be seen in the French Directoire designs, but it was Napoleon who aroused full expression of this new style. Napoleon took the symbolism of Rome seriously, re-enacting the career of Caesar and posing with laurel leaves and all. The first Roman-style furnishings, in fact, were commissioned by

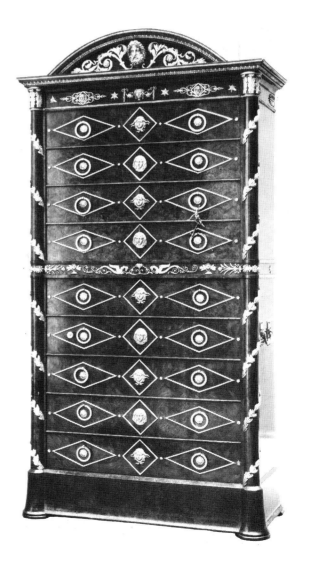

Desk, Empire style, Paris, 1805–15, made of amboyna wood with ormolu mounts. Empire design generally involves heavy proportions, strong contrasts and classical motifs. Parisian examples have the best-executed bronze mounts. Later nineteenth-century bronze is apt to be thin or badly detailed.

the painter David for background in his portraits.

This Empire style developed in a truly imperial manner, with designers Percier and Fontaine creating furniture-to-order for the Emperor Napoleon. Curiously, Empire ultimately became the most enduring middle-class style of all time, lasting until 1850. In France, Empire was a sharp shift from earlier notions of classicism. The scale of furniture from this period is large and heavy, as the delicacy of earlier neoclassicism gives way to monumentality. Huge expanses of rich dark wood are decorated in gold, and Roman models are used wherever possible; the much drawn-upon klismos becomes the basis for side chairs and armchairs. Ornaments are Roman, too, with caryatids, lion's head columns and a host of other motifs decorating pedestal tables and chests of drawers.

Ironically for modern buyers, the later nineteenth-century revival of Empire was a little lighter, a little less ponderous than the original. The ormolu is more delicate and the pieces themselves more slender. Thus, before buying an outrageously expensive chair purportedly from the room of Napoleon himself at Malmaison, you should try to make sure that it is not from the revival period.

The English version of Empire is called Regency, after the Prince Regent's reign from 1811 to 1820, but the furniture itself is usually considered to date from about 1800 to 1830. The English style is lighter than the French, and is a continuation of the English furniture-making tradition that combines an emphasis on fine woods with restrained but fine design and construction. Regency furniture seems to encompass some unusually flamboyant work as well as some that is particularly simple. Besides Greek and Roman forms that follow the boldest Greco-Roman models, often painted a blackish green to suggest antique bronze, there are colorful Chinese designs. The Empire period saw extensive importation from the Orient, and the imports included furniture. Oriental bamboo pieces competed with false bamboo made in England; on both, lacquer panels are inserted in cabinets. In either phase of the style, parlor sets were popular, and various embellished and decorative cabinets were introduced. A taste for strong contrasts was expressed in brass inlay and painted or stenciled ornament on the very dark rosewood that was used as often as mahogany.

Since much of this furniture is painted, it is important to be cautious about what the paint covers. English dealers believe in making things pretty, and they do not care how original the surface of a piece may be. When I complained about the newness of almost every detail on a cabinet I was trying out in a London apartment, the dealer scoffed at me for being a purist—and his shop was on Bond Street, where the going prices are gold.

Before 1830 there was extensive production of simple but stylish pieces that can often be found at bargain prices today. Well made but plain furniture, cut in just the right classical patterns, is well worth looking for, if the form suits you.

The German-Austrian version of Empire design furniture was dubbed Biedermeier by a later generation that equated the furniture with one Papa Biedermeier, a comic character used in Viennese newspapers as a caricature of the well-to-do bourgeois; he was a synthesis of everything middle class and tasteless. The style is actually much better. Although some belated examples were dull and badly made, between 1810 and 1830 the classical design was handled as well in the German-speaking world as anywhere. German and Austrian designs may be a bit flashier than English or French, and tend to have thicker ormolu, with more detailed designs that glow just a little extra against very dark woods. In plainer examples, the basic shapes are usually exaggerated.

opposite
Center table, mahogany base with specimen marble top, Empire style, by A. G. Quervelle, Philadelphia, about 1830

American Empire is a period where a new collector can make very interesting discoveries. Empire-style examples are somewhat more readily available than earlier work, although interest is now great enough for the really fine and elaborate pieces to be well above the bargain level. A rare white marble-topped side table, with handsomely carved legs, is tagged at $22,500. An important sideboard with stenciled decoration brings $5,000. Still, tall, marble-topped tables designed to go between windows—pier tables —can be found for a few hundred dollars, and a number of other plain examples can be found at comparably low prices.

Among the most elegant American works in the Empire style are examples attributed to Charles-Honoré Lannuier, who came to America from France at the beginning of the nineteenth century. He favored elaborate caryatid and swan supports and applied lots of ormolu representing mythological subjects. Elegant sets of parlor and bedroom furniture by Lannuier evoke their French counterparts, but the restraint so evident behind all the glitter shows a distinctively American touch.

American Empire furniture is often elaborately carved in classical patterns. Sofas with scroll-ends and curving feet are frequently embellished with cornucopia, lion's-paw feet and acanthus leaves, all of them quite thick. Imposing but a little too narrow to be comfortable, this classical sofa design is common. The Empire-style version of the klismos, a bit thicker and plainer than the earlier version, was popular and is still relatively common. Both chairs and sofas were often reproduced in this mode at the turn of the century, and more recent models are easier to find than early nineteenth-century ones. One form that is often a bargain, because it is hard to use today, is the wardrobe.

The most neglected phase of Empire style is the very plain furniture made from about 1830 to 1860. These pieces have monumentality and simplicity. The parts look as if they had been cut out with minimal effort, and there is neither carving nor other embellishment. When properly finished, these pieces are elegant; but, too often, when they do turn up, they are in bad shape. If the veneer is secure, you sometimes only have to remove old varnishes to show a fine piece. There are some notable values in plain Empire furniture, because much of it still costs less than new furniture.

VICTORIAN

Victorian is a catch-all phrase. The monarch who gave her name to this era reigned from the 1830's to the early twentieth century, and furniture styles inevitably went through several phases in a period that long. Since the nineteenth century was one of great artistic turmoil, marked by many attempts to revive earlier styles, the picture is further complicated.

Most of the period was marked by historical awareness, and the waves of revivals of earlier styles are linked to this. Early in the period, Gothic revival was a prevailing mode, and the reformers who spurred it were affected by a contemporary religious movement that was fighting what appeared to be the heathen influence of ancient Greece and Rome. These reformers, spearheaded by the English designer Pugin and by John Ruskin, saw Gothic as more functional and natural than neoclassicism or Empire. But despite their philosophical beliefs, they had little real impact on the basic concept of furniture; most of the Gothic revival is seen in the ornamentation. The pointed arch, tracery and other Gothic architectural elements were simply applied to Empire forms. They were also used as a basis for more innovative designs, which have the small scale and intricacy of most work done in reaction to the Empire. Either way, the reformers must have been aghast—their arguments for simplicity and functionalism were completely ignored.

By the 1840's there was an interest in reviving seventeenth-century styles, although examples of this impulse are easier to find in architecture than in furniture. This revival, called Elizabethan, included a number of elements, such as twisted columns, found in late seventeenth-century work.

The most popular revival style of the early Victorian period—about 1830 to 1860—is the rococo. This furniture, mostly in rosewood, is a very free adaptation of French Louis XV design; the scale is small, and many of the newer objects are more practical. Also clearly a reaction to Empire, these later rococo shapes tend to be exaggerations of eighteenth-century models. Carved ornamentation, which was usually executed with the aid of a machine but finished by hand, was frequently in high relief. Parlor and bedroom sets were made, but have rarely survived intact. The mid nineteenth-century parlor commonly had matching chairs of various sizes, a couple of sofas, a round or oval table for the center of the room, and an elaborate set of shelves for bric-a-brac. Chairs are found more often today than sofas or tables, and sets of shelves are rare because it was easier to break them up than to move them.

The rococo revival ranged from the very elaborate to the very simple. Extremely fine examples have details carved with a disarming realism; the most primitive carving is detailed, but is in the spirit of folk art, or perhaps just vaguely rendered. John Henry Belter (1804–63) is the most famous name of the rococo revival. He was an American furniture manufacturer who patented a process for bending laminated wood. Belter's

74

Cabinet, Renaissance revival, by Alexander Roux, New York, about 1866. The effect is impressive with details that are more schematic than on earlier pieces. Less important examples have incised gilded lines but neither the inlays nor the plaques.

*Center table, rosewood base with marble top,
rococo revival, American, possibly by J. H. Belter,
about 1850*

furniture is of layers of veneer elaborately carved and steamed into shapes suitable to rococo design. Despite his patent, Belter had many imitators. But his curves and fine carving are hallmarks of his distinctive work.

Reformers deplored the rococo revival. It was showy and replete with sham, and the latest mechanical devices were used to ease its production, an affront to those espousing handwork. In a sense, the rococo revival was a return to eighteenth-century elegance, but most people who chose it as their means of reclaiming a lost grandeur were far removed from the "great families." If you want to look at it that way, rococo revival is one manifestation of the increasing availability of luxuries during the nineteenth century.

Folding chair, by G. Hunzinger, New York, about 1866, made of walnut. The stamped patent mark suggests the date. Patent chairs are relatively easy to find but rarely with the original upholstery.

Another Victorian style that did little to cheer reformers was the Renaissance revival. It was based mainly on French models of the 1500's, with added elements from eighteenth-century neoclassical styles and from ancient Rome. This revival was at a peak as the rococo revival faded. Renaissance revival furniture comes in a broad range of designs since it was made expensively by traditional cabinetmakers in New York, London and Paris, as well as mass-produced by factories in Grand Rapids. The earliest examples are ornamented with carving—hanging game and fish on a sideboard, for example. Later, surface decoration became more important, with patterns of inlay, ormolu and porcelain plaques featured on more expensive pieces, and inscribed linear decorations, highlighted in gold, used on mass-produced items. Walnut predominates over the darker rosewood of the rococo revival.

The nineteenth-century fascination with gadgets and inventions gave rise to a number of patent chairs—spring rockers and folding chairs of every variety. Since it was deemed something of a coup to obtain a patent, a number of manufacturers stamped their patents on everything they made. G. Hunzinger, for example, won several patents for folding chairs, and so now one finds the numbers and dates of those patents even on plain, straight chairs that will crack if they are folded.

The tubular bentwood chair is a nineteenth-century design that has never looked antique because it is still made and used in quantity. Bentwood has been used for making tables and chairs since the 1830's. The largest early manufacturer was the inventor Michael Thonet, whose factories were in Austria-Hungary; distribution was extensive, so his products might as easily be found now in Ceylon as in Wisconsin. The most popular form is the rocker, and examples made between 1880 and 1900 seem the most decorative, with tubes twisted into the delightful patterns needed for strength. A lot of bentwood is still being made in Italy these days, but old pieces command a premium because they are better looking. The Italian version is a flattened imitation put together sloppily. Even Thonet's own modern products are a little too plain, but at least they are substantial.

MORRIS, EASTLAKE AND LATER

The reaction against revivals that was strong in the 1880's can be traced back to about 1860, when the English reformer William Morris (1834–96) began campaigning for good design. Morris was upset by the prevalence of sham and the wide use of machines to counterfeit fine work. He decried the flamboyance of the rococo and Renaissance revivals, and his solution was to return to simpler medieval and Gothic designs—although his writings make his vision seem virtually Bauhaus. The wooden-framed easy chair with an adjustable back that is named for Morris may be considered representative of "Morris design," though he himself was personally responsible for the execution of only one of them. The style was still being used extensively at the turn of the century on both sides of the Atlantic. In fact, one early Sears, Roebuck catalogue—in a burst of misplaced patriotism—referred to Morris as "the American Chippendale."

Charles Eastlake's book, *Hints on Household Taste*, published in England in 1867, popularized the Morris philosophy. Eastlake's book is a guide to practical application of Morris's ideas to the problems of furnishing a home. Its designs betray a variety of Renaissance and Gothic influences, but the style it augured was soon to become a much more ambitious combination of disparate elements. This style, now called Eastlake in the United States, is called Cottage Queen Anne, or just Queen Anne, in England, although it arose a good century after the Queen's time. The Queen Anne designation came about because cottages of the early eighteenth century helped to inspire many of these nineteenth-century designs. Eastlake-Queen Anne employs Near Eastern and oriental motifs in designs having something of a Gothic quality. Wood textures are exploited through use of thin strips of wood in straight or herringbone patterns. The more elaborate efforts included decorative panels of inlay or pottery tiles, with ebony sometimes being used on the richest of these works.

This furniture was mass-produced in quantity, so the collector's only really serious problem today is to find examples that have not been remodeled.

At about this time, a group of art furniture manufacturers began producing elegant pieces in roughly the same taste. Japanese and Near Eastern influences can be discerned in some of this work, and the craftsmanship is quite fine. Continental and English examples are easier to find than American.

Even while Eastlake was inveighing against meaningless revivals of early styles, the United States entered an era of affluence that set off a splurge of houses in Renaissance and baroque styles. This change set furniture-makers to producing designs of Renaissance taste, replete with ostentatious carving. This work is closer to the original than was the revival of a few decades earlier. The pieces are large, the carving is impressive, and—for a bonus—the prices today are still low: $50 for a table, for instance. Where the work is on a smaller scale it generally dates from the 1920's. The best-known architects of the

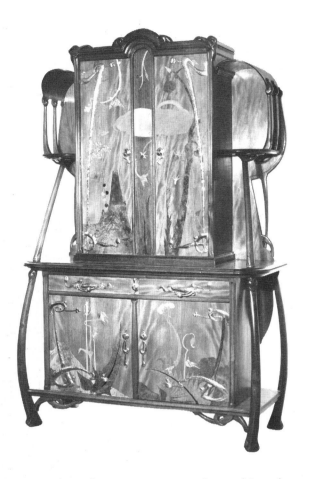

Cabinet, Art Nouveau style, by Louis Bruhot, Paris, about 1900, made of walnut with exotic inlays. New shapes have been introduced in a number of details, such as the backs of the shelves, the legs and the brass drawer pulls and hinges. The inspiration for most of the motifs is flowers.

period, such as McKim, Mead & White, designed houses with rooms in many styles. The Breakers, built in Newport about 1898, has rooms ranging from the Renaissance to Louis XVI. And the excellent furniture made for it is closer to the original styles than anything earlier, though there are interesting variations. Similar furniture of varying quality turns up occasionally, but as second-hand furniture rather than as antiques.

While the traditional designs of the turn of the century are generally ignored these days, work in the style called Art Nouveau is more expensive and coveted than almost anything else from the nineteenth century. Prices for Art Nouveau begin at about $200 for a chair and rise to nearly $10,000 for a par-

ticularly unusual cupboard. French Art Nouveau commands the highest price, because it is the style's most elegant manifestation. Louis Majorelle, Hector Guimard and a host of others created sinuous forms elaborately decorated in inlays and carving that expressed perfectly the decadence of the end of the century. German, Austrian, and even Eastern European versions of the style are more angular and much less elegant. Works from these countries have the same elongated forms; although lacking fine carving or inlays they have their own kind of charm and have been coming on the market at much lower prices than the French.

An American named Gustave Stickley made furniture of note at the beginning of the cen-

Cabinet, Art Deco style, by E. J. Ruhlmann,
Paris, 1926, made of macassar ebony and ivory.
Louis XVI design has been simplified but
craftsmanship is superb in the inlays and
veneers. Other Art Deco pieces are apt to be in
more innovative shapes and more simply made.

tury, following the Morris doctrine. Straight and simple oak pieces by Stickley show construction traits similar to those of medieval times. Stickley began his career as a furniture manufacturer, and his later role as a reformer was affected by this. Stickley expressed his ideas in a magazine that he founded called *The Craftsman,* which offered workable designs for those who preferred making their own furniture to buying his. Although Stickley used the name Craftsman for his designs, his style became more popularly called Mission because it was considered appropriate for California missions. The connection is vague, but the name stuck. Between 1905 and 1915, manufacturers in Grand Rapids produced large quantities of pieces similar to Stickley's but not so carefully constructed. Mission-Craftsman is usually made of oak and it looks strong.

Elbert Hubbard, another reformer influenced by Morris, founded a group called the Roycrafters around the beginning of the century. The Roycrafters produced furniture in the Craftsman style, among other things. Both Craftsman and Roycrafter examples have been collected seriously and are now rare.

Oak furniture made by large manufacturers in the United States and on the Continent was sometimes fashioned in the same spirit and at other times was completely eclectic. It is easy to find and often amusing to use. The prices are about equal to those for decent modern furniture.

And now we are not talking about antiques at all, but about furniture familiar to us from our childhoods. Collectors find it hard to get interested in work this close to them. The bedroom furniture your parents bought when they were married, you are perfectly sure, has no place in your home. You may reason that, after all, design was in a sorry state at that time—but you can be sure your attitude is quite the same as that of the children of 1800, 1750, 1910, or any other moment in history. It seems to take a generation or two of aging for designs to pass from being merely out of date to being a wonderful rediscovery. By and large, Granny's dresser is more interesting than Mother's. The rare exceptions to this rule are occasional radical departures and unusual statements—Art Nouveau and Art Deco for two—that were mostly ignored when new.

Think carefully, look closely and for a long time before you start collecting furniture. Try to dissociate sentiment from design; a house you were happy in may have contained grisly furniture, while your dislike of another might have blinded you to enduring examples of good design. A change of heart in furniture can be very wearing, especially if you have to move your mistakes by yourself.

Dressing table, Art Deco style, by Albert Rateau, Paris, 1925, made of bronze. The peacocks supporting the mirror frame have been simplified in a way typical of the 1920's. Occasionally the designs are bolder and more geometric. Iron as well as bronze was used for elaborate furniture.

Textiles

RAGS TO RUGS

Collecting textiles is not so easy as it was thirty years ago, when a group of genteel New York women known fondly as "the rag ladies" sold yardages of antique fabrics for use in decorating. The supplies have dwindled, most of the women are gone, and only the fabrics themselves seem to have changed little. The draperies Marie Antoinette used at Versailles will hold their color much longer than the new ones you bought last year; chemicals introduced into the dying process in the early 1800's resulted in more fugitive colors. Fragments of fabric that have survived several centuries will carry on for quite a while yet if they are kept clean and are not scrubbed into oblivion—or seized, as a prized linen sheet of mine almost was, for Halloween costumes by children.

The collecting of textiles, from rare silks to cotton to tapestries to needlework wall hangings and patterned wools and rugs, should really interest more people than it does. Textiles document the evolution of taste as well as any type of old objects, and they are durable and compact.

Blue-resist printed cotton, an eighteenth-century example whose origin is unknown. Samples have been found in New York, but the material was not made there. The possibilities of English or Indian manufacture have been raised.

FABRICS

Old fabrics are most likely to be found today in pieces about the size of a table. At the turn of the century, when the idea of collecting antiques was just coming into fashion, old fabrics were popular as table scarves; many larger pieces were cut up and fringed or hemmed and used as an embellishment for big or little tables or the piano. Most of these scarves are silk, but wool, linen and cotton were also important fibers when the fabrics were first made. Sometimes the pattern was woven in reversibly, in a damask, or just on one side, in a brocade; sometimes it was embroidered on after the fabric was woven. Some of these fabrics seem uninteresting today, but others can remind even experts of elements of design that have otherwise been forgotten.

A simple example is the evolution of the pomegranate motif. The Renaissance pomegranate of the 1500's appears on silks as a staid-looking and symmetrical fruit. In the 1600's the baroque designers added a suggestion of shadow and life. In the 1700's it acquires graceful flourishes that give it a more realistic look. The pomegranate fell from favor in the late 1700's but reappeared in the 1800's with some perspective added.

Although there are other motifs that can be traced in this way, it is probably a more interesting exercise to concentrate on elements of design that are peculiar to their time. For example, scroll, leaf and flower combinations in the rococo spirit of the 1740's and 1750's appeared again when the rococo was revived, from the middle of the

Brocaded velvet, Italian, 1450–1500. The flower and rosette motifs are typical of the fifteenth century. Small-scale patterns were also important in the sixteenth century. Velvet is a pile fabric with patterns made by cutting away the pile.

1880's on. Trellis designs and small repeating flower motifs were first popular in the 1770's and 1780's. From 1800 to 1840, large-scale classical motifs had their day. Picking up these fragments that have been made into table scarves is not a costly pursuit; $10 to $50 is the price range. You may find yourself exploring some curious hideaways as these fragments grow more scarce.

Fabrics with printed or painted decoration seem never to have found favor as table scarves; these have usually survived in smaller pieces. The fabrics were more often created for upholstery or for wall hangings. Sometimes prized examples were later framed and hung. Many of the designs are exotic and can be traced to a tree pattern that was commonly used on fabrics made and hand painted in India for export to the West. These popular Indian designs inspired the French and English fabric makers, who used woodblocks and later copper-plate printing to render the tree in reds, deep purple, greens and blues that come close to capturing the spirit of the originals. The tree, usually called Indian Tree, with leaves, flowers and birds that are curiously distinctive, forms the large center motif on a typical hanging. When the tree motif was used on upholstery or dress material, it was condensed into an over-all pattern. Examples from India from about 1700 will be priced at $2,000 and over; nineteenth-century pieces are $100 to $300.

Printed textiles also frequently have pictorial decorations, and in the eighteenth cen-

Silk brocatelle, Spanish, seventeenth century. Flowers enclosed in a kind of floral wreath are typical seventeenth-century motifs. Designs become more complex and less forceful in nineteenth- and twentieth-century reproductions.

Cut and voided velvet, Genoese, about 1700. A polychrome floral design relatively smaller in scale reflects the approach of eighteenth-century designers. Patterns are more complex than in the previous century but not as detailed as in later ones.

Brocaded satin, Venetian, 1700–50. Rococo fantasy inspired scenic designs with ships or figures. In the brocade the pattern is woven into the individual sections so that a group of loose threads is seen on the reverse side.

*Block-printed cotton, English, about 1780.
The trees and flowers were obviously borrowed
from the painted cottons of India. Both French
and English cottons of the eighteenth century
repeated Indian designs.*

Copper-plate printed cotton, English, about 1785. French and English cottons were made in a variety of patterns, with scenes and figures reflecting the taste and political sentiments of the time. Reproductions have been made for many years, but recent copies are smaller in scale than original designs.

tury the French and English cotton manufacturers used copper-plate engravings to create scenes that often make a political statement. American Revolutionary War heroes appear on some. Other samples are more in the rococo or neoclassical mood. In the nineteenth century glazed fabrics were used for colorful patterns that reflect the taste of the period. In hunting these fabrics the trick is to find a piece large enough to give a clear idea of the pattern. This was easy from 1900 to the 1930's—you could have upholstered an entire room in what you found. Now you have done your work if you succeed in unearthing a sample that documents the style. Small pieces often cost less than $100.

LACE

If you were to walk into an antique shop today and say you are a lace collector, jaws would drop in wonderment. However, not so long ago there were quantities of old lace available, and pieces that have significance do emerge from time to time. Although lace-making attracts little attention these days, as recently as the 1930's many shops were making lace by hand. The result was sold along with the machine products, which were first introduced in the middle of the nineteenth century.

In the sixteenth century lace designs were based on published embroidery designs. For all practical purposes the sixteenth century offers just about the oldest gems, although the origins of lace can be traced to ancient

Brussels lace (part of flounce), about 1700. The small-scale over-all pattern is characteristic of the time. Bobbin lace gets a bit thinner later on. Repeats in the pattern will show variations each time a motif is used.

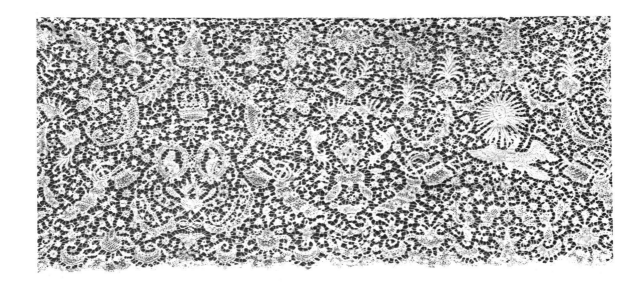

Brussels lace (corner of coverlet), 1805–15. Bobbin lace at the beginning of the nineteenth century was made in precise bold patterns. While the flowers have come from Indian cottons, the border is classical and in the spirit of the Empire style. The same details have been applied in needlework.

times. Early designs tend to be thick, almost schematic and in classical patterns. Early lace, called needle lace, is generally made by a simple technique: a single stitch is worked with a single thread on a parchment or heavy paper bearing the design. One type of needle lace, Punto Tagliato, is applied on a linen ground, but most are stitched freely in patterns that are essentially linear. A later technique, bobbin lace, is more complicated: many threads, each wound around a bobbin or small spool, are worked on a pillow by imaginative intertwining of the threads. The results are more elaborate, and often there is a ground of fine meshlike lace under the ornament. The ornament itself includes classical figures and architectural elements. Whether abstract or naturalistic, lace patterns are richly varied. Many reflect trends in fashion, but often the virtuosity of the maker is dominant. Although borders and small panels made by hand form a special group that is very much admired, there is less disdain now for the better machine work and it is beginning to become important. Prices are difficult to estimate on lace; there is not much competition for even fine examples. The range is about $20 to $200, but top dealers may offer much costlier pieces.

TAPESTRIES

One of the many areas where current prices suggest that we are just a little late is tapestries. Only ten years ago dealers found it hard to sell tapestries and the prices were a fraction of what they had been in the nineteenth and early twentieth centuries. When tapestries were popular there was constant talk of the rarity of good examples, but in the 1940's and 1950's there was no market at all and tapestries were virtually discarded. In 1959 a decorator was about to have a fine eighteenth-century example glued onto a screen for my brother, because it was cheaper than wallpaper, and he desisted only when I protested. Not long after that incident, interest in tapestries began to revive in Germany. This concern spread quickly over the Continent and to the United States. Now try to find a fine example at less than the price of wallpaper!

Tapestries, cloth woven in a design that is usually pictorial, are most often found in wool, but there are examples in silk, linen and cotton. The technique is ancient, although documented examples from the earliest times are all but impossible to find. One early type that does sometimes turn up, usually in fragments, is Coptic tapestry. This Egyptian work, from the third to the sixth century, characteristically has borders of stylized classical animals in roundels. Aside from the Coptic fragments, the earliest tapestries the collector is likely to find are the fifteenth-century Gothic examples. These are made on a large scale with interesting figures against schematic backgrounds. Lavish use of

Tapestry fragment, Coptic, fifth to sixth century. Abstracting classical motifs such as dancing figures was typical of Coptic workmanship. Small pieces from private collections turn up, although Coptic fragments are rare.

Tapestry representing the Annunciation, Flemish, early fifteenth century. Gothic tapestries in good condition are rare. Scenes should be simple and consistent. Late nineteenth-century copies have more intricate details. Another problem is afforded by pieces that have been cut down and parts of scenes rewoven or painted to look like a unit.

Tapestry with coats of arms of France and
Navarre, Gobelins, late seventeenth century.
The fleur-de-lis and chain border make up a
frame that is as thick as the prominent moldings
around chimneys of the period. The juxtaposition
of cupids, garlands, draperies and arms suggests
the classical mood then fashionable.

trees and flowers and over-all floral patterns characterize these works.

The Renaissance brought classical ornament into tapestries. In Italian examples bold, colorful fruit garlands often form the border and the figures in the middle are bold and forthright with carefully worked details. The French examples are much like the Italian and can usually be distinguished only by experts. The baroque tapestries of the seventeenth century generally have classical subjects and classical details. The designs seem to have more suggestion of movement and more grandeur than those of the century before. The borders are spiral-turned columns or lavish swags of drapery or garlands that drip into the center. The scenes, often from Roman history, seem dramatic because all of the figures appear to be in motion, rather than posing. Some seventeenth-century tapestries have symbols or marks in the corner to denote the maker.

The tapestries of the eighteenth century are lighter in scale; the borders resemble picture frames and the scene takes up proportionately more space or is broken up into small pictures that are carefully arranged, as on a wall. The great tapestry houses of France—Gobelins, Aubusson and Beauvais—make their appearance at this time and the quality of their craftsmanship has kept prices of their works high. Eighteenth-century tapestries were often based on paintings—both seventeenth-century and contemporary examples. Where the source is the seventeenth century—Dutch genre paintings, for example—the tapestries seem weak to our eyes. In the 1920's such tapestries brought $12,000, but today they are more likely to go for $3,000. A tapestry based on a Boucher painting of a mythological subject seems more appealing to us and consequently it costs more. The verdures, plain green landscapes of the eighteenth century, represent another field that seems to have a lesser appeal today. These are not so dull as they seem initially and can represent a good buy.

Today's most neglected tapestries are those of the nineteenth century. At the start of the twentieth century one writer noted that Americans were paying $500 a pound for tapestries not 100 years old. These pieces were not all bad and bear investigation at the more reasonable prices they now bring. The spirit of most of these is seventeenth- or

Tapestry, "La Collation" from "Fêtes Italiennes," a series after François Boucher, French, 1762. Eighteenth-century tapestry weavers translated design to wool by adroitly omitting details. Nineteenth-century copies are often more detailed but less carefully rendered.

eighteenth-century, but many of the designs are innovative and distinctive. The only tapestries of the nineteenth century that have commanded conspicuous attention lately are those from Merton Abbey, a house founded by the reformer William Morris, whose influence is felt extensively in the decorative arts. Morris had been thinking about tapestry as a modern medium for some time before he finally founded the works, training the craftsmen himself to avoid using anyone who worked in the traditional manner, which he typically considered decadent. He wanted to escape the Gobelins approach and get back to the fourteenth- and fifteenth-century Gothic mood. He most particularly opposed the scenery found in the verdures and sought the use of figures. Morris used some artists from the Pre-Raphaelite school, notably Burne-Jones, and the results do echo the Gothic. Nonetheless, Morris was thwarted, as he often was, in at least one instance: Merton Abbey made a tapestry that was a reproduction of Botticelli's *Primavera*. The Morris examples go in the thousands when recognized, but sometimes they are just thrown in with less respected nineteenth-

century examples that sell for under $100.

Several American tapestry makers are recorded in early twentieth-century histories, among them the Baumgarten Works of Williamsbridge, now in the northern Bronx. This house was founded in 1893 and won prizes at several international shows. The tapestries hand-made there were intended for the big houses being designed by McKim, Mead & White and Richard Morris Hunt. Baumgarten depended heavily on tradition—Gothic, baroque, rococo and neoclassical—but the interpretations have a fairly fresh look. These works have often been discarded as being too recent to be of interest, but a Baumgarten would be a worthwhile prize for its quality and as a document of an age that seems utterly remote from modern America.

An interest in tapestries has a certain prerequisite: you must have some wall space. An old house with high ceilings will often turn its owner into a tapestry aficionado, and soaring modern houses take surprisingly well to them. You may not find a sixteenth-century Renaissance work for $500 to fill the space, but you can probably locate a fine example in good condition from a later date.

NEEDLEWORK

The needlework most frequently encountered in antique shops today is in the form of nineteenth-century pictures. Typical is the mourning scene, where a doleful damsel under a weeping willow leans on an urn bearing the name and dates of the deceased. Generally this is of silk embroidery on a satin or plain silk ground. Equally popular but more likely to be found in a thrift shop than at an antique dealer are ambitious Biblical scenes popular from the 1820's to the 1850's. These have an over-all surface of stitches following a design that had been printed on the cloth ground. Both types were most often made by skilled amateurs working in the spirit of their time and are usually boring. Needlework, whether of earlier or later date, can be much more interesting when it is less standardized. Despite current shortages, examples of fourteenth-century religious work are discovered from time to time. Religious vestments have been collected since the beginning of the 1800's and they occasionally appear on the market. These often have minutely sewn delicate figures in elongated renditions characteristic of the Gothic. Details are suggested with minimal fuss. The contrast between the original work and nineteenth-century imitations is dramatic: The revival pieces have meticulously rendered details that make the work too elaborate.

Framed needlework pictures of the seventeenth and eighteenth centuries do turn up. One popular type interprets paintings or other pictures in such a way that the individ-

Needlework picture, mourning scene, American, 1803. The weeping willow was a favorite element in these scenes. Often some elements are stitched and others painted or printed on the silk ground.

opposite
Needlework picture, English, about 1710, in frame of about 1800

opposite
Chasuble, silk and gold embroidered on velvet,
English, 1300–30. Late nineteenth-century
collectors were able to find Gothic needlework
occasionally. Even though examples are
exceedingly rare, studying the design helps
clarify the approach of later craftsmen.

Stump-work frame, English, seventeenth century.
Figures were put in relief by backing; elaborate
stitches add the third dimension to wreaths
and wigs. In the eighteenth century similar
relief figures were sewn onto costume prints.

ual stitches are almost invisible. Much more attractive to modern eyes are the pictures that have a quaint charm because the boldness of the stitches has added amusing distortions. Sometimes the figures are done in relief, and then the technique is called stumpwork. The quaint pictures have also been used as the decoration for jewel boxes and frames. These were particularly popular in seventeenth-century England and have been appearing in increasing number in shops. Their prices are in the thousands. The eighteenth-century embroiderers did a kind of folk picture that also has great charm. The subjects are generally rustic or rural, with cows and possibly a river scene where fishing is the important activity. These were popular in England and were also made in the Colonies. The prevalence and durability of seventeenth- and eighteenth-century needlework is suggested by the number of bedhangings that have survived. Using designs based on the early painted cottons of India, embroiderers executed bold over-all tree patterns that were embellished with flowers, birds and at times animals. These are more often found in wool than in silk. In the 1700's those who continued making crewel, or wool, hangings worked in more delicate designs. The motifs were reduced in size and the amount of visible cloth increased. Occasionally, instead of a unified pattern, the motifs were sewn on in rows. Although it is difficult to locate whole sets for beds, pieces of crewel or silk embroidery can be found; a flower or branch and a bird or ani-

Sampler, wool on linen, Pennsylvania, 1827. Patterns showed off a young girl's skills with a needle. The most attractive examples have houses with good details. The most desirable samplers are from eighteenth century, but they were common into the mid nineteenth century. Samplers were made all over Europe and are not exclusively American.

mal will make an impressive picture when framed.

Samplers were a device for showing the sewing skills of young girls. The earliest examples are now rare, but there are quantities of nineteenth-century examples. Americans have always been too eager to concentrate on the American product; English and Continental pieces reveal great skill and have charming small pictures along with the usual alphabet and numbers. While the early work is a delight and quaint, there is much to be said for the more fashionable efforts of the 1800's. If one is prepared to pay hundreds for what was once priced at merely $40, there are some early examples available. The nineteenth-century works cost much less.

COVERLETS

Quilts and coverlets are a field filled with variety. Patchwork quilts come to mind first, but there are any number of types of bedcovers. The earliest examples are often made of patterned textiles that can be distinguished as covers only because they were cut to fit beds. There were also embroidered bedcovers with designs tailored to the bed. More significant are examples made in techniques that were devised exclusively for beds. All-white coverlets embroidered in patterns that are put into relief by stuffing, a process called candlewicking, are distinctive. The eighteenth-century examples are hard to find, but nineteenth-century versions, which have simpler patterns, are available. The all-white was particularly popular in the early

Quilt, calico patchwork, American, nineteenth century. The patches of printed cotton are an index of the age. The small patterns of dress fabric date from the 1840's and the quilt was probably made within a decade after the fabrics were new. Designs vary and so do the dates of quilts. Eighteenth-century examples are very rare.

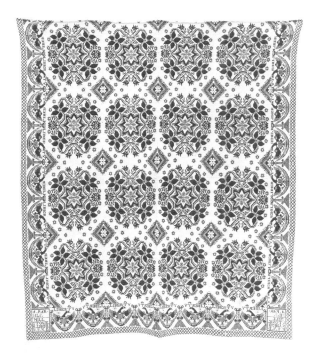

*Woven coverlet, by A. Parsils, American, 1838.
Cotton and wool were woven into reversible
patterns that frequently include patriotic
motifs. Blue is the most common color, red
next and rare examples have green
as the dark color.*

1800's. In addition to embroidering, both amateurs and professionals used a weaving technique for a geometric kind of pattern that combines raised relief ornament and flat background. Early coverlets are priced between $100 and $500. Woven coverlets made on simple looms in the early nineteenth century are another type that has become very well known. Using wool or wool and cotton, the weaver made double-width damask in a wide variety of geometric patterns. Occasionally the corner that has a signature and date will also include some additional element such as a flattened schematized landscape. For the collector who gets caught up, the designs can be carefully traced and called by name. Again, $100 will buy ordinary exam-

ples, with the rarer pieces priced much higher.

Patchwork quilts are at their peak of popularity these days. There is an interest in reviving the craft of quilt-making and a fervent quest for early examples. The quilts seem as American as pumpkins, but are not always. There are English and Irish examples that come close to the American versions. In most instances it is a good idea to forget about trying to date a patchwork quilt.

The use of odds and ends of material for decorative quilts goes back to the eighteenth century, and there are handsome examples of that period. But quilt-making has never ceased. When the farm household stopped producing, the arts and crafts studio took

Bed rug, American, 1790. Embroidered in a looped stitch, this is a very rare example of a type of bedcover that should be kept in mind by collectors. The next one will turn up in a farmhouse attic in Montana.

over. Those who know textiles can frequently date a quilt by examining the scraps and catching what they think is the latest piece. It is best to relax and simply not pay for age and rarity but for the ingeniousness of the pattern. The early examples of the eighteenth century have interesting scenes with figures. Although some exceptional nineteenth-century examples with figures exist, the more popular versions have geometrical patterns that have also been given names. Most designs were used and reused and are indigenous to many places.

RUGS

Rug collecting is changing. Even the most dedicated and knowledgeable collectors are learning to be enthusiastic about nineteenth-century examples because the sixteenth- and seventeenth-century oriental ones are so rare. Students are beginning to see that even late nineteenth-century examples have a distinctiveness and charm of their own. There is a contrast in oriental rug traditions that can help make seeking rugs simpler. Today, as in the seventeenth century and earlier, Persian carpets seem to work well and elegantly with gilt furniture. Those who like rougher execution, who prefer country furniture to fancy urban design, will find Turkish and Central Asian carpets more to their liking. Normally both are pile carpets, although the Persian is

Hooked rug by Lucy Barnard, American, nineteenth century. Cloth scraps, preferably woolen, were drawn in loops through a linen, cotton or burlap backing in a pattern. Simple, primitive landscapes are a popular subject. Often patriotic statements are included. Some date from the twentieth century, but it is design and not age that determines value.

likely to have many more threads to the inch and to seem smoother and more delicate.

Persian carpets or rugs (the terms are most frequently used interchangeably although some can make a distinction) have more naturalistic designs, with the leaf and tree patterns frequently recognizable. Curving elements are used to create abbreviated gardens. Turkish and Central Asian designs are essentially geometric. The flowers and trees are reduced to a linear pattern that is often very exciting. Close analysis of the patterns discloses, however, that the garden theme is as important in the Turkish examples as in the Persian.

In both areas rug-making took on regional characteristics, and patterns are generally

Carpet, Savonnerie, French, seventeenth century. A former soap factory became the site of the royal carpet factory in the seventeenth century. Pile rugs were made and patterns generally followed Western fashion. Flowers were realistic but in classical design rather than abstract Eastern fashion. Savonnerie carpets come in eighteenth- and nineteenth-century designs, too.

Detail, wool needlework rug, by Zeruah H. G. Caswell, Castleton, Vt., early nineteenth century

Carpet, Kazak, Caucasian, about 1900. Collectors are discovering that traditional geometric patterns are as strong in some recent examples as in early ones. Carpets of the turn of the century have a distinctive palette and distinctive designs, but they can be as successful as the seventeenth-century pieces.

Carpet, Indian, seventeenth century. Indian flowers are almost realistic in carpet designs.

named after regions where they were made. The question gets complex and a bit inaccurate in later examples, because influences crossed back and forth between centers. Also, since earlier rugs are considered more respectable than later, these newer rugs were named for earlier centers. Learning names is a lot less important than learning to look and enjoy. If you are a nut on symmetry, be careful about getting a rug with a design that is just mildly off center. The nineteenth-century craftsmen worked fast to feed their families and they were not fussy about centering designs or making them fit within the area of the rug. This adds to their charm and distinction. It is important to be careful about the condition of the rug, since repairs can be costly. At the turn of the century when many of the rugs were brand new, some people sought to make them look older. Baths with harsh chemicals were an easy way to fade a rug, but they did not help the strength of its fibers. Avoid buying an example that has obviously been antiqued with chemicals. Among the nineteenth-century examples there are many flat-woven rugs. These often have just about the same patterns as the pile carpets, and it is strictly a question of taste because the belief that pile makes a rug sturdier is debatable.

Even rarer but important are the Western-made carpets. Needlework examples from the eighteenth century occasionally turn up, but there were extensive factories for both pile and flat-woven examples in France and England in the eighteenth and nineteenth centuries. Some designs were obvious adaptations of the Turkish carpets that were admired; others were in patterns that are completely occidental. The names Aubusson and Savonnerie are linked to flat-woven and pile carpets in classical and neoclassical modes, but those two looms merely head a considerable list of weavers active all over the Continent and the British Isles. Actually most of what is available in the Louis XVI taste was made after 1850 and has more of the Victorian in it than many collectors are willing to admit. Occidental rugs made by amateurs constitute a field that offers some great finds. Needlework examples of room size are the kind of rarity to hope for but not expect. The smaller examples in primitive hooked designs are closer to reality. These were first made in the late eighteenth century, but those being made today may well be in antique shops in five years. It is not easy to date the rugs, so you should not pay a premium for age. Simply buy what is attractive at a price appropriate to the quality of design.

Ceramics

Earthenware jar, Connecticut, about 1800

CHALLENGES AND REWARDS

The art and technique of ceramics have not developed in a straightforward or logical way. The field is full of throwbacks, survivals and parallel tracks. Plain earthenware, which represents an early stage of development, is still being made; old stoneware in simple, useful forms may command remarkable prices; a porcelain cup without saucer may go for rummage.

If the story of ceramics were to be written from the standpoint of its technology, the history would be complete by the ninth century, when porcelain was developed in the Orient. Porcelain—thin, elegant and translucent—represents the greatest refinement in ceramics, an art that has not evolved substantially since that time. But the most sophisticated collectors do not necessarily concentrate on porcelain. And there is no consistent correlation between cost and either age or quality.

The area of ceramics thus provides a collector with a full range of selection, both in price and in mood. As an added attraction, there are surprises—what ought to be rare sometimes turns up for little.

The search is exciting; even the smallest town will have a barn or shop full of "old things" or rummage from people's basements that can yield a real find. Once you get away from the burnished, window-washed antique row in a town, you may find the thing you seek lying in a heap of old Mason jars. A scout in New England has discovered that increasing numbers of antique dealers, new to the trade, are so fascinated

Jar, earthenware, Egyptian, predynastic (3600–3400 B.C.). Unglazed surfaces have been decorated from earliest times. Shapes were determined by needs. The same plain reddish body is found on primitive wares made by Indians in the nineteenth century and simpler pieces of modern manufacture.

Footed cup, Etruscan bucchero ware, 610–560 B.C. Blackened terra cotta was familiar both in Greece and on the Italian peninsula from the seventh to the first century B.C. Plain or decorated in reds and whites, ware is thin and is made in a broad range of shapes.

with Gone With the Wind lamps that they don't recognize country stoneware as anything but junk and price it accordingly.

Even in the most knowledgeable shops, factors other than value affect prices. Supply and demand—and local tastes—have an impact. A late nineteenth-century American vase may be priced at $1,500, while an ancient Greek pot, simple and small but authentic, may go for $50. A rare eighteenth-century porcelain tureen from China may be $30,000, but a funerary urn from 2000 B.C. will be $3,000. Saucers without cups and other small objects from the eighteenth century may turn up at $20 to $50 in shops that put price tags of $200 on unimportant but decorative nineteenth-century pieces.

Another factor affecting price is the usefulness of an object as interior decoration. A vase unimportant in itself will be more expensive if it can be turned into a lamp base.

Objects with writing on them—a date, or particularly, a place—seem to fetch higher prices. Objects associated with a particular area are generally higher priced in that area. A vogue for a particular color may mean that the same dish in another color will be cheaper.

The novice collector should absorb two vital principles as he sets his foot upon the road. The first concerns markings, which are not the final word some dealers would like you to believe.

Pottery and porcelain, from early Chinese to recent American, often bear makers' marks in an underglaze blue, scratched in plain lines or painted over the glaze. But not everything was marked at the time it was made, and it is not difficult to add a mark later to make a piece seem rarer than it is. In the nineteenth and twentieth centuries, for example, standard symbols of major eighteenth-century factories were plagiarized to exaggerate the importance of some relatively dull work. Marks from other periods are also sometimes outright fakes.

One fact to keep in mind regarding marking is that after 1891, United States Customs required that the country of origin be noted on imports, so the indication "Made in ———" is usually a sign that a piece was made during the last eighty years.

In short, a mark can help you confirm what you have already gleaned from your examination of the piece, but you should be able to recognize authenticity without depending upon the mark.

And this is the second vital principle for the novice: Descriptions—even photographs —in books are no absolute basis for judgment. The only way to know what you're getting is to know, and there is no instant course in this. If you own an item you like or one you know is authentic, you should become intimately familiar with its feel, weight, coloration, sound, shape and detail. This heightened awareness—when you look at it you can almost feel it—will enable you to recognize its mate easily, regardless of marks, price or dealer. You simply know it is right or wrong.

This guideline is already part of the knowledge of the collector who has owned an authentic piece and a copy. With time, the too-regular surface of the fake, or its inappropriate irregularities, became obnoxious. The collector does not make this kind of mistake again.

An example is eighteenth-century German porcelain. A real piece is worth thousands; copies should sell for a couple of hundred dollars or less. The nineteenth-century copyist concentrated on emulating the earlier work and he tried to conceal any evidence that colors, firing techniques and other technical factors had evolved in the meantime. But the copyist inevitably eliminates a little detail or unconsciously changes elements just the same. If the copy and the real thing are closely compared, the authentic porcelain will demonstrate itself. But do not misunderstand. There are honest approaches to nineteenth-century design that pay homage to earlier work without counterfeiting, and these are worth collecting in their own right.

In visiting a shop it is important to look closely at everything available and to handle and feel the objects. Some shops have a policy of buying things back at the same price; the collector can take an object home and live with it to experience its qualities.

Whatever has integrity is worth collecting, very old or not so old, delicate or coarse. But ascertaining integrity takes knowing, takes time.

TERRA COTTA

The word ceramics covers all objects made of clay, shaped by hand when soft on the potter's wheel or in a mold, and hardened by heating. Generally, the thinner the ware, the higher the temperature at which it was fired, or hardened.

The simplest pottery is made from locally dug clay, shaped and baked in the sun or over a fire. At the dawn of history, men made containers by this method; some primitive tribes still do. This simple ware is called terra cotta—literally, cooked earth. This unglazed ware, because of the necessarily low heat at which it was fired, is very brittle, and few old examples have survived. Terra cotta jugs are still being made in Mexican villages today, and these occasionally turn up in shipments of antiques.

The simplest forms of terra cotta, with patterns scratched into the surface, afford an interesting range of possibilities to those who admire rough textures and the boldness of plain shapes. Shops that offer primitive art will often carry examples of contemporary American Indian or African terra cotta that look much like examples dug up at the sites of ancient cities. These are not fakes or copies but rather represent the continuation of a long tradition.

Terra cotta is subject to one basic variation: the surface can be polished to reduce porosity. Ancient Greek and Roman potters covered surfaces with a clay paste before they burnished or polished them.

Terra cotta flask with relief decoration, Roman, about 300 A.D.

GLAZED EARTHENWARE

The next step that the potter took to reduce the porosity of his vessels was to cover them with a glassy surface. The earthenware body of reddish brown, green or yellow was covered with a metallic oxide combination that, when fired, fused into what we know as a glaze—hard, shiny and nonporous. This process can be traced back to the ancient Middle East; the Ishtar Gate of Babylon, which dates from the sixth century B.C., has a glass glaze.

Lead was the main ingredient of this early glaze—which was still being used at the end of the nineteenth century—and when it was fired it was transparent. This transparency enabled the potter to apply decoration under the glaze. A coat of whitish slip—a pure, light clay thinned out to a heavy liquid—was applied over the clay body, and a decoration was scratched into it, or worked in relief, or painted in the varying colors of slip. This lead-glazed earthenware is most frequently called simply redware.

Bowl, earthenware, covered with green glaze, Roman, first century B.C.–first century A.D. Green and blue glazes were applied to Roman wares. Relief ornament is common, either in a vine or with figures in relief. The glazes were later used in the East on examples that look more exotic.

REDWARE

The tradition of redware is long, so differentiating between ancient and modern requires a little study. In the beginning, earthenware was the best ceramic material available and it was handled as such. By the nineteenth century it was one of the roughest materials and was used primarily for strictly utilitarian containers. The redware body is relatively thick and no matter what its age, the shape is likely to be simple and decoration bold and sparse. Cast pieces of ancient Roman origin are covered with green or golden-brown glaze. They have bands of figures on shapes that were inspired by the work of metal artisans. Incised or scratched decoration was also popular in ancient times.

There are few opportunities to find redware made before the Christian era, but small pieces such as bowls do turn up. Most collectors find the eighteenth- and nineteenth-century wares the most challenging and appealing. Because of the demand, premium prices are asked, so careful study is advisable.

To Americans, the most interesting glazed earthenware is of Pennsylvania German origin. It was made from the middle of the eighteenth century to the end of the nineteenth, with the peak of production about 1800 to 1840. It is evidence of the craft tradition, the work of small shops in which age-old techniques such as throwing on the potter's wheel were used. The patterns are distinctively outlined against the pale slip coating, which often has green spots. Where there is no glaze, most American examples show a reddish brown body, but the body can be greenish or a rather pale buff that darkens when dirty.

For all the century and a half of their production, these pie plates and jars—made in Pennsylvania in the spirit of European peasant ware—remain exceedingly rare and expensive. A good plate with a tulip or bird pattern (the eagle, especially) scratched into the slip will bring $2,000 or $3,000 when it turns up.

A few American potters continue to produce the traditional ware, and their work is collected for its good quality if not for its age.

European examples of redware are more often molded than the American ones. The molded forms are straighter and more regular. The European potter may use more variety in applying green or brown slip, and his decoration may be more casual. European examples are considerably less expensive and rarely go for more than $50 a plate, a worthwhile thought for the budget-bound.

Peasant wares were still being produced in Europe at the end of the nineteenth century. Caution is important in collecting the European examples because some factory imitations crop up among these later works. The work from factories is of more refined clays fired at higher temperatures. The ware is thinner, the exposed clay paler and the glazes are smoother than the handmade samples.

Ordinary pie plates—round, deep dishes with a regularly crimped edge—are readily

Pie plate, brown-glazed earthenware with slip decoration, American, about 1810. Simple reddish-brown glazed pieces were as popular in the nineteenth century as centuries earlier. The prized examples show signs of having been made on a potter's wheel, but molded examples with straight sides and a flat bottom are more common.

Dish, earthenware, by Thomas Toft, English, about 1675. Yellow slip is often applied to plain earthenware pieces. Extraordinary decoration and signature make this important, but plain mugs and bowls of the same body and glaze are easier to find. Staffordshire was a center for their manufacture in the seventeenth and eighteenth centuries.

Pie plate, earthenware, by Samuel Troxel, Pennsylvania, about 1820. Scratching linear designs through the surface of slip and glaze is a technique mastered by the American potters of German origin who worked in Pennsylvania. They preferred primitive patterns to the more complex designs followed on the Continent.

available. These are covered in a reddish brown glaze and the more choice examples have a buff-colored slip decoration. Linear designs are dripped on and sometimes so is a greeting such as "Happy New Year." These plates were made to the very end of the nineteenth century in simple small potteries all over the United States.

ANCIENT EGYPTIAN CERAMICS

Long before even the Ishtar Gate, at the time of the Old Kingdom (3000 B.C.), the Egyptians were making ceramic objects with non-porous glazes. These, however, were not of earthenware, but principally of a siliceous sand mixture. The body was covered with a glaze that was a combination of silicic acid (quartz sand) and a flux that caused the glaze to fuse with the body during firing. The usual fusing agents were alkalis such as potash and soda. Metallic oxides were added to the glaze to color it.

The early output of the Egyptian ceramists was mainly small figures that had religious significance and were used in funeral rites. Typically they were light blue. After about 1300 B.C., the palette was broadened to include green, a purplish blue, violet, orange, red and white. Varied sorts of containers from the later period are also found.

These Egyptian objects have been of interest to collectors for over a century. But by the end of the nineteenth century, there was considerable experimentation in learning how this ware—which was incorrectly called Egyptian faience—was made. The results were objects that imitated the Egyptian pale matte finishes. There is a second cause for a number of nonauthentic objects. Egypt was on the Grand Tour itinerary of many wealthy American and British families, so there was a good market for "a little something" to take home. Thus, small inexpensive pieces of "ancient Egyptian faience" should be suspect.

Cup, "faience," Egyptian, Eighteenth Dynasty, 1580–1350 B.C. Egyptian "faience" was used for small figures as well as containers. Many reproductions were made at the turn of the century, so caution is important.

EARLY OPAQUE GLAZES

At least as early as 500 B.C.—about a century after the appearance of the transparent lead-based glazes—tin-enamel glazes, which are opaque, came into use. There is almost no hope of finding ceramics with opaque glazes from this period. But Near Eastern tiles and bowls dating from the ninth to the twelfth century can be found, and they provide evidence of the long tradition of opaque glazes.

The early Near Eastern wares have a special grace. Long-necked bottles and plainly curved bowls became the inspiration for later craftsmen and designers, who in turn created models for factory production. White-and-blue tin glazes and bronze- and copper-colored backgrounds were used on the earthenwares, and the decorations appear to have been drawn on adeptly and rapidly. The designs are often calligraphical, and the inscriptions have the beauty of abstract patterns to those who cannot decipher the Eastern script. Figures are sometimes applied with delicacy and at other times are defined by thick lines. The designs are clearly the work of craftsmen who could simplify with such skill that no vitality was lost.

Iran is one source of these wares, but potters all over the Middle East produced tin-glazed wares of strength and charm. Fakery abounds, so it is important to be cautious and to become familiar with the types of wares that one likes.

Restoration is also a factor that must be considered. When a piece is newly restored, the patchwork is invisible, but trouble can develop later because the restored section

Bowl, earthenware, Rayy type, Persian, twelfth to thirteenth century. Luster and blue used over a white glaze are found on one type of Persian pottery. Decoration often includes calligraphy, but even when it doesn't there is an easy flowing line to define forms in the decoration.

Mosque lamp, earthenware, Turkish, sixteenth century. The influence of oriental porcelain is evident in the floral and leaf patterns. The shape is determined by the function of the piece.

will discolor and the piece will be more brittle at the point of repair.

Architectural tiles, originally incorporated into walls, are most frequently decorated in relief. Collecting them requires caution because they have been faked for over fifty years. When reliefs are very flat and have linear highlights to point up elements that should have been detailed in relief, one should suspect recent manufacture.

Metallic lusters were introduced by Near Eastern potters as an additional way to decorate in opaque glazes. The luster colors vary from silver and gold to copper. A wide range of luster-decorated pieces was made in the Near East, first in such centers as Rakka, Rhages and other potteries in Syria and Iran.

The Spanish potteries then started using luster decoration while under the Moorish influence; by the end of the fourteenth century they were supplying this decorative ware to the whole of Europe.

The early luster technique was continued by Spanish potters, and even the nineteenth-century samples seem to represent the survival of the technique rather than a revival. Perhaps for this reason, the term Hispano-Moresque is used to describe lusterware made in Spain at just about any time, even though the Moors had been expelled by the end of the 1400's.

As a rule, the early Spanish lusterware is subtly decorated in fine, complex interlacing patterns. Primitive forms covered with

Dish, earthenware, Spanish, 1400–50. Lustered decoration appears on the so-called Hispano-Moresque wares that are in the tradition of much earlier Persian pottery. The decoration is fairly delicate on early examples. By the eighteenth and nineteenth centuries luster is much more thickly applied.

crudely defined luster patterns are often of eighteenth- or nineteenth-century origin. But producing luster was a difficult task for the early individual artist-craftsman, so sometimes the work of the late nineteenth century, in its crudeness, can be confused with the early Hispano-Moresque.

Victorian luster is worth investigating on its own. Outstanding designers such as William Friend de Morgan, an associate of William Morris, the most important design reformer of the nineteenth century, produced signficant interpretations of lusterware.

MAJOLICA

The Near Eastern and Spanish wares had long been known in the West before the Italians in the fifteenth century began a serious attempt to produce distinctive decorative wares themselves. The Italian products were of two kinds—a ware glazed in tin-enamel with luster decoration, and another having an undercoat of slip with a design scratched into it, covered by a lead glaze. Both of these Italian wares were called majolica, the Italian name for Majorca, the Spanish island port through which the Hispano-Moresque wares were being shipped to Italy. By extension, the term majolica is sometimes also used to describe all sorts of earthenware products that have been covered with a dark opaque glaze.

Jar, earthenware (majolica), Italian, Faenza, early sixteenth century. The tin glaze provided an off-white ground decorated in floral patterns applied adroitly but schematically. The flowers are reduced to flat elements but they are composed in a way that captures the idea of flowers. The nineteenth-century decorator put in more but was less convincing.

132

Dish, earthenware (majolica), Urbino, mid-sixteenth century. An over-all picture based on an engraving of the period was the decoration for the istoriato ware. The later versions are in more carefully drawn perspective.

The earliest Italian majolica has bold and simple patterns as well as a few variations of flower designs, peacock feathers and fish scales. These patterns were adapted to the Italian taste by being simplified and enlarged.

In the course of the fifteenth century these Eastern influences gave way to the Italian style then evolving. The scrolls, urns, garlands and other patterns that the Renaissance elected to revive from ancient Greece and Rome begin to appear on majolica. The portrait profile became a central decorative theme for both vases and plates.

In the sixteenth century istoriato—storytelling—decoration became popular, with the scene forming the over-all decorative theme of a piece, in the manner of eighteenth-century toile printed fabrics. Each of the Italian centers that were producing majolica developed a particular style and group of color preferences, so advanced students of Italian majolica can often attribute an unmarked piece to a specific center.

By the seventeenth century the classical designs of the Renaissance were less fashionable than the oriental patterns that appeared on the wares being imported into Italy. In addition, new sources in the West were producing majolica. Nonetheless, elaborate classical pieces were still being turned out by the makers in Italy. In the eighteenth century important or ambitious examples became rarer and the Italian potteries began to lighten their designs and make the decoration more intricate.

Like the Hispano-Moresque wares, majolica continued in production long past its peak period, the sixteenth century. By the nineteenth century the Italian majolica was a conscious revival of the earlier efforts. As early as 1850, in fact, reproductions of the famous sixteenth-century wares were being made.

This can mean confusion for the collector, because something now already a hundred years old was made to look still older. Sometimes these reproductions are not easily distinguished from their originals, but signs of the later workmanship may be found in over-pretty detailing or touches that seem more appropriate to the Pre-Raphaelite nineteenth century than to the Renaissance of the sixteenth. The ceramic body may provide no clue, but an early piece, closely observed, is found to bear a decoration that accentuates the shape, while the later piece may be ornamented in a way that has no bearing on its shape.

In the sixteenth century, at the peak of its popularity, majolica was being made in France, the Netherlands and what is now Germany. Some of this work is close to its Italian inspiration, but there were local developments that can indicate origins.

At several potteries in France, wares were developed in the French Renaissance spirit as well as in the Italian spirit. Two of the most distinctive French wares of the sixteenth century are not actually majolica but lead-glazed earthenwares. They both reflect the furthest advance of the French Renaissance style.

Platter, earthenware, manner of Bernard Palissy, French, late sixteenth century. Palissy's name is associated with dark lead-glaze colors and Renaissance design. The sea-life motifs were important, but since Palissy has been prized throughout the nineteenth century, reproductions are common. Look for clear definition of details and simply rendered forms.

The best known, Palissy ware, takes its name from the most important French potter of the period, Bernard Palissy (c. 1510–c. 1590), who worked mainly in Saintes, near Bordeaux, and in Paris. In common with many of the foremost names in antiques, he wrote a treatise describing his technique of making molded lead-glazed wares in unusual blues, reds, greens, and yellows. Since there are few documented examples of Palissy's work, distinguishing it from the work of his imitators is difficult. Most attributions are made on the basis of quality; the best work in the Palissy style is assumed to be his.

Palissy ware is characterized by a broad interpretation of the Renaissance motifs—obviously classical figures in mythological

Jug, hafner ware, earthenware, workshop of Paul Pruening, Nuremberg, about 1548. Renaissance influence is suggested by the Venus-like appearance of Eve and the cupid holding the frame around the arms. Earthen colors were used in the lead glazes of the German potters, and, again the connoisseur discerns a simple forcefulness in the sixteenth century that is not visible in the later repetitions.

or religious contexts, and naturalistic fruit and fish. Grottoes of lizard crabs and murky seascapes on some of the Palissy platters are of the sort that make the queasy squirm. Palissy's molds were used long after he died, but they grew worn. Thus, pieces of early concept with ill-defined details are probably newer products of older molds. In addition, there was a Palissy revival in the nineteenth century, and these reproductions abound.

The other notable French ware is St. Porchaire, named for the site of a pottery that operated between about 1525 and 1560. This pottery, in western France in Deux-Sèvres Department, produced an unusually thin earthenware that is creamy in color. The decoration, in a variety of classical patterns,

was inlaid rather than painted on. Early St. Porchaire ware follows models that are typical of metalwork, while later work includes naturalistic designs like those on Palissy ware. Chances of finding original St. Porchaire are slight, but nineteenth-century interpretations do appear from time to time.

German potters of the sixteenth century also produced a lead-glazed earthenware in the Renaissance style. These products were called hafner-wares, meaning oven-makers' wares, because the potters were particularly adept at making tiles for stoves.

Typical hafner-wares are of earthenware lead-glazed in warm earthen colors. Renaissance details such as the round arch and related classical architectural decorations—as well as figures that may be based on classical models—appear on this ware.

Hafner-wares are boldly schematized and the colors are loud. Naturalistic elements such as leaf patterns and realistic portraits also appear. Working in majolica, the Germans also produced close copies of the Italian istoriato wares.

The term majolica is also applied, curiously, to several wares that have their origins in the nineteenth century. In Staffordshire, England, the most famous local pottery, Wedgwood, capriciously called its revival of eighteenth-century earthenware majolica. Use of the term spread to various glazed colored products being offered in the middle of the nineteenth century. Around 1880 in the United States several companies began making imitations of the eighteenth-century wares as well as more complex variations of the designs. Pink and blue were added to the earthen colors. These later wares look brighter and more sensational.

Late majolica is enthusiastically collected by those who admire the designs of the late nineteenth century. Another factor that probably creates popularity is that anything of this type is under $50. Marked examples of American majolica show it is often from Phoenixville, Pennsylvania.

DELFT

Although the blue-and-white design says "delft" to the casual viewer, it is the material under the glaze that sets it apart from other ceramics. This European earthenware was wildly popular in the seventeenth and eighteenth centuries and was widely made, not just in the Netherlands.

Delft objects from the peak period are relatively thick-looking, but not so heavy as their appearance would indicate. They are most commonly decorated with blue and white glazes, but delftware is also found with yellow, green, red and purple designs on white. The white glaze is shiny and uneven, and the bare surface at the base of a piece is porous and is reddish brown, greenish brown or buff.

Landscape plaque, tin-enameled earthenware, by Frederick van Frijtom, Delft, about 1670. Van Frijtom was a painter and potter. Other potters tended to adapt well-known engraved views. The seventeenth-century landscapes on pottery are as generalized as those in oil. Tile landscapes of the nineteenth century are much more intricate and sometimes inept.

Bottle, tin-enameled earthenware, from Adriaen Pijnacker factory, Delft, seventeenth century. An oriental porcelain form was the model for the shape, but decoration was as occidental as eastern in inspiration.

The town of Delft in the Netherlands owes its pre-eminence in the ceramic world to the collapse of its first major industry, the brewing of beer. Sometime in the early 1600's, the town fathers realized that beer exports were no longer producing the revenues of a century before. Rather than struggle to regain the market, these officials decided to devote the town's labor and resources to the production of pottery. Some clays were available locally, and others could be shipped in.

The city fathers were not making a wild guess. The prospering of the Italian cities that made majolica was well known, and the European demand for decorative ceramics was still at high tide. Imports from the Orient were filling most of this demand, so

Delft saw its opportunity and gave an early demonstration of a complete retooling. Kilns began replacing vats in the unused breweries and, around 1650, delftware was born.

The Delft innovation was in design rather than technique. The clay mixture that the Dutch potters used was quite close to that used in producing majolica and faience. Although there were some variations, it is this similarity that tends to cause the term delft to be interchanged with majolica and faience. For their new pottery, the Dutch first adapted the forms that were selling well in oriental porcelains, but they soon offered a variety of designs as dictated by public demand.

Blue dash chargers, English delftware, about 1700

Plate, tin-enameled earthenware, Delft, about 1750. The floral pattern in orange, blue and brown is called the peacock design. The colors can be fired at low temperatures.
Pale and more varied colors required special treatment and were introduced later. Peacock plates were a popular form made in a number of Delft factories.

Butter dish with lid, tin-enameled earthenware, Delft, 1750–1800. A simple wooden tub inspired the shape, and rococo engravings were the source of the ornament. The cow is appropriate on a cover for butter, but dog finials borrowed from Chinese porcelain are more common.

The colors were circumscribed by the firing techniques. Having chosen a white tin-oxide glaze, the artisans could use only colors that would stand up under the high temperatures needed to set the white. Blue was easiest to handle, but red, purple, yellow and green could also be used. A second firing, which added to the expense, was needed for further colors. Hence, a more varied palette was not introduced until after 1760, when competition from German porcelains drove the Dutch to it.

Among the earliest known objects of delftware are landscape plaques, which show all the attention to detail found in the Dutch paintings of this period. Another form is the tile, found either with an independent de-

sign or as part of a larger design. The tiles were used as borders for fireplaces or were placed at the baseboard of a wall. Landscapes, Biblical scenes and floral designs were popular subjects for tile decorations.

Some of the designs that launched delftware continued throughout its period of production. But new forms constantly appeared, inspired by contemporary European silver or porcelain shapes as well as by the oriental imports. Many of the simple, curving forms of bowls, vases or pitchers resulted from the adaptation of oriental designs to the limitations of the potter's wheel and large-scale production.

Later delftware decorations have a distinctive quality, although an expert can be

Harlequin from Adriaen Pijnacker factory, tin-enameled earthenware, Delft, 1750–1800. The competition of the German porcelain factories was met by making similar figures. Earthenware is not for delicate work, and the best potters were able to exploit the grossness of the medium. The harlequin is rendered with charm and a minimum of detail.

fooled. The illustrations are rendered summarily, as if the artist wanted to capture the spirit of the subject with a minimum of detail.

Delftware plates most commonly have floral motifs. A circular border of small flowers may enclose a large central bouquet. Some plates are divided into panels decorated with flowers, birds or human figures. The peacock feather was introduced in the seventeenth century and it became a standard ornament for simpler items in the eighteenth.

Classical motifs are found on bowls and vases; these include illustrations of baroque fountains and formal gardens. Other forms of pure ornament such as arabesques of classical scrolls and garlands appear to have been borrowed from contemporary engravings.

By 1750, changes in taste caused the Delft potters to turn to smaller pieces and novelties. Asymmetric rococo designs—free adaptations of classical motifs—began to appear. The small whimseys, the pottery violins and shoes, also began in this period.

At the same time, porcelain began to make inroads on the pottery market, and the makers of delftware started to copy the figurines and small ornaments that were selling so well in porcelain. Some difficulties were encountered, however. For example, the earthenware body was too thick to be readily adaptable to the delicate arms of a ceramic shepherdess. The pressures of the mar-

Chimney garniture, tin-enameled earthenware, from the pottery of Lambertus Sandus, Delft, about 1760. Rococo decoration transformed vases based on Chinese porcelain models. These forms have often been copied in the last fifty years. The modern ceramic is lighter when pieces are reproductions, but if intended as a fake the body is heavy. Decoration is less schematic on recent work.

ket also made richer colors imperative. Costly special kilns were needed for the second firing.

For purists, the inappropriate imitations of porcelain and the new colors spell the end of the "classical" period of delftware. But others find the clumsy smaller pieces are enjoyable to collect. Their awkwardness has some of the appeal of the provincial furniture of the eighteenth century, and they are often displayed together.

The delftware that was made outside of the Netherlands is generally simpler and less fashionable than the Dutch original. To many Americans, the most appealing of the non-Delft delft is the English version. English production in the 1600's centered on London,

but included Bristol and Liverpool. The English product is decorated in a manner that is as often Middle Eastern in feeling as it is oriental.

One popular item is the blue dash charger—"charger" being an archaic term for a large platter. This plate derived its name from its border design, a series of short blue stripes. The center decorations—flowers, scenes of Adam and Eve, or royal portraits—are bold and schematic. Bowls in simple oriental shapes were decorated with floral motifs, after the models from Delft, but exceptional new pieces with colorful flower ornamentation were developed in Liverpool. Oblong, brick-shaped containers for flowers came from Liverpool and Bristol.

Dish, blue dash charger, tin-enameled earthenware (delftware), Lambeth or Bristol, about 1700. Sponge decoration and plain blue brush marks are employed as elements of a succinctly drawn portrait of King William. The same form was used for a series of portraits of traditional figures, including Adam and Eve.

Puzzle jug, tin-enameled earthenware (delftware), Brislington or Lambeth, 1689. Openwork necks are found on jugs that were meant to challenge a drinker. The same form appears on other earthenware in the nineteenth century.

The delft period ended by 1800, when porcelain and the more durable earthenwares of Staffordshire crowded delft out of the market.

Buying delftware from the 1650–1800 period requires caution. Reproductions and outright fakes abound. A first check is the color of the unglazed portion of the surface. It should be a buff or brown, because it was fired at temperatures that are low by today's standards. The higher firing produces a white body. If the forger fakes the old color, the piece will weigh more than it should.

The delft items most often found are tiles, plates, bowls, vases and pitchers. Some delftware is signed on the bottom, often with the name of the former brewery in which it was made—the Young Moor's Head, for instance, or the Golden Flowerpot. But, as always, signatures are easy to copy, so this evidence is not definitive.

Similarly, elaborate pieces at bargain prices should arouse suspicion. Some delft items may sell for thousands, but such prices are for rarities. An ordinary bottle-shaped vase can cost as little as $50 (when you're lucky), and plates for $30 are not unknown—just hard to find. The best course for the beginner in delft is to concentrate on common, inexpensive plates and small vases because, like pennies, they are not worth forging.

FAIENCE

The name faience is French, and it derives from Faenza, an Italian city that was a sixteenth- and seventeenth-century pottery center. The name was originally applied because local wares were created to imitate—or replace—wares that had been coming from Faenza. Sometimes the term faience is applied to *all* glazed earthenwares, but it is usually interpreted to mean the tin-glazed earthenware made from about 1650 to 1850 that was highly popular in France and Germany.

Faience is little different from majolica and delftware, although its designs generally followed the fashion of the moment while the two others are more traditional. Italian majolica is in the main based on Renaissance models; the inspiration for delftware was primarily oriental porcelain. The designers of faience first followed silver and then European porcelain in an effort to remain stylish.

Faience was made all over Europe, with regional pecularities in design that experts can usually spot, although they sometimes disagree, and violently, about origins of particular pieces. For those less than expert, a feeling for the evolution of the designs and an awareness of some twentieth-century imitations will serve as safe guides.

Faience forms are often heavy, and relatively thick, interpretations of porcelain. The designs are bold and have a rusticity that harmonizes well with country or provincial furniture. If a piece is light or thin, it may well be a later copy. For about forty years,

Ewer, tin-enameled earthenware (faience), Rouen, 1700–20. The major difference between faience and delftware is in design. Faience is often more sophisticated. The shape of this ewer is very close to those in silver. The decoration is derived from contemporary books of decorative engravings. The nineteenth-century reproductions are a little more evenly potted, with decoration that appears more mechanically applied.

Tureen, tin-enameled earthenware (faience), by Joseph Fauchier, Marseilles, about 1750. The best efforts of the faience potteries have elaborate floral, scroll and animal decoration. More modest examples are restrained, but include some of the same decorative elements as are shown here. Rococo borders were used on thin-bodied nineteenth-century pieces.

there has been a revival of faience-making and some of the older of these new examples may appear much like their eighteenth-century prototypes. The later work can be recognized by examining the ceramic body itself—it will be more highly refined and lighter. To conceal recent manufacture, a piece may be made needlessly thick, but often potters do not bother to conceal recent manufacture. When the fake is intentional, the maker may apply a seventeenth- or eighteenth-century date. While some faience from those centuries is dated, the prospective buyer should be more cautious about dated faience than about the rest.

France was the first important center of faience production—hence, the French name. In the first decades of production, starting about 1650, the makers followed in the majolica tradition—oriental designs were as important as the classical.

At Nevers and Rouen in the seventeenth century the two sources of inspiration ran neck and neck. Nevers is best known for varied forms based on Persian imports, with a blue ground and white decoration. In Rouen, the work was more typically stylishly baroque and silver forms were the source for most of the shapes. Blue decoration on a white ground was typical. The forms were classical and patterns were often in the spirit of the late seventeenth-century "ornamentistes" who offered designs that were combinations of classical motifs. The early examples have a special elegance that comes from the crispness of their appearance.

Until the middle of the eighteenth century the palette was limited to high-fire colors—blue, green, red and yellow—and the forms, whether Eastern or Western, were bold and simple. Heavy round moldings based on architectural details were used on shapes with the same inspirations. Pitchers and bowls are the most common examples but vases, plates and a whole repertory of ceramic forms were made. The decorative details have a more precise, linear quality than they do on delftware.

After 1750, faience blossoms out in such rococo motifs as the asymmetric shell. Simple scalloped-edge plates were popular. The obvious influence was the porcelain-makers, and both colors and shapes are interpretations of spectacular examples of the artistry of the best porcelain.

About 1770 the technique of firing the faience a second time, at a lower temperature in what is called a muffle kiln, was developed. Thus, the palette used in faience became as varied as the colors used on porcelain.

Examples of the most complex faience designs—lavaboes, tea sets and decorative plaques—are very rare, but simpler pieces do turn up, often at sensible prices. Plates of eighteenth-century origin will bring $50 or less in many shops. However, no one should pay this price if authenticity is dubious.

In the late 1700's and early 1800's there was a naturalistic trend in rococo faience; tureens in the form of cabbages, cauliflowers, animals and fish were popular.

In Germany, faience seems to appear in two main forms—and at extremes in design. At one end is the remarkably traditional work: jugs and pitchers in shapes that go back to medieval prototypes, but decorated with designs of chinoiserie in blue and white, often capped in pewter. The forms look as if they had been made on a potter's wheel, and the shapes are the same as those of dark, lead-glazed wares of an earlier vintage.

At the other extreme is the work influenced by the fashionable porcelain factories. These objects are occasionally quite ambitious—elaborately shaped and decorated faience bowls or tureens in rococo designs. Often fashionable faience came from factories that were also producing famous porcelain.

By about 1800, finer clays were being used and slightly thinner wares were made in modified shapes. These were formed more quickly than before, using an early version of the assembly line.

There were thousands of potteries in operation in Germany in the 1700's. Their main objective was commercial, so these potteries pirated successful designs. In general, the influence of Rouen was felt first; blue-and-white wares in classical shapes were the most popular. Later, rococo porcelain was the major inspiration. Characteristic colors and designs of each pottery become known to collectors as they develop experience.

Scandinavian potteries were more conservative and rarely produced elaborate work. Bowls in the shape of bishops' hats are curiosities that seem to have been unique to Scandinavia, but these seldom turn up. The best-known pieces are subtle variations of designs based on early eighteenth-century silver or porcelain.

Since faience potteries operated all over Europe, great variations in design are found. Before 1850, however—and despite regional differences—the wares were fairly consistent. In examining these objects, bear in mind that a very smooth white body is likely to be a recent imitation, while bodies with varying colors under the glaze—darker at the beginning of the eighteenth century and lighter later—are more likely to be the real thing.

HIGH-FIRED EARTHENWARE OR FAIENCE FINE

The English potters of the 1700's worked harder on improving the earthenware bodies of their ceramics than their Continental competitors. Porcelain, which had been coming from China for some time, was now also being made in the West, and the English wanted to create a ware that would be as thin and hard as porcelain but not as expensive. And they succeeded.

The potters in the Staffordshire region used special pure clays that enabled them to fire their wares at higher temperatures. The result was a stronger body and thus it could be worked thinner than faience. On the Continent, this product was called faience fine. Today this high-fired earthenware is known as Staffordshire, which was where

Teapot, lead-glazed earthenware, Astbury type, Staffordshire, about 1740. Thin earthenware pieces were introduced in England in the 1730's. Shapes are rococo or oriental. Applied decoration was popular in fairly flat, almost abstract designs. Later, realism is an influence on decoration.

most of it was made. Creamware and modern earthenware are other names for it. The body is porous and opaque, but it is a step ahead in earthenware and it made England the foremost pottery-producer in the West.

The Staffordshire region produced some prominant potters—especially Whieldon, Astbury and Wedgwood—and many objects from other places have been attributed to this big three, right along with their actual products. The problem of dating some of the simpler work from the Staffordshire region is just beginning to be solved.

Another confusing element is that the earliest work was an effort to make real porcelain and the results were sometimes earthenware and sometimes turned out to be stoneware, the next step to porcelain. And technically, the earliest of the thin wares are not faience at all because the glazes were made with lead, not tin, and the familiar earth colors predominate.

John Astbury (1668–1743) is generally credited with making some of the earliest thin-bodied earthenware pieces. Typically, their dark-brown glazed bodies have white or light buff relief decoration. Teapots of this type turn up at prices from $100 to $400. The varied small oriental shapes of these pots seem to indicate that they were made over a long period of time.

Thomas Whieldon (1719–95), another of the Staffordshire giants, produced the colored ware named for him and is also associated with the development of the thin white stoneware body called saltglaze. Whieldon ware is a thin product, often covered with a glaze that suggests tortoise shell or agate and that ranges from brown to blues and greens.

Plaster-of-Paris molds began to be used by English potters such as Whieldon to make fairly elaborate teapots, sauceboats, bowls and plates. Basket-weave borders, sometimes interspersed with a name or motto, appear on plates glazed in tortoise shell. These plates are among the most reasonably priced articles attributed to Whieldon, ranging from $70 to $300. Sauceboats based on contemporary silver designs and teapots based on Chinese porcelain are much rarer and keep getting more expensive; the finest pieces may cost $1,000 or more.

Making high-fired earthenware look like porcelain with a white or cream-colored

Plate, lead-glazed earthenware, Whieldon type, Staffordshire, about 1750. Greens and a variety of mottled colors appear on pottery associated with Thomas Whieldon. Molded designs are often the same as those for saltglaze.

Teapot, lead-glazed earthenware, by Josiah Wedgwood, Staffordshire, about 1760. Cauliflower- and pineapple-patterned pottery was made by Wedgwood just before he perfected creamware. The colors should be plain greens and off-white (or yellow). When lusters and pinks appear, the examples are late nineteenth-century adaptations.

Pierced vase, creamware, Leeds, about 1780. Wedgwood's 1760 development, creamware, was adopted by potters all over England within a decade or two. Leeds is a center associated with pale yellowish pieces often pierced in over-all patterns. Late nineteenth-century examples are frequently crude.

glaze is an achievement credited to Josiah Wedgwood (1730–95). Wedgwood began making creamware—named after the color of its glaze—in about 1760, and every potter in Staffordshire was soon doing so, too. Wedgwood's creamware was also called Queensware, in honor of Queen Charlotte, and this name is still used by Wedgwood.

The early examples of creamware were made in molds that repeated patterns used on porcelains. The creamware was sometimes decorated with hand-painted scenes or scenes applied by a process called transfer-print decoration. Essentially, this transferred an engraving to the pottery surface. Rococo engravings were a favored source of inspiration—frames made up of leaf, scroll and ribbon motifs, and intimate scenes of lovers in a garden or a family at tea.

Although early sets of creamware can be amazingly expensive, single pieces can be found in the range of $50 to $100. Straight tubular mugs, cups and saucers, casters for condiments, and bowls were made, along with the complete services. Handsome display pieces of creamware with intricately pierced sections are often attributed to a pottery at Leeds, England. Creamware was also made at French and German potteries.

Liverpool, a port town that maintained potteries to make ceramics for export, also produced creamware. A simple curved pitcher with a transfer-print decoration showing, for example, a patriotic American theme was a typical design. The Liverpool jug was common enough on the American scene for Paul Revere to have copied it in silver. Plates and platters made in Liverpool have scalloped edges with a color—usually dark blue or green—brushed around the edge.

Creamware was also used for small figures and for mugs and pitchers in human form. The familiar Toby jugs, which honor Toby Fillpot, the nickname of a noted eighteenth-century toper, were first created by Ralph Wood, a Staffordshire potter. But Toby jugs have never diminished in popularity and they are still being made. In searching for early examples—a good one may run you $500 to $600—the warm earthen colors of the 1700's are a good guide. The detailing should also have good quality.

Shortly after 1800 a white glaze was developed for earthenware. The most famous

Toby jug, "Rodney's Sailor," by Ralph Wood the younger, lead-glazed earthenware, Staffordshire, about 1780. The figural or toby jugs head a list of English ceramic figures. Colors on the eighteenth-century examples are warm, but blues and more harsh metallic browns dominate the early nineteenth-century examples.

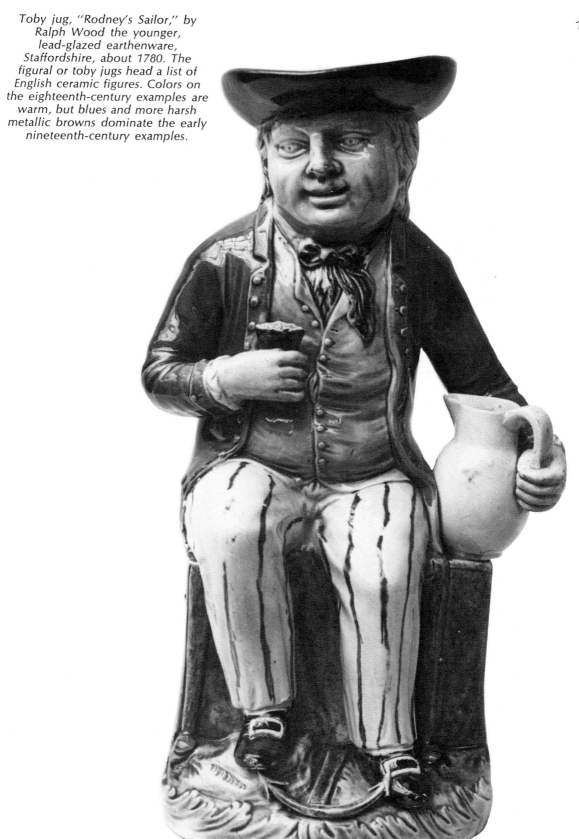

products using this white glaze have all-over transfer-print patterns, and these ceramics form the much-collected group that is generally called Blue Staffordshire. Typically, there is a richly detailed floral, scroll or shell border with a scene in the center. From about 1820 to 1840, an extensive series of American scenes was made for the American trade.

The Staffordshire potters used a wide variety of scenes, from the most famous monuments of large cities to almshouses in towns so small they are almost impossible to find on a map. Collectors of Blue Staffordshire, like stamp collectors, prize certain peculiar scenes for their rarity. A view of an Ohio or Michigan town will fetch $3,000 to $4,000,

Plate, earthenware, by J. & R. Clewes, Staffordshire, about 1830. Often called Deep Blue Staffordshire, this transfer-print decorated ware was at its height between 1820 and 1850. American subjects were popular. The early ones are dark and decoration is simple. The late are lighter in color and more complex in pattern. In reproductions, the decoration is applied by a photographic process, and close scrutiny discloses this.

Pitcher and mugs, matte-glazed earthenware,
Rookwood Pottery, Ohio, 1905

Teapot, Rockingham ware, designed by Daniel Guentbach, Jersey City, about 1840. Brown-glazed ware was popular after 1820, first in Staffordshire and then in the United States. This early rococo revival piece is a rare American example, and it suggests the variety possible.

Sugar bowl, earthenware, by Lyman Fenton & Co., Bennington, Vt., about 1850. A patented "flint enamel" mottled glaze with blue mixed into the browns is a telltale sign of the Bennington examples that are sometimes called Rockingham.

while a familiar view of New York can be found for $50 to $100 and romantic scenes of nowhere in particular are less. A very rare American example from about 1840, made by the American Pottery Company of Jersey City, shows an imaginary view rather than a scene, but the rarity of this sample makes its price the exception to the rule on made-up scenes.

The darker blue prints are generally more desirable because they are older; as the transfer process was improved, the prints got paler. Toward the end of the nineteenth century the whole process of making transfer prints was simplified, and photographs were used instead of engravings. A careful examination of the design will disclose if it is one of these later plates, even though the title may be one prized by collectors in its earlier version.

The earthenware body was constantly improved in the 1800's. Clays were purified further, and firing at higher temperatures became possible. Some of the improvements led to a ceramic body that was technically closer to stoneware, and by the middle of the nineteenth century, ironstone had appeared. Ironstone is somewhere between stoneware and earthenware in consistency. This sturdy thick pottery was molded in a number of shapes. Whole dinner sets in late Empire or simple rococo revival designs are on the market. Although most were left plain, some bear small transfer-print decorations. These items tend to be fairly inexpensive when available.

Poodle, earthenware, by Lyman Fenton & Co., Bennington, Vt., about 1850. A popular subject on both sides of the Atlantic, poodles have been reproduced continuously. The customary Bennington glaze is rarely duplicated by the later potters.

Mass production in Staffordshire resulted in reasonably priced, durable, graceful wares that wiped out country potters all over the Western world. As small potteries closed, the mass-producers began to make popular, folksy wares to take the place of the true folk pottery. Plain and mottled brown glazes were used on molded wares, decorated with rustic country and hunting scenes.

One name for the brown-glazed wares is Rockingham, after a pottery operated by the Duke of Rockingham, where it is believed to have originated. Americans tend to call the ware Bennington, after the Vermont town where some of it was produced. Actually, a host of United States potteries was turning out Rockingham ware from 1830 to 1890. Pitchers are the form most often found in Rockingham ware, but it was used for teapots, odd-shaped decanters, candlesticks, bowls and purely decorative figures as well.

Rockingham was made in quantity in England. But after about 1830 some English potters migrated to the United States to try their hands at making the ware here, and the familiar English subjects begin to emerge from factories in New Jersey, Ohio and Vermont. Distinctively American scenes were also produced—primitive views of boats or fire engines.

Rockingham ware is occasionally marked on the bottom but more often not. Some of the wares of the U.S. Pottery Company at Bennington may be identified by a special glaze, called flint enamel, which was introduced in 1849. This has strokes of blue in the brown-and-buff mottling.

Earthenware production has thrived right up to the present day. For those interested in collecting less popular types, where prices remain low, there is an enjoyable challenge in finding distinctive late nineteenth- or early twentieth-century wares. Part of the challenge is weeding out the novel from the preponderance of bad imitations of earlier works.

There were ambitious efforts to create contemporary designs in England, on the Continent and in America, and these are worth seeking. For example, Wedgwood produced some fascinating late Victorian designs with the help of the craftsman-potter William Friend de Morgan, and at the beginning of this century, the Buffalo Pottery in New York veered from complete schmaltz to interesting Art Nouveau designs, now much in demand. There were hundreds of factories active, and it's a matter of tracking down an area that still represents good design and hasn't been clambered over by everyone else.

STONEWARE

Nonporous glazes had been used for centuries before potters discovered how to make the ceramic body itself impervious to liquids. This achievement came almost simultaneously in the Far East and in the West, in the sixth century. Potters used purer and purer clays that finally created a ceramic body that could be fired at temperatures of 1,200° to 1,300° F. The result, compact and waterproof, is known as stoneware. In the East, stoneware was a step in the development of porcelain—which was created there in the ninth century—but in the West, stoneware was more than a way station and had an importance of its own.

Despite its close kinship to porcelain, stoneware is commonly thought of in the

Tankard from the Eigesteiner pottery, salt-glazed stoneware, Cologne, about 1540. Color is buff rather than white. The relief decoration of a woman with trees and animals is northern Renaissance in spirit. Ornament is sometimes more obviously classical on other sixteenth-century pieces, but it gets more primitive in the eighteenth century.

*Tureen, salt-glazed stoneware, English,
about 1740*

Jug, salt-glazed stoneware, German, seventeenth century. The shape goes back to medieval models. The relief head of the bearded man on the neck was thought to have been a caricature of Cardinal Bellarmine, who was strongly anti-Protestant. The jug was used for ale in taverns during the sixteenth and seventeenth centuries.

form of large gray jugs and jars, and examples of all sorts can be found in the simpler, barn-like antique shops in shabby sections of cities or on gloomy country roads. From the beginning, stoneware's practical appeal was that it could hold liquids without sweating. The bulk of the late nineteenth-century objects to be found now reflect this; they reek of sacramental wines that were made during Prohibition, or they still smell of pickles.

There is only the slightest chance of finding stoneware that dates from earlier than the nineteenth century. If you see a Chinese example in the shop of a specialist, you may not recognize it because it will probably be smoothly glazed rather than have a saltglaze,

that orange-rind texture we generally associate with stoneware.

The medieval forms, using saltglaze, were made as late as the seventeenth century in European potteries. One jug that does turn up occasionally is the Bellarmine, which has a medieval, almost globular body and a narrow neck topped by a bearded head. A Bellarmine costs a few hundred dollars when it does appear.

German potters of the sixteenth century used stoneware as a medium for items with relief decorations that are sophisticated in the Renaissance spirit. The finest examples are off-white. The simpler are grayish or brown, and the gray examples frequently have blue decorations as well as details in relief. Excavations at Williamsburg, Virginia, have uncovered German and English eighteenth-century stoneware.

By the end of the seventeenth century the English potters in Staffordshire, seeking the secret of true porcelain, began making a white stoneware that they optimistically called porcelain. This stoneware is now called salt-glaze, and it was mass-produced as an inexpensive substitute for porcelain in the period from 1720 to 1780. Often the Staffordshire potters used stoneware to produce the same shapes that they were making in high-fired earthenware—there are samples of Whieldon work in both. This English stoneware has been used as the model for reproductions by Colonial Williamsburg, which, like the reproductions of all responsible museums, are carefully marked to prevent their being passed off as the real thing. But the huge quantity of mediocre saltglaze turning up these days makes one wonder if there isn't an industry out there someplace.

Americans began working in stoneware in Philadelphia in the 1730's. Most of the early examples have disappeared and—even in museums—it is hard to find American stoneware made before the Revolution. However, nineteenth-century American stoneware is a good field for collectors, and some late eighteenth-century examples can be found. The prices are under $100.

Examples that date from the late eighteenth century were turned on a potter's wheel, which produces a more interesting shape—curved from bottom to top. But by the middle of the nineteenth century a growing number of stoneware pieces were molded and have plainer, more regular shapes. The putting-down, or preserving, crock is an example of molded work.

The maker's name and sometimes the town are often found on stoneware jugs or large pans. These tend to be more expensive in the areas where they were made.

Early nineteenth-century examples have delicate ornaments in the form of drapery swags, flowers, birds or other devices. Among the most coveted are those with an eagle, colored blue. Later rarities have deer or houses applied with the naïve charm of folk painters. Most later work skips the decoration altogether, the seams of the mold show in the clay, bespeaking their destiny—to hold food in the cellar or backyard.

Teapot, salt-glazed stoneware, English, about 1745. The thin white salt-glazed ceramic body was made by English and French potters from about 1720 to 1780. Some designs were inspired by oriental porcelain but many were distinctive. The house is one of a number of forms the teapot took in saltglaze.

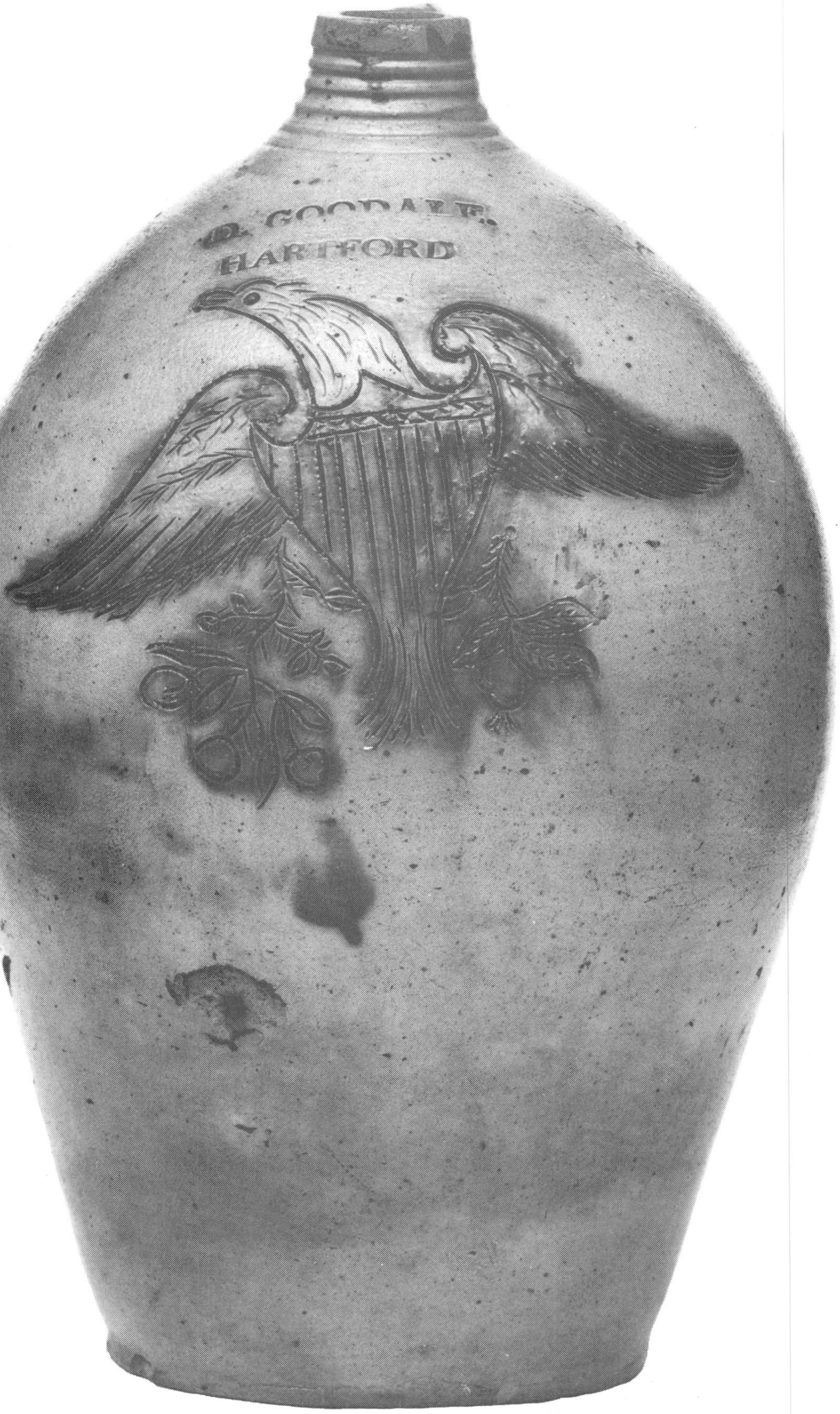
HARTFORD

opposite
Jug, salt-glazed stoneware, by Daniel Goodale,
Hartford, Conn., about 1825. The thick gray
stoneware body occasionally decorated with a
combination of incised line and blue is well
known for functional American wares throughout
the nineteenth century. The eagle motif
was favored early.

Covered urn, yellow jasperware, by Wedgwood,
English, about 1885. The delicate stoneware body
developed by Josiah Wedgwood in the
eighteenth century has been popular ever since.
Late nineteenth-century examples are often well
made but some lack the precise detailing
characteristic of the best work.

Wedgwood also produced stoneware. His version, which is in black or pale colors, looks like biscuit porcelain. He named it jasperware after the stone because it is a stone-like material and he treated it much like the semiprecious stones that were used for jewelry.

The standard pale-colored wares, with their white neoclassical relief decorations, were at their height in the 1780's and the first decades of the nineteenth century. But they were made long after—are still being made, in fact. The more recent creations have fussier designs, but are otherwise much the same as the older. Wares marked with the Wedgwood name became more common after 1820, but not all Wedgwood was marked.

PORCELAIN

In the Tang Dynasty, about 900 A.D., the ingredients that were used to produce stoneware were being mixed with more precision, and porcelain was the result. Porcelain is made of kaolin (the Chinese called it kao ling), a very pure white clay, and pentuntse, a feldspar. Fired at a high temperature, these ingredients fused, or vitrified, to make a translucent white body that was far less brittle than the stoneware that is its clumsier brother. Porcelain's resistance to shocks allowed the potter to work it thinner and thinner.

It was not until the eighteenth century that Westerners were able to make true porcelain, although there were attempts to imitate it with mixtures of glass and pottery. The gap between the evolution of porcelain in the East and its evolution in the West gave rise to porcelain's other name—china—which it was given in the seventeenth century.

Collectors who love a challenge love porcelain. The examples most in demand—from the eighteenth century—are quite expensive, but every porcelain collector makes a great discovery now and then because even the experts can be confused over what is real. Fakes, reproductions and bad contemporary imitations of the best all make hasty buying a great gamble.

The first principle to follow, here above all, is to remember that the object and not the mark should dictate selection. The copyists and fakers have been at work for over a century. Many marks, such as the crossed swords of the Meissen factory, have been put on just about anything because of their identification with excellence.

A good second principle is to try to avoid the period that has attracted the most collectors—the middle of the eighteenth century. Curiously, the most expensive samples, other than the very early ones, are those turn-of-the-century American wares that are collected avidly by residents of the areas where they were made. The late nineteenth-century works of Knowles, Taylor & Knowles in East Liverpool, Ohio, provide examples of prices in the upper reaches.

Buying porcelain should begin at a fine shop where you can talk to a dealer who knows what he has. Although they may seem high, his prices will be fair and you will be

Coffeepot with cover, porcelain, Doccia, Italy, about 1760

able to associate makers and dates with typical output. Once you can distinguish early work from imitations, you will be able to make discoveries on your own. Nonetheless, chances are that the really great additions to your collection will continue to be purchases from the best dealers, who have a lot more time to search out rarities. It is fun to find a rare eighteenth-century German cup and saucer for $30 in a shop that is displaying, with a $2,000 price tag, an 1890 Knowles, Taylor & Knowles urn that is sought by collectors from Cincinnati to Cleveland.

Porcelain is the hardest, thinnest, most colorful and most useful of ceramic wares. Although we think first of its delicacy and whiteness, it can be thick and richly colored, too. Since its development in China, porcelain has been made to suit a wide variety of tastes.

CHINESE AND CHINESE EXPORT PORCELAIN

The Chinese did not differentiate between stoneware and porcelain, so early descriptions are not helpful. The Chinese were interested in handsome forms that gave resonant sounds when struck, and you can get a very fine "ping" from stoneware. Grayish blues and reds were popular in the early period, and some early examples have interesting gradations and crackle in the glaze. Even the familiar blue-and-white wares that had a strong influence on the West have a thickness that surprises the people who are more familiar with late nineteenth-century oriental wares.

Oriental ceramics constitute a special field, and it takes a lot of conviction and a lot of money to delve into it. The finest examples

Cup and saucer made in China for the Western market in about 1740. Coats of arms were a popular form of decoration on such porcelain.

of seventeenth-century, late Ming Dynasty porcelain bring over a hundred thousand dollars at auction.

Admiration for wares of the early period was great in the nineteenth century, so reproductions are common. If you see a delicate long-necked bottle that looks tenth-century and resembles a picture in a book, compare it with something proven old, or pay no more than you would for the lamp base it might originally have been.

As a rule of thumb—and you'll need lots more if you're going to specialize in early oriental porcelain—objects of extreme delicacy are more likely to be nineteenth-century, and sloppy designs were not prized in the Orient. By the late 1800's, the Western influence on Chinese work is obvious; traditional designs are rendered in a virtuoso manner.

Chinese porcelain made for the European and American markets is a field that interests many. These wares have been called Trade Porcelain, Compagnie des Indes, Chinese Export and most confusingly, Lowestoft. The last name arises from a mistake. An early book on the subject assumed because one piece of Chinese porcelain had been decorated in the town of Lowestoft, England, that it all had. That was, in fact, the only case.

Export porcelains were made in great quantity in a few centers in China. Other porcelains for sale abroad were made in Japan. The work is of a quality that was not considered to measure up to the more precious decorative and ceremonial wares made to be kept at home. The surface is frequently shiny and textured, and the white has a greenish cast that is obvious once you recognize it. Further, the object was business, and the makers thus kept copying themselves so long as their output was selling.

Occasional sixteenth- and seventeenth-century blue-and-white pieces are considered to be in the category of Export, but the bulk of the output is of eighteenth- and early nineteenth-century manufacture.

Export has a distinctive charm, despite its second-class category in the eyes of collectors of oriental ceramics. It appears in simple oriental shapes, as well as in oriental interpretations of standard occidental shapes. Dinner and tea services that met the needs of modish Westerners were popular. The early plates are simple octagonal forms with polychrome floral patterns. Sometimes a tureen will appear that reflects the influence of the fanciful rococo models that were made all over Europe in the period from 1730 to 1770.

Several distinctive patterns were well known on the American scene between 1780 and 1830. One is Fitzhugh, a complex leaf-and-scroll over-all pattern. Also well known were simple border designs with family arms or monograms in the center. A dinner set of this sort commands a price in the thousands.

The blue-and-white landscape designs represent a curious case. These were once the least desirable of the Chinese exports—George Washington used this ware in the kitchen, and it was a party setting only for lesser folk. Huge quantities of the blue-and-white have survived, and with a Fitzhugh dinner set in a rare green going for $30,000, it should be no surprise to find elegant contemporary tables set with the humble old blue-and-white. The blue-and-white is called Nanking or Canton, depending upon the border: the latticework of Nanking is more intricate. The two are from the same period and both were made as late as the 1840's.

Rose Medallion is a pattern that was ignored until about ten years ago. It has a predominantly green and red over-all pattern that includes figures. This was made between the War of 1812 and the end of the nineteenth century in imitation of the more subtle eighteenth-century Famille Verte, a pattern applied to fine wares, with green, red and gold figures and pictorial decoration.

Prices on export wares have increased fantastically in the last few years. For this reason, flea markets and lesser dealers are apt to carry a variety of substitutes. Badly made repetitions of good eighteenth-century designs seem to move better when depicted as wares intended for export to the Indian market, but one wonders why the Indians are saddled after the fact with such poor taste. The late nineteenth-century repetitions of Imari—a bright red, orange and gold design on dark blue—are sold as Japanese Export, which is true enough, although the date of import seems to be fairly recent. Hong Kong reproductions of Export wares have the proper textures and imperfections, but disclose their newness when stared at long enough.

Tureen and platters, Fitzhugh pattern, Chinese,
late eighteenth century

EUROPEAN PORCELAIN

When Europeans first tackled porcelain, they couldn't quite master it. Their first products, which are from the fifteenth century, combined clay and glass, or the ingredients used in making glass, to create a thin translucent body that approximated the whiteness of true porcelain. Although true porcelain is glazed before firing, these early European efforts, called soft-paste porcelain, were fired and then glazed. This makes the glaze more evident and the surface glossier than on true porcelain. Soft-paste is also fired at a lower temperature and is thus more brittle and generally a bit thicker. It tends to scratch more easily, but the materials were ideal for the delicate designs that are characteristic of European porcelains.

Porcelain vase made at Meissen, 1725-30. Oriental shapes and decoration were an important source of inspiration for porcelain manufacturers, early as well as late.

Flowerpot, soft-paste porcelain, St.-Cloud, 1720-30. The imitation, or soft-paste, porcelain is frequently glassier looking than the true porcelain. It may also have imperfections in the form of black spots. French potters used metal designs as models for early pieces.

Soft-paste porcelain was first made in the late fifteenth century in Venice. In the sixteenth century the so-called Medici porcelain was made in Florence. It was not until the late seventeenth century that any extensive production began, when the pottery at Rouen, France, started to produce a blue-and-white ware. True porcelain did not appear until the beginning of the eighteenth century, when the factory at Meissen, Germany, cracked the Chinese secret.

In France and England, soft-paste porcelain continued in production through a good part of the eighteenth century. It was used most successfully by those who understood the esthetic of the glassier, thicker material and created bolder and more generalized pieces than would be suitable for true porcelain.

Also notable is the English potters' lack of royal patrons, who made their Continental colleagues' lives easier. The English thus produced to sell. The utilitarian shapes and the transfer prints favored by the English suggest that these were relatively inexpensive porcelains the first time they were sold.

Because of these esthetic watersheds, perhaps, porcelain collectors almost always work exclusively in the wares of one country. Once they develop a taste for French, German or English work, they find they no longer like anything else. The national traits persist through style evolutions: French porcelain reflects fashion, German is flamboyant and technically right and English more compromising with imperfection.

French Porcelain

Because of its concentration on the mode of the moment, French porcelain captures the fullest essence of each style. Although we may think of the most elaborate rococo efforts of the eighteenth century as typically French, there are fairly simple examples of the late seventeenth and early nineteenth that are just as successful in embodying their time. Since design and not technology was uppermost, French porcelain is not always chemically perfect. These imperfections, however, are rarely evident because of the art that concealed them.

This fixation with design probably explains why the French were the first to begin considerable production of soft-paste porcelain. Other potters were satisfied with their heavy interpretations of Chinese porcelain in delftware. But the French knew how they wanted their work to look and, after fruitless efforts to divine the Chinese secret, settled down to create their simulation.

The first factory to produce soft-paste in France—Rouen—was also making faience. The first soft-paste creations from Rouen are impossible to find. When you see them in a museum, you will find that they combine classical and oriental shapes. Handsome fluted forms, familiar in silver of the same period, are decorated either in the classical or Chinese manner in blue.

A factory in St.-Cloud, just outside Paris, produced similar wares at the turn of the seventeenth century and as late as 1730. The body is ivory-toned and glassy, and the

motifs are of oriental inspiration. Work from St.-Cloud is rare, as is the work of the next important factory, Chantilly. At Chantilly there was more work in the Japanese spirit. Small figures and varied forms for serving tea were made in designs often based on Arita models—a Japanese pattern.

The early work from Chantilly has a tin glaze instead of the usual lead glaze. After 1760 the Chantilly work, while often interesting, was rarely innovative or outstanding. Soft-paste wares continued to be produced in Chantilly until 1800, and the main factory continued in business until 1830. Another factory in Chantilly made true porcelain from 1820 to 1870.

Another name of importance in France in the early years is Mennecy, a pottery established by the Duke of Villeroy in 1732. The soft-paste made there was a handsome milk white, and the forms follow the trend of the times. In the first thirty years, the influence of Meissen was strong. Later the Japanese Imari patterns were often copied. Mennecy operated at several places until the beginning of the nineteenth century, but a pottery has operated there recently, so there can be confusion.

Sèvres, France's most important porcelain manufacturer, was first under royal patronage and then under government sponsorship. The pottery was the fruit of an effort that started in the Château de Vincennes in 1738 and moved to Sèvres in 1756. After 1760 the King of France was the proprietor. It was at this time, coincidentally, that the factory gradually changed from soft-paste to true porcelain.

When the factory was at Vincennes, it produced the fashionable designs based on Chinese models. It then moved on to rococo designs. Scenes by the painter Boucher were a source of patterns, which were painted in single colors, or polychrome. Porcelain flowers were a specialty. Plain unglazed porcelain, called biscuit porcelain, was introduced at Vincennes.

When at Sèvres, the factory was responsible for the most elaborate and colorful of French porcelain. Rococo design at its best emerged from the factory until the neoclassical Louis XVI style overwhelmed the rococo. The rich colors and elaborate gilding

express all of the shifting styles almost perfectly.

Sèvres remained a force in design through the nineteenth century. The director of the factory from 1800 to 1848, a man named Brogniart, was a chemist rather than an artist. But the staff of designers that worked under him kept up with the fashions of the day as the ceramic body was constantly improved. Empire designs were succeeded by the waves of revivals that appear in other decorative fields.

The number of modern and relatively old imitations of Sèvres is great. As a guide, eighteenth-century colors are more subtle than recent colors, and even the brightest of the eighteenth-century colors, such as Rose Pompadour, is grayish in comparison with something such as a shocking pink from the 1860's. In that decade the factory seems to have had fun making rococo and Louis XVI revival pieces with blue inscriptions in the underglaze. The names for these mock presentation pieces are plucked from history books, so only famous counts and princes are mentioned. Lots of fancy porcelain that is preserved as a treasure from Madame de Pompadour should be properly dated a century later, and inspection would disclose this disparity.

Independent potteries in Paris provided a significant amount of porcelain in the nineteenth century. Names such as Nast, Dagoty, Darty and Guerhard are found on fine examples of the Empire style. These pieces are often simple, bold shapes painted with elaborate decoration. The Parisian potters tended to be conservative in the 1830's and 1840's, continuing to make Empire shapes but executing them with verve and decorating them skillfully. Jacob Petit, whose shop was active between 1830 and 1865, experimented with more fantastic forms.

French porcelain design in the 1800's is not very well known. There is a quantity of rococo-revival work that looks nothing like real rococo. Flat, molded forms in elaborate floral patterns were typical. More appealing today are the products of the late nineteenth century, which reflect the desire for something new. These are often in dark colors with luster patterns added to heighten the dramatic effect. The designs indicate some

study of Near Eastern work. There are also Art Nouveau porcelains from Sèvres and the smaller potteries.

Frankly, little of the nineteenth-century output has an instant appeal, so the task becomes to decide what will be satisfying after a period of ownership.

German Porcelain

The first true porcelain factory in the West was founded in the eighteenth century at Meissen, a town in Saxony outside Dresden. Early production was experimental; continuous production dates from 1713. Meissen—sometimes also called Dresden—looks harder and smoother than soft-paste. It has an elegance that differs

left to right
Chocolate cup decorated by Herold, beaker with cover, tea caddy, sugar bowl, tea caddy, all Meissen, Germany, about 1735.
Rococo ornament was used for all kinds of small forms in the eighteenth century, but the collector's problem is that the later repetitions can be confusing. Early work is less complex.

radically from the French work because the best examples are brash and less subtle.

The first Meissen designs are close to the Japanese and Chinese models that inspired the original effort to find out how porcelain was made. By the 1720's, rococo was a stronger influence than the oriental.

From the practical point of view, a collector might begin with more ordinary tea cups and saucers, since the more elaborate work is both rare and expensive; good examples of flamboyant bowls go for thousands, and sometimes tens of thousands, of dollars. In the simpler pieces, the virtuosity of the maker as demonstrated in the modeling—as well as the intricacy of the decoration—are prized.

Meissen spawned an extensive network of German potteries, each, if the stories are to be believed, started by a refugee from Meissen or someone who got a factory manager drunk and pried out of him the secret of true porcelain. While the basic approach—concentration on a fine ceramic body and showing off of technical abilities—is constant, there are local differences.

Besides the production of the factories that Meissen unwittingly spun off, there are also conscious copies of Meissen wares. For the collector, the difficulty lies in deciding whether a modest version of an elaborate idea came from a smaller German factory or came from a nineteenth-century copyist. Since even experts can be puzzled, it is best

176

opposite
Ewer, porcelain, Lycett Manufacturing Company, New York, about 1890

Plate, soft-paste porcelain, Chelsea, England, about 1750. English porcelain was even more gross than the French, but it has charm and appeals to many collectors. Rococo patterns are simplified in the best English efforts.

Teapot, soft-paste porcelain with transfer-print decoration, Worcester, about 1765. Use of engravings on porcelain suggests that English product was less precious than Meissen or Sèvres. The forms are often simple and the body less than perfect in what appears to be the middle-class rococo.

to pay the nineteenth-century price whenever it is possible a piece is not truly old.

The Meissen factory was active all through the 1800's and, as at Sèvres, there were efforts to keep up to date. The famous Blue Onion originated as a classical pattern in the nineteenth century.

A number of other factories thrived at the same time. The best known are the Royal Porcelain Factory in Berlin and the Nymphenburg factory. Also popular, but only from the late 1870's, was the output of Rosenthal.

English Porcelain

Like French and German porcelain, English porcelain has its separate set of esthetic standards. A number of factories that began in the eighteenth century, without royal patronage, started with a soft-paste that was less perfect than the French—black spots are occasionally encountered. English designers seemed to take a tongue-in-cheek approach to the problem of making porcelain and were not distressed by the impurities. The best designs show simplicity and strength.

Chelsea, in 1745, was making shiny, glossy figures and plates that seem rough compared with Vincennes or Meissen, but they have a special charm. Modified versions of the rococo also have a particular appeal. Bow, Derby and Worcester are among the important names for early English porcelain. **Tea**

Porcelain vase, by Marc Louis Solon for Minton, English, about 1875. The cameo technique of decorating porcelain called pâte-sur-pâte was used extensively in the late nineteenth century. It made a special delicacy possible.

Pitcher, soft-paste porcelain, by William Ellis Tucker, American, about 1830. The body has a greenish cast when held up to the light. The reeded base and plain form are typical of Tucker products.

sets and a limited number of dinner services were made in the ever popular blue-and-white and in polychrome decoration.

The device of using relief ornamentation goes back to the eighteenth century, but the flowers are rendered with greater detail in the nineteenth. Some feel the rendition is a bit too real, but the prices for the most elaborately detailed nineteenth-century wares frequently surpass those for earlier pieces.

By 1860, neoclassicism was more important than rococo as a source of inspiration. For the more conservative, Louis XVI designs were carefully reproduced. For the adventuresome, older models were adapted, mostly becoming more delicate. In the 1870's and 1880's, Near Eastern models were used as the basis for new designs that showed off the delicacy of the porcelain body. Elaborately pierced sections of vases and ewers exploited the eggshell-thin porcelain. Pierced work, particularly in a cream color, was favored at the Worcester factory.

Minton, following the lead of Sèvres, introduced a fine, elaborately decorated ware called pâte-sur-pâte, literally, paste-on-paste. Layers of porcelain were applied and cut away like a cameo to create delicate relief ornamentation. Solon, a French craftsman hired away from the Continent, signed the best examples of this work, in which white relief figures close to those in sentimental classical paintings appear against a dark background.

American collectors often patriotically seek the rare Tucker porcelains. These porcelains, produced in Philadelphia from 1826 to 1838, have a white body that is marked—like Chinese Export—by a greenish cast. Pitchers were an especially popular form, but many other objects were produced: dinner services and tea sets, decorative vases, scent bottles—and right down the line. Tucker, a relatively simple ware, resembles the more restrained work of Paris shops. When Tucker pieces are recognized, the prices are high—close to $1,000 for a good pitcher, for example.

Commemorative vase, porcelain, Union Porcelain Works, American, 1876. Designed to celebrate the centenary of American independence, this vase is evidence of the abilities of American potters and a reminder of the fact that design was occasionally unusual.

BONE CHINA, BELLEEK AND PARIAN

In ceramic technology, the great contribution of the English in the nineteenth century was bone china. It was developed in about 1800 by Josiah Spode, a major English potter, as an inexpensive version of true porcelain. The composition of bone china is close to that of true porcelain: bone ash is added to kaolin and feldspar to make a paste that is more easily controlled in the kiln. Although Spode's goal was to reduce expense, bone china turned out to be a distinct improvement over porcelain—it was lighter, whiter and more receptive to bright colors than either true porcelain or soft-paste.

After Spode's breakthrough, most of the major potters in Staffordshire started making bone china, as did some of the minor factories. The names Spode, Minton, Coalport, Rockingham and Worcester are notable in this field. Much of what was made was marked at the time so that it is not difficult to identify the makers.

Although it comes from many factories of the nineteenth century, Belleek is named after the town in Ireland where the ware was first produced in the 1850's. It is a thin porcelain with a glossy glaze. Shells and undulating forms were used to show off the thinness of the ware. Much Belleek was made late in the nineteenth century and even into the early twentieth, when souvenir cups and saucers were popular. Belleek was made in Trenton, New Jersey, and the names Ott & Brewer, Ceramic Art Company and Lenox

Part of bone porcelain table service, Crown Derby, English, about 1820. Dark colors and lots of gold were used on early nineteenth-century English porcelain.

Dish designed by Joshua Poole, Lotusware porcelain, Knowles, Taylor & Knowles, East Liverpool, Ohio, about 1890. The specially thin body was used by a number of potters in the late nineteenth century. It was first introduced in France in the 1860's. This is close to what is called Belleek.

Pitcher, showing Niagara Falls in Parian ware porcelain, by U.S. Pottery Co., Bennington, Vt., about 1855. Unglazed, or biscuit, porcelain was used in the eighteenth century for a variety of neoclassical designs. It was revived in the 1840's by the English potters for figures, and by the mid nineteenth century Americans were also making a biscuit porcelain called Parian because it supposedly resembled marble. The subject reflects nineteenth-century interest in nature.

are associated with the American output; Lotusware, with a slightly thicker body, was produced by Knowles, Taylor & Knowles at the turn of the century.

About 1845 the Copeland factory in England developed a biscuit porcelain, a porcelain without a glaze, that was a bit less expensive to make than the earlier biscuit ware. Copeland's motive was to respond to a revived demand for small decorative figures.

Copeland's formula was quickly taken up by Minton, which called the new ware parian, and this has become the generic name for it. However, Wedgwood sold it as carara. Parian was used for copies of famous statues, as well as for such popular themes as crying children, frolicking dogs and famous people of the time. The English versions are realistic or sentimental.

Parian was produced in the United States, notably in Bennington, which made not only the figures but also pitchers, cups and other small objects. Slightly later, other potteries in New Jersey and the Middle West entered the field. Parian continued in production until the end of the nineteenth century. These wares, of the common English variety, can be found for $20 to $30; Bennington products will be ten times higher, or more, if the figure is considered a rarity.

LATER CERAMICS

At the turn of the century, Art Nouveau became the style. Pottery and porcelain strongly show this influence, with some of the samples suggesting the rococo in their elongation. So great was the vogue that art potteries sprang up and expanded on the basis of the demand. But many of the traditional potters tooled up and pursued the trend. Rozenburg, a turn-of-the-century Dutch potter, produced fabulous angular shapes in thin porcelains that add a dimension to Art Nouveau; Rozenburg wares are costly.

Villeroy & Boch in Mettlach, Germany, famous for late nineteenth-century steins, also made a variety of objects in the Art Nouveau manner. Thin porcelains in elongated forms, decorated in naturalistic floral

Teapot, porcelain, Rozenberg, The Hague, 1900

or relief patterns, or in geometric motifs, emerged from many Continental factories.

A recent outgrowth in ceramics is the cubist work of the 1920's and 1930's. Angular shapes, resembling the simplified forms found in the work of Léger and Picasso, were characteristic of what is now called the Art Deco style, named for an exhibition held in Paris in 1925, l'Exposition International des Arts Decoratives.

The Art Deco style, evoking the magic period of the movie idols and new skyscrapers, finds favor with a group of adventuresome collectors. Examples were being made at most of the important porcelain factories, but these are hard to find.

Collecting later ceramics has few pitfalls in the way of fakes. The only problem is to decide what's good.

Pictures

Oil on canvas: After the Ball *by Alfred Stevens, Belgium, 1874*

MINOR ART

You'll find no lost masterpieces by Rembrandt or Van Gogh if you do your picture-hunting in antique shops. Antique dealers carry pictures to fill up the spaces between tabletops and ceiling rather than as vehicles for significant esthetic experience. Nevertheless, a lot of what the antique dealers choose in pictures—oil paintings, watercolors, drawings, and prints—embodies fine craftsmanship and has strong charm. Even if they do not represent high-water marks in the history of art, the pictures reflect the changing tastes of past periods.

As a picture hunter you should heed two caveats. First, remember that your goal is decorative and not profound and there need be no long palaver on the qualifications of the artist if you don't think the picture will enhance your room. Second, recognize that even connoisseurs have trouble determining the nature of something framed and under glass. Most glassed-in pictures are on paper and they might be drawings, fine early prints or modern reproductions. If you cannot examine the work close up, pay no more than the frame is worth to you.

PAINTINGS

By and large the paintings hanging in antique shops are of eighteenth- and nineteenth-century origin. Countless portraits of nameless worthies by Continental and English artists, equally anonymous, turn up for sale. When these are sufficiently stylized they are often more interesting than works more carefully rendered. If you are looking for an ancestor to go with a favorite piece of eighteenth-century furniture, an anonymous portrait may be just the thing. Look hard and be sure you find the person appealing, because few things are more annoying than being stared at daily by a gentleman or lady you abhor. Usually, however, English and Continental portraits of the eighteenth century are generalized enough to keep you from feeling you have an enemy in the house.

American portraits and landscapes of the eighteenth and nineteenth centuries tend to have been stylized more ably than the Old World examples. The American painters brought to their canvas the same forthright qualities and fondness for simplicity that the furniture-makers did, and the results are much in favor today. The market for American art of every kind is rising; the best portraits of the eighteenth century and landscapes of the nineteenth century have brought over a hundred thousand dollars recently. Works this expensive are from a select group that is closely associated with important artistic tendencies; you would recognize the names of artists or styles. When viewing works of the kind more often en-

countered in shops, be wary of something described as American without any corroborating evidence; the attribution itself raises the price. When the work is distinctively American, prices usually move quickly out of reach: a good but unknown eighteenth-century American portrait will cost over $10,000, while a fussier product from Europe will go for a few hundred. Not everything American is dear, however. You can still find simple stylized nineteenth-century landscapes for a few hundred dollars.

If you find you like the effect, simple primitives are a worthwhile field. In the late eighteenth and early nineteenth centuries, the works of primitive artists, now sometimes called naïve painters, were internationally popular. Usually they took as a model a work by an established academic artist, modified the composition to accommodate their talents—omitting details, emphasizing overall shapes, sometimes abandoning perspective—and produced pictures of great charm. The late modern primitive artist "Grandma" Moses would paint in the green on a number of pictures in one day, and the black the next, to avoid wasting paint. While such an approach makes academic artists cringe, it never hurt her sales. The works of earlier primitive painters sometimes suggest the use of similar methods. Collectors who favor the virtuosity of eighteenth-century craftsmen over folk or experimental works tend to buy traditional academic-genre paintings—pictures of everyday life—and landscapes by trained artists of the nineteenth century.

American works of this type are priced in the upper reaches, but European examples are moderate. A few hundred dollars will buy a Swiss mountain, while a Catskills scene is likely to be $15,000 or over. An amusing incident of hunting along the Mississippi will be $40,000, while the same scene in a Rhine Valley setting will go for $400.

When you encounter bargains in neglected fields, remember that the best possible examples are the wisest buys from the standpoint of investment. In fields that attract little attention, a signature on a painting will barely affect the price. But if such an area of, say, nineteenth-century art should begin to be an object of attention, the signed work will be worth more than the unknown one. The price differential between fine and mediocre pictures in a neglected field is slim; you might as well buy the best you see. If you collect in popular fields and spend a lot, beware the faked signature. You can generally tell when the picture has been signed over old paint, but the picture that has thus been "improved" is usually of not very great quality; this should warn you off right away. There has been some fakery in the less important folk pictures. A man rumored to be living in Pennsylvania has recently been creating early nineteenth-century folk pictures. But he doesn't try too hard and there are bloopers in details—such as the number of stars in his flags.

Most paintings in antique shops are on canvas. But there are other types. One can find small sixteenth- and seventeenth-century paintings on copper that are often school repetitions of works by great painters of the period. Although rarely important, these are sometimes appealing. With some research, you can often find out what painting was being copied. In the Renaissance painters often worked on wood panels. Such paintings from the eighteenth and nineteenth centuries, however, usually turn out to have been signs, parts of furniture or pieces of paneled walls. These decorative panels, like the pictures on copper, were frequently inspired by famous painters' works. American examples are both rare and expensive; some of the European peasant pieces have great charm and cost less.

Paintings on glass were a novelty that was popular in the eighteenth and nineteenth centuries. Most frequently the picture is

Mercy Harvell, by E. E. Finch, oil on canvas, Maine, about 1840. American folk art has a strong appeal. Stylized, simplified and the work of unschooled craftsmen, the portraits capture the spirit and vitality of the subjects. The cautious collector makes sure no restoration will be necessary.

Liberty Supporting America, *Chinese painting on glass after an engraving by Edward Savage, about 1790. Chinese paintings on glass use American and European engravings as a source of inspiration. In England the print was actually applied to the glass and colored after most of the paper was removed.*

based on a print. The print was applied to the back of the glass and the paper rubbed away, leaving an outline that was then colored in with paint. Generally some paper is left behind; when, as in many eighteenth-century examples, this is a sizable amount, the color is affected. In some nineteenth-century examples the images are simply stenciled on the back of the glass in the bold masses typical of folk art. An additional primitive effect is produced because the artist, working in reverse, had to apply the eyes and mouth before he painted the head.

Chinese artists painted on glass for export to the West late in this period. These works often appear to have been rather free renditions of popular prints: portraits of Washington, for instance, or, more often, of ladies of fashion. There were also a certain number of Chinese landscapes on glass. One Victorian variation of paintings on glass involves a backing of tinfoil or tinsel that shows through in unpainted places. Tinsel pictures are most frequently still lifes of fruit or flowers, but there are other subjects as well. An unno-

ticed tinsel picture will sell for less than $50, but good examples are getting closer to $500.

Watercolor, popular in the eighteenth, nineteenth and twentieth centuries, was a medium for amateurs as well as professionals and some pretty odd things turn up. Mediocre examples—a wedding present from Uncle Eddie?—sometimes turn up magnificently framed. Fine efforts by significant painters can also be found, forgotten in notebooks that have been lost for a century or so. They sometimes turn up unframed in a portfolio of prints. The price range for watercolors is astounding: great examples of nineteenth-century virtuosity are $20,000 and much more; good, routine work by respectable recognized artists will go for $300. Many collectors favor amateur studies that have the naïve charm of folk work. Watercolorists seem to have done everything—from vases of flowers to landscapes and interiors of all sorts. The exploring is fun and the size of these works makes them easy to take home.

DRAWINGS

Drawings—pencil or pen work in a single color on paper—are almost identical to watercolors from the collectors' standpoint. Amateur and professional work abounds. Works by known artists are expensive and simple; unsigned, undated works can be had for little. However, the area where drawings and calligraphy overlap is today of considerable concern to collectors. The calligraphers, or writing masters, of earlier times did penmanship exercises using their elegant swirls and flourishes to create deer, men on horseback, birds and fantastic creatures. Americans tend to prefer the local product, but these works were created all over the Continent and the curves are just as flamboyant and the results just as amusing for a lesser price.

A Bower of Mulberry Trees, by Hannah Cahoon, an inspirational Shaker drawing. Poetry and design were combined in works by members of the Shaker community. The drawings were motivated by strong feelings and were unusual in communities that proscribed pictures as decoration.

When they weren't teaching, Pennsylvania calligraphers of the eighteenth and nineteenth centuries got the business of their town writing certificates: birth, baptismal, wedding—whatever needed to be attested. At the beginning of this century Dr. Henry Mercer made a pioneer study of these certificates and called them fractura, reviving a term from the sixteenth century. Fractura combine lettering and pictorial embellishment in a way that shows they are the last gasp of a tradition of lettering going back to the Middle Ages. Not surprisingly, the work of Pennsylvania German calligraphers is particularly prized in the United States. Good fractura cost thousands of dollars, but there are small examples and figures without the

Birth certificate, fractura, Lancaster, Pennsylvania, 1820. In watercolor or engraved, the Pennsylvania German certificates are the last form of manuscript illumination. Fine lettering and appropriate motifs are integrated in strikingly decorative pieces.

Silhouette of members of the family of Count van Loewenstern of Riga, by Peter E. Rockstuhl, German, 1785. Cutouts of figures, or figures simply painted in silhouette, were a popular form of portraiture from the late eighteenth century until about 1850. Usually small, they can be collected in quantity.

lettering that are $50 to $100. The European versions, virtually ignored, are priced at $100 or less.

Silhouettes are outline drawings filled in with black or another solid color. They were drawn and painted, or cut out or made with a mechanical tracing apparatus. Portraits were most popular, but landscapes and pictures of people in action are also found. Silhouettes were at the height of their popularity from 1800 to 1850. Galleries making them flourished in all major cities on both sides of the Atlantic.

PRINTS

Aside from the sort of remarkable find reported on the front page of the newspaper every five years or so, the most important pictures to be discovered in antique shops are the fine prints. These prints, as distinguished from reproductions, are made in a deliberately limited number, usually under the guiding hand of the artist who created the original picture or under the control of a craftsman who has been chosen to translate the work. Such prints may be numbered and are sometimes signed. The making of fine prints began with fifteenth-century woodcuts and has continued to the present, using modernized techniques—etching, engraving and lithography. Because a print is made in quantity does not mean it is necessarily inexpensive. Although there are prints of all kinds selling for $10 or $20, many others are priced in the thousands. Neither age nor quality are consistent factors in price; Rembrandt etchings are costly, but so are important nineteenth-century views of American cities. A collector may be seeking the artist, the subject matter or, in some cases, the refinement of the technique.

If a collector is willing to search and is content to buy items for which there is less demand, he can find bargains. An Albrecht Dürer print went at auction recently for $14,000, but equally authentic examples of the great German artist's work are available for $200. They are small, the subjects are not so thrilling and the prints not so carefully made, but they are Dürers all the same and the genius of his work can be discerned.

Similarly, views of towns can be astronomical or modest. An 1820 view of a south German town will cost less than the sales tax on the view of a major monument in New York or Philadelphia, made at the same time with the same skill.

In hunting for these sorts of bargains, try to avoid later prints made from early engravings. Many of the blocks or plates for early work were preserved and then reused from the 1700's on. There are several ways of determining if a print falls into this category. The color of the newer paper usually makes the print look peculiar; this is the easiest giveaway. In addition, the plates were sometimes so worn that those who revived them worked on them a bit—usually refurbishing the foreground. For example, when nineteenth-century artisans revived the plates of the eighteenth-century views of Rome by Piranesi, they did a little doctoring on the conspicuous parts, but the backgrounds have gone misty. The effect is pretty, but the originals have more vitality.

The earliest kind of fine print is the woodcut, which dates from the 1400's. In this technique a design is created on a block of wood when the background is carved away. Woodcuts are thus usually characterized by bold, plain, heavy lines. Late Gothic examples are few and far between, but woodcuts from the 1700's on can be found. Most eighteenth-century broadsides—advertisements, announcements and poems—are woodcuts and these frequently include simple, bold pictures. Many nineteenth-century

Woodcut, Flight Into Egypt, *by Ludolphus de Saxonia, German, 1495. Elongated forms in the Gothic spirit, drawn with a minimum of detail, are found in early book illustrations. Nineteenth-century folk artists had a similar approach to making woodcuts.*

Engraving: Adam and Eve, *by Albrecht Dürer, German, 1504. The engraving technique is much more practical for artists interested in precision. Tiny crags and correct botanical specimens can be recorded more readily in an engraving.*

folk prints are also woodcuts; the schematic rendering of simple statements seems perfect for folk art. Not all woodcuts have the heavy-line look, however. Some are relatively complex compositions with shading and textures created through density or sparseness of the lines. The German artist Hans Baldung Grien and the Italian Titian were two masters of the sixteenth century who made intricate woodcuts. Many simple eighteenth- and nineteenth-century woodcuts cost less than $20; woodcut illustrations removed from eighteenth-century books are $10 to $50 depending upon the popularity of the subject.

The technique of engraving came fast on the heels of the woodcut, in the fifteenth

century. It is really a reversal of the woodcut, with the line that is to be printed cut into a metal plate, usually copper. This incised, or intaglio, line is more delicate than the line created in the relief work of woodcuts, and engravings can be more detailed. The lines are sure and free, but somewhat stark, and were considered too plain for the baroque expressions of the 1600's. But artisans of the period did engrave portraits, often for books, and these are available today. A century later, a variety of instructive illustrations and simpler portraits and city views were engraved. In the eighteenth century engravers made exceptional use of the technique to create copies of the fashionable painters of the day. Expert engravers translated works by Boucher,

Engraving: Anne of Austria *by P. de Champagne, engraved by J. Morin, French, seventeenth century. Portraits were popular in the seventeenth and eighteenth centuries. Able engravers adapting the efforts of the best artists produced fine work.*

Engraving: scene from Marriage à la Mode, *by William Hogarth, English, 1743. Satirical prints of the eighteenth century occasionally document the objects as well as the spirit of the time. Hogarth was particularly adept in setting scenes accurately. He published several series that were reprinted in the nineteenth century and were pirated even when new.*

Engraving: View of Piazza del Populo, *Rome, by Giovanni Battista Piranesi, Italian, 1750. The Piranesi views recorded Rome successfully enough to have stayed in demand for many years. Reprints from the original plates were made. The late repetitions are not as consistently clear as the originals.*

Watteau, Fragonard and others into black-and-white prints, which were sometimes hand-colored; these were fervently collected in the 1920's. Because they are ignored today, this is an area of worthwhile bargains, and a beautifully framed example of this sort can sometimes be found for less than $100. There are also outstanding English and American eighteenth-century engravings, Hogarth works among them. The outstanding American examples include historic scenes such as the Boston Massacre, by Paul Revere, an artisan versatile in several fields. The American works, including portraits, tend to be plainer than the English or Continental. Less important views are around $100; the more noteworthy cost well above that.

At the beginning of the 1500's, etching, a refinement of the engraving technique, was developed. Acids were applied to the plates to cut the lines, and it became possible to increase the detail and nuance in the picture. While the first dated etching is marked 1513, the work of Rembrandt, born a century later, is the work one thinks of in connection with this technique. Etching was ideal for the subtle control of light that is characteristic of Rembrandt's work. His etchings are generally costly, but there are later prints from the original plates that are priced in the hundreds—roughly the same price asked for early, but imperfect, Rembrandt etchings. In the eighteenth century, etching was employed in combination with engraving for

Hand-colored engraving: Boston Massacre, by Paul Revere, American, 1770. Although Revere borrowed this design from a competitor, Peter Pelham, the Revere print is his most famous engraving. Revere and Pelham are two of a number of engravers whose work has the charm of folk art.

a

c

b

a
Etching: Faust in His Study, *by Rembrandt, Dutch, 1652. Rembrandt worked on the etching himself rather than using the services of a special craftsman as in other print media. The qualities are implicit in every scratch. The Rembrandt plates were reused long after he died. Because of wear and inept restoring, the later editions are not so great as the early. Paper differs in each century, but so does the over-all appearance.*

b
Engraving: The Governess, *by Chardin, engraved by Bernard Lépicié, French, 1739. Engravings of famous paintings were important in the eighteenth century. Able craftsmen worked on the old masters as well as on contemporary work but were more successful with the contemporary. Lépicié engraved Chardin's work soon after it was completed.*

c
Mezzotint: Lt. Col. Tarleton, *by Joshua Reynolds, engraved by J. R. Smith. Planes or whole areas are rendered flat and in shades closer in effect to paintings than engravings. The English engravers adapted the work of the most important painters in the mezzotint technique.*

numberless simple views—landscapes and cityscapes. Etching used alone was the technique for the popular views of Rome by Piranesi, and these are available in a wide range of quality. Some can be found for $5, but the best examples are over $1,000. Views of Rome from "unimproved" plates go for about $500.

In England at this time the most characteristic print was the mezzotint. The mezzotint, invented late in the 1600's, is another refinement of the engraving technique, in which whole areas rather than just lines were incised. The result is a print of greater subtlety. The portraits of eighteenth-century England were more often published as mezzotints than as either engravings or etchings. Paintings dear to the lives of the educated English were also made widely available this way. Before 1930 these prints were much collected, but interest has faded since then. There are good chances of finding fine examples if one avoids famous heroes; John Paul Jones will be $750, but an unknown lady might be $40.

About 1770 a Frenchman, J. B. Le Prince, invented another refinement on engraving, the aquatint. Like the mezzotint, it defined areas rather than lines, and by the end of the 1700's it could be printed in color. Many neoclassical subjects were executed in aquatints; the English satirist Rolandson depicted the lurid side of life of the time in colored aquatints. Goya is one of the outstanding artists whose works were often executed in this technique. Like mezzotints, aquatints were more important to collectors forty years ago than today; good buys are to be had.

All of these techniques—woodcutting, engraving and etching—continued in use through the nineteenth century. The skill of the nineteenth-century printmakers, who were often the artists themselves—Daumier notably among them—was amazing. A number of prints were published in relatively small editions; others were illustrations for books or periodicals of wide circulation. Daumier's work, for example, is usually found on pages cut from periodicals. Prints by Impressionists are generally quite expensive, but etchings by the landscape artists of the Barbizon school can sometimes be purchased inexpensively. Works by masters of the technique, such as Charles Meryon, who had an impressive eye for detail, are worth seeking.

Although these earlier methods continued, the preponderance of prints in this period were done using the technique of lithography. About 1796, a German, Alois Senefelder, invented this chemical technique to supersede engraving. Lithography is based on the principle that oil and water do not mix; a stone is treated so that the areas that are to hold the oily ink are greasy, and so that the other areas reject the ink and the paper is left white. Senefelder devised the lithographic technique while he was looking for a cheap way to print his plays, and its use for pictures was an afterthought. The earliest work in lithography reflects this: the artists often used lines alone rather than availing themselves of the chance to record degrees

Etching: Le Stryge, *by Charles Meryon, French, about 1850. The nineteenth-century revival of etching was the work of artists interested in showing off their skills by working directly on the plate. The etcher was able to pick out the smallest details. Meryon's pictures of Paris are strangely personal at a time when more ordinary views were standard.*

Etching: Limehouse, *by Whistler, American, about 1860. The American virtuoso of etching and lithography, Whistler created works that range from well-composed views to moodily expressive pictures. Although quite well known, he is but one of a long list of artists who produced fine etchings after 1850.*

Lithograph: French fashion plate, late nineteenth-century. Pictures of clothing that were intended as inspirations to tailors and dressmakers make delightful period decoration. These were published in quantity from the start of the nineteenth century. The figures are anonymous, and the details of the costume dominate.

of light and shade. The process was relatively inexpensive, making it a boon to such popular expressions as cartoons and advertisements that relied on line rather than shading. But lithography was also used from the beginning for purely artistic work, notably old-master drawings. Lithographs by Goya, Delacroix and Gericault represent the serious efforts of the early period.

Artists prominent in the first half of the 1800's, among them Bonnington and Isabey, created lithographs of French landscapes. Experiments in color lithography began as early as the 1830's, and some of these landscapes are in color. Although these works were much prized by collectors at the beginning of this century, they tend to be ignored today. With the exception of such works as Goyas, some of the output is rather fussy and the picturesque views seem rather staid to modern collectors. Thus, the area is a good one for the bargain hunter, who need only avoid the more recent copies, a task easily accomplished if the age of the paper is examined. In contrast to the neglected fine lithographs of the early nineteenth century, the popular political works of the period are in intense demand today. The French journalists favored a satirical approach that seems quite pertinent now. Daumier and Gavarni are two notable names in this kind of work.

American lithographs tend to be more commercial than artistic. The best known by far of the nineteenth-century publishing

Lithograph: The Old Homestead, *by Nathaniel Currier, about 1855. Currier & Ives employed a large number of artists but achieved a consistent appearance because the lithographers rendered everything in about the same style. Until the 1880's Currier & Ives lithographs were hand-colored. Reproductions are common.*

houses is Currier & Ives, a firm active from 1834 to 1906 under several names. This New York house published all sorts of American views, records of important events, sailing vessels, sentimental scenes and much else. Although these prints were originally priced at a few cents to a few dollars, they have been collected avidly for fifty years; many of the rarer examples have risen in price to a thousand dollars or more. Because of their popularity they have been reproduced extensively, and the more popular the scene the more frequent the reproduction. It does not take too long, however, to study some early versions enough to be able to recognize a modern copy. The beginner should be wary of any paper that indicates that the print has been produced photographically.

The work of Currier & Ives stands out among the work of other American lithographers of the period, partly because of its typical nineteenth-century look and partly because of its naïve quality. Although the firm used artists who probably were fairly sophisticated, the result is generally primitive. The pictures are simple, descriptive and folksy—perfect as pictorial records that put no intellectual strain on the buyer. Other kinds of works by some of the Currier & Ives artists point up the special spirit in the lithographs. George Henry Durrie, for example, did careful renditions of detail in his oil paintings, but there is no sign of this trait in his lithographs. Among the notable competitors of Currier & Ives are Kellogg and Sarony & Major. Works from these houses can often

Wood engraving: Our Army Before Yorktown, *Va., by Winslow Homer (from* Harper's Weekly), *American, 1862. Homer's magazine contributions are easily available to collectors. The wood-engraving technique was used for the first comic strips.*

opposite
Detail of poster for the New York Ledger *by H. B. Eddy, American, about 1900*

NEW YORK LEDGER

PRICE 5¢

FROM A DESIGN BY H.B.Eddy.

be found at better prices than the Currier & Ives.

Lithography was also a boon to the poster makers. There are examples from England and France that were made before 1850, but the collector who favors American work will find that most of what he wants dates from the late 1800's. Color lithography techniques were markedly improved in the 1860's, so there was an upsurge of posters after that. The bold compositions and imaginative ideas found in these posters appear to foreshadow modern advertising. Some posters are schematic representations of factory towns, others are more usual commercial arguments. Theatrical posters reflect more advanced graphic work; elongated organic plants characteristic of Art Nouveau designs were well known in posters for the theater long before they appeared elsewhere in the decorative arts. But those who like posters generally have a hard time quitting at 1900; adventuresome efforts continue into the twentieth century, some quite radical for their time.

Print collecting can be fun, but there are three approaches and you should be clear about the category to which you belong. You may want prints of the style and time of the furniture you collect; then date and authenticity are vital to you. You may be most concerned about subject matter—transportation, or a particular city. Or you may make your selections on the basis of artistic merit, regardless of period or subject. If you cannot decide which of these three factors is the most important, but want pictures that qual-

Colored lithograph: Opening of Brooklyn Bridge, *poster by Currier & Ives, American, 1883. Posters to announce just about any occasion and to advertise every type of product were increasingly common in the late nineteenth century. Some have the quaintness of folk pictures while others reflect latest artistic trends.*

ify on all three criteria, you are probably going to find everything you want is priced out of reach. Once you have settled your priorities, you will find satisfactory examples in all price ranges—it's only a matter of pursuit. As an example, there are for sale 1920's re-creations, honestly updated, of famous 1820 views of Philadelphia and 1760 New York views. Many collectors are delighted with these because they offer the right subject matter at a practical price—$200, or a tenth of the price of the original. If you avoid the example so inexpensive that it looks like a steal, you can find what is important to you in prints—style, subject or virtuosity—at a price that suits you.

Metals

BASE AND PRECIOUS

Collectors of metals are a diverse lot. A collector of antique gold keeps his priceless collection in a locked glass case in a room designed to set off his prizes. Another collector covers the walls of the cellar of his Iowa farmhouse with primitive farming tools, from post-hole diggers to sieves. Both are serious collections and their owners each knowledgeable about his field. But it is hard to imagine people with less in common, except that they collect metal objects.

Gold is by no means the most expensive field in which to collect; demand disturbs the concept of precious metal versus base. A fine small gold box of eighteenth-century Continental origin may cost $150, whereas an eighteenth-century American pewter tankard may run to $10,000. Demand creates other anomalies. Sixteenth-century Italian brass or bronze mortars cost about $50; signed American brass of the 1780's runs into the hundreds. Silver, brass and pewter in the Art Nouveau style have attracted considerable attention, and these objects are likely to be more expensive than work dating from earlier in the nineteenth century. Objects stamped with the Tiffany studio mark are the highest priced of all recent work. But simple modern silver of the 1920's, which is acutely rare, has begun to carry away top honors in the price department.

As in any field of antiques, the distinctive work of each era offers the greatest challenge. Take, for example, the endless silver reproductions made in the 1920's and 1930's. These pieces are probably a good practical

Chalice, silver gilded and enameled with jewels, Freiburg, 1225–50. Gothic-period craftsmen often used the round rather than the pointed arch for decorative effects. Elaborate surfaces were created with applied ornament. The squat lines and almost primitive simplicity of early work is much less slick than examples of the nineteenth-century Gothic revival.

investment; the prices are often considerably less than those for comparable new silver, and the collector may find them a good compromise in taste. Living with this silver, however, he may find it of less interest than something original in concept and execution. The reproduction follows the original in every detail, but the modern techniques used to do the job create some obvious differences that most students find annoying. It is only when the differences become great enough that the new version becomes distinctive and can be appreciated for its own merits.

In metals other than silver, reproductions are of less interest. While the metal objects of the eighteenth century are still the most coveted, there is a growing awareness of later examples. The metalwork of the late nineteenth century, often ignored, includes distinctive designs that will come into great demand as the pendulum swings back toward a taste for elaborate decoration.

PRECIOUS METALS

Silver and gold have always been prized, not just for the rarity that has made them mediums of exchange but for the ease with which they are tooled into decorative pieces. In fact, silver and gold are so soft that they cannot be used alone, and another metal must be added for strength.

Sterling is the term that is applied to relatively pure silver. The standard for sterling was set in England in about 1300, and it requires about 925 parts pure silver to 75 parts copper. The workable gold alloy has varied. Silver and copper have generally been added; if copper alone is added, the gold has a greenish hue. Pure gold is 24 karats. In the eighteenth century, 22-karat gold was first regarded as standard, then 18-karat became popular, but 14-karat is popular today.

In England precious metals are tested by government assay offices and marked to show that they meet official standards. The English marks, in use since the fourteenth century, are the best known and most easily recognized, although a number of Continental centers of the eighteenth and nineteenth centuries also tested metals. Until 1798, silver and gold were marked in the same way.

Of the marks shown in the illustrations those of most concern to the collector are the ones applied to English silver since 1784, because collectors encounter this silver most often. Starting in 1784, five marks have been hammered onto silver, usually in a row. A crowned leopard's head signifies London quality, which means that the piece meets the sterling standard. A letter connotes the date of manufacture. A lion passant—walking rather than standing—also signifies sterling and was evidently introduced in 1544–45 as a way of confirming the purity of work assayed after a period in which a lowered sterling standard was used. A stamp containing initials, a name or the first two letters of a name and a symbol tells who the maker was. A profile head of the reigning sovereign showed that the duty had been paid. Duties had been imposed on silver earlier, but the payment was not recorded on the piece until December, 1784. The duty mark was not used after May 1, 1890, when the duty was lifted. Before 1784 all but the sovereign's mark were used. For the period between 1697 and 1720, when a purer sterling was made, a seated figure of Britannia was used instead of the leopard's head. The Britannia mark was also used between 1863 and 1875, and if the date marks have been erased, it is possible to mistake a simple 1863 piece for a 1716–17 piece.

When marked, American silver of the seventeenth to the nineteenth century is stamped with a maker's name; after the introduction of mass production a number was sometimes included, which rarely has any significance for the collector. Between 1814 and 1830 the Maryland assay office applied four marks: one for the town, another for the assayer, a third for the maker and the fourth for the date. At about this time, several New York silversmiths used meaningless marks to make their silver look English.

Makers' marks are initials or initials and a symbol.

Mark of origin
In England each regional assay office had
it's distinctive mark.

A typical English mark has four or five stamps.
The single letter is a date mark.

Typical Parisian marks.

Typical American marks.

The question of plated silver versus sterling often makes the beginning collector feel uncomfortable; he is afraid of displaying his ignorance by asking the dealer outright. But where the ware is a product of the eighteenth century, the question is far from naïve. In the eighteenth century a factory method of applying sheets of silver to copper was perfected, and this lower-priced ware was made and bought in quantity. If the object does not bear one of the emblems for sterling, however, it is probably plated. On ware made after about 1840, when a chemical plating technique using electricity replaced the earlier mechanical process, the question usually resolves itself. A gray alloy was sometimes used for the base instead of copper. Dark dull spots that look like dirt or tarnish, but that will not polish off, make this later plated work easier to distinguish.

Because of the darkening that neglect produces on metal objects, there are moments when it is all but impossible to recognize even which metal an object is made of. Those who frequent garage sales and smaller auctions where objects are sold before cleaning and testing should ever be optimists, hewing to the mottoes "all that is gold need not glitter" and "all that is silver need not shine." An acquaintance bought half a dozen 1890–1910 napkin rings in a lot that included a small bowl that might have been Mexican and looked as if it might be useful for nuts or olives. All were black. Cleaning disclosed the rings to be mediocre silver, but the bowl revealed itself as a $12,000 example of New York sterling. It is now in the Minneapolis Art Institute. At about the same time, my wife was delighted to turn up, also blackened, what she was sure was an Art Nouveau silver vase. For $3 and three hours of vigorous rubbing, she got a pewter vase that leaks. And not so long ago, a perfectly ordinary pair of chalices turned up in a design that was typically mid nineteenth-century American. The design was of no particular importance and the assumption was that the chalices were gilded. A jeweler's examination showed them to be pure gold.

The collector who haunts places where junk is sold can often achieve one of these great disappointments, even if he can't manage a great find. The job of the specialist is to do the hunting for you; although the price is correspondingly higher, the incidence of disappointment is less.

Gold objects are quite rare, in the junk heap or on the dealer's shelf. Through history, until well into the eighteenth century, the craftsmen who fashioned objects of gold and silver were all known as goldsmiths, but they worked in silver most of the time. The "gold" objects most often found are thus likely to turn out, under jewelers' tests, to be gilt silver. Gilt silver was produced by two processes. One method was for the gold to be melted, mixed with mercury, brushed on and the mercury burned away. In the other method a mixture of linen ashes and gold chloride was brushed onto the surface. Either technique produced a thin, delicately colored surface much less harsh looking than later gilding, which was accomplished by electrolysis. Gold applied to a base metal such as bronze or copper is generally a fine color but the object is relatively thick looking. Because of the sophistication of these processes, the only way to find out if an object is gold is to submit it to jewelers' tests. Most of the time the gold will prove to be brass.

SILVER

The process of fashioning silver into forms by hand begins with a sheet of silver that is cut into appropriate flat shapes. The shapes are then hammered—a technique called raising because the sheet is raised to create a three-dimensional form. To facilitate the hammering, the metal is heated constantly. This produces a scale of black, which is burnished off. Early silver shows irregularities that resulted from faint hammering marks and discolored spots where the burnishing did not completely erase the black. Late nineteenth-century efforts at reviving hand processes exaggerated the marks of raising; mass-produced objects were sometimes finished with a regular pattern of hammer marks.

Silver is decorated by three techniques, used singly or in combination. The first is engraving, in which linear embellishments are scratched into the metal. The second is chasing, whereby the surface is worked upon with a blunt-edged instrument creating a design by depressing areas of the metal. And the third is embossing, by which higher relief is created through broad sweeps made on the inside of the piece. At times decorative elements are cast and then soldered on.

Later silver-making techniques have been simpler and quicker. The slower hand processes were replaced by stamping, in which the sheet metal was pushed into a form by machine, and spinning, in which the third dimension was added when the metal sheet was held against a turning lathe. The products of these later techniques give them-

selves away; there are no marks of a craftsman's tools and the spinning marks show.

Although the chance of finding silver made before 1700 is virtually nil, it is worthwhile to note that the ancient craftsmen used decoration that was larger in proportion to the form than those who worked later. Further, Gothic design of the 1400's is much more intricate than the late Renaissance efforts of the sixteenth century, whose smooth classical forms depend more for effect on the quality of the metal than on the decoration.

Practically speaking, the collector can start his consideration of silver with the work of the seventeenth and eighteenth centuries. There are bargains in the simpler works, but these works may be so simple as to be dull. The most interesting of these simple objects echo medieval forms or they are plainer versions of the designs then fashionable. Most of the bargains are unmarked pieces that cannot be easily associated with particular centers. The price rises steeply if the piece is marked and can be identified; unfortunately, the most interesting work is marked.

Georgian English Silver and American Silver, pre-1850

By the eighteenth century the work of English and American shops diverged from the work on the Continent. Continental craftsmen were still concerned with silver as a medium for elaborate decoration, but the American and English began to concentrate on ways of exploiting the richness of the metal by keeping the surface

Silver porringer, by Benjamin Wynkoop (1675–1751), New York, about 1710. Handle designs vary from complex to simple. Continental examples often have two handles that are thinner and solid.

relatively plain. This American and English work is highly favored by collectors, and a consideration of specific objects from the period is appropriate.

The porringer, known to English collectors as a cupping or bleeding bowl, is a plain vessel with a pierced handle that is simple and flat. It was introduced in England in the 1600's and was one of the more popular pieces produced in America all through the 1700's. The disparity in name demonstrates how little we know about the function of these old objects, but marked pieces in quantity prove the design was common over a long period and that it was probably used for display more than anything else.

The design of the handle varies, but the variations are not indicative of the date of the piece. The best indication of age is the way the bowl is fashioned. Early examples are plain; eighteenth-century examples tend to have distinctive turned-out lips and plate-shaped bases. Conceivably the more elaborate shape could be raised more swiftly with the aid of additional tools. The latest examples are of the nineteenth century and these seem to be fashioned of several pieces soldered together. Reproductions, made for over forty years, were created by stamping and have a sharpness that is distinctive. No signs of handwork are evident on the twentieth-century examples.

Mugs and tankards, or mugs with lids, are also notable. Aside from a few exceptions, the standard early types were squat tapering cylinders with minimal ornament. The han-

Silver tankard, by Cornelius Kierstede, New York, about 1695–1705. The flat tapering cylindrical form was used in England in the seventeenth century. American craftsmen employed it throughout the eighteenth century. The elaborate border around the base and the relief decoration on the handle are signs of New York craftsmanship.

dles were sometimes flat sheet silver, but more often they were cast in curving shapes that were occasionally embellished with cast decoration. In the eighteenth century the cylinder was gradually replaced by the pear-shaped form. On early examples of tankards, lids are flat, but they later grow dome-shaped. Account books of early silversmiths disclose an extraordinary amount of silver-repair work. The mugs and tankards evidently got knocked around and new covers or handles were often put on. In the nineteenth century spouts were added to tankards to make them into pitchers, and these pieces constitute a peculiar problem: they don't look right with the spouts and they rarely look right if the spouts are removed.

Silver tankard, by "W. F.," London, 1765–66. Not every maker's mark can be identified. The curving sides and domed top were in fashion after 1750. Mainly English, this design was used by several Americans at about the time of the Revolution.

English tankards and mugs tend to be much less expensive than the American examples because collectors of English silver prize more fashionable objects than these practical items.

Spoons are a form falling somewhere between functional and decorative silver. Although obviously designed to be used, spoons have also been vehicles—albeit limited—for expression of the current mode. A spoon collection can thus illustrate in detail, and in a small space, the evolution of silver design. Spoons tend to be inexpensive because of their small size, but early examples are prized and cost in the hundreds of dollars. One of the most coveted forms, the Apostle spoon, gets impossibly expensive in sets of twelve. It is tricky, as it was widely reproduced in the last century. The basic design of the Apostle spoon is merely a variation on the seal-top spoon of the sixteenth and seventeenth centuries: it is small, the handle square in cross section and the end of the handle is topped with a seal or an Apostle's figure. The bowls are thin and tear-shaped. It is easier to find a simple seal-top spoon than an Apostle spoon, but there are many reproductions of both.

Toward the end of the seventeenth century spoon handles were flattened rather than squared and were cut in varied patterns. Some curve along the sides, while others have trefoil ends displaying early efforts to create flowing designs. The new forms were embellished with engraved decoration at the point where the bowl joined the handle.

Silver spoon, by Tunis D. Dubois, New York, about 1797–99. Original engraved linear decoration is neoclassical, a sign that piece dates from the late eighteenth century. Over-all design for spoons was simplest close to 1800.

Sometimes reinforcement was added in the form of a narrow rat-tail; an extention of the handle under a portion of the bowl. Designs continued in use for some time, so it is not easy to date simple unmarked examples. Later examples are better integrated, with less of a division between bowl and handle. The change was brought about by the use of a mold in which spoons were cast in a single piece. Mid eighteenth-century examples are plain, but the forms are curved in three-dimensional patterns that capture the essence of the rococo style then in vogue.

Sometime after 1760—depending upon the modishness of the craftsman—neoclassicism superseded the rococo in silver designs. Spoons became simpler and appeared in more angular patterns. Sharp engraving in delicate designs was characteristic. Thereafter, each of the succession of nineteenth-century styles appeared on spoons, and a wide range can be accumulated by the collector. The prices are more moderate than for, say, teapots, and will be even more reasonable if English rather than American work is the focal point of the collection.

The parallels between English and American design are clear, for London was the center for the English-speaking world. However, differences are also apparent. English craftsmen, particularly in London, were more adventurous than their American counterparts in keeping up with fashion. Although there are many examples that can cause confusion, in general the English work is more elaborate and the American more functional. Those who assert that they can spot American work at forty paces maintain that American craftsmen did not permit the decoration to overwhelm the form, no matter how ornate, while English designs can become all decoration. On either side of the Atlantic the evolution of style can be easily traced in elegant examples made for display. Two-handled cups, tea equipment, tureens, casters, dish stands and boxes all reflect the developments of their time, from the monumental efforts of the 1600's to the more intimate, light designs of the late 1700's.

Prices for seventeenth- and eighteenth-century silver are bizarre, with quality of design only one factor. Americans prefer American silver and pay a premium for their taste, particularly if the object is marked. Big names mean a lot and the creations of crafts-

men who have a large body of work surviving fetch fancy prices. Equal efforts, sometimes almost exact duplicates, by unknowns will cost a fraction of what a big name brings.

Paul de Lamerie (1688–1751) and Paul Storr (1771–1843) are two English silversmiths whose work is most coveted. Lammerie worked in various phases of eighteenth-century style, from the restraint and symmetry of early classical design to the exuberant rococo, which is asymmetrical, bold and unrestrained. Storr worked mainly in the bold Empire style that was almost as monumental as Renaissance design, using classical motifs and mythological figures on forms inspired by a study of ancient design. There is justice to the prices the work of these two

craftsmen brings because it is handsome, significant and the best expression of its period. Hester Bateman (1709–94), on the other hand, headed a shop in London that produced work ranging from good to mediocre. But collectors become irrationally intrigued by the notion of a woman craftsman bending over a hot forge, and the prices for some of her work are out of line.

Paul Revere is the best-known American silversmith. Before the Revolution he produced some of the finest rococo teapots along with traditional mugs and porringers. After the Revolution his neoclassical efforts were among the best. Nonetheless Longfellow and that midnight ride have affected Revere prices, and the most routine skewer

Teapot and tray, silver, by Robert Hennell, London, 1784–85

a

a

*Silver teakettle, by Paul de Lamerie, London,
1744–45. This represents the English rococo at
its height. Scrolls, cupids, shells, flowers and
even a palm tree have been incorporated into
the relief pattern on a shape based
on a Chinese model.*

b

*Centerpiece, silver gilt, by Paul Storr, London,
1810–11. The beginning of the nineteenth
century was an era of classical design. The
figures supporting the basket and each motif can
be traced back to ancient Roman models.*

c

*Sugar bowl, silver with blue glass lining,
by Mary Makemeid, London, 1774–75. A
contemporary of Hester Bateman, Mary
Makemeid also made the simpler kind of
neoclassical silver that was occasionally
shoddily executed.*

b

c

Teapot, silver, by Paul Revere, Boston, about 1782. The simple oval or circular pot with a straight handle is characteristic of neoclassical silver design. Revere was one of the first Americans to introduce the style. In later examples the relief borders are more delicate.

from his shop commands a sum that boggles the mind. A tea set that might be worth $5,000 if the maker was an unknown will bring $100,000 if it is a Revere.

Because a mark on a piece of silver has such an extraordinary effect on price, it is not surprising to find that the forging of marks has been developed to the level of high art. A maker's mark can be recreated by making a cast of an authentic example and stamping it on good unmarked pieces. The way to detect this type of forgery is by being alert to fuzzy marks that are a trifle larger than they should be. Also, if wear scratches do not extend into the marks, one should be suspicious. An easier way for a forger to make a mark is to buy a small piece such as a spoon, cut out the mark and solder it on a teapot or some larger piece that will then appreciate in value many times over. Most silversmiths had sets of marks, scaled to size so that they could put the appropriate one on each object they made. The spoon marks are too small for tureens and one should be suspicious if the letters seem out of scale.

Collectors' over-optimism can also send prices out of reason. A piece of silver marked "PR" could be by Paul Revere, but it could just as easily be by Peter Reed. To be sure a mark indicates the right maker, you should compare it with a documented example. This can be difficult at times. All the same, if I were offered a Revere tea set at $95,000, I would like to see the tea set listed in a Revere account book before I bought it.

Continental Silver

Although a collector will almost never be able to acquire a piece for himself, the silver of Nuremberg and Augsburg is the most important of Renaissance craftsmanship. Silversmiths in those two German cities produced work that was superb as decoration and the finest expression of the Renaissance ideals—actually surpassing the sculptors and painters of the time. The great examples from these cities were made for monarchs and the like, and most remain in royal collections and museums, so there is little hope for the private buyer. Beginning in the 1500's, however, the traditions of Nuremberg spread to a large part of Europe, including the cities of Danzig, Riga and

opposite
Tea set, silver, by Paul Revere, Boston, about 1790

Hot-water urn, silver, by Tijmon Suyk, Amsterdam, 1733. The three-spigot urn (only two show here) seems to have been Dutch exclusively. The emphasis on the plain surface, interrupted only slightly by ornament, suggests that English influence was stronger than the Continental.

Budapest. The influence was at its height in the 1600's, and still had not passed by the 1700's. Under the inspiration of Nuremberg, craftsmen used silver as well as gold for elaborate pieces, decorated in relief, that were intended essentially for display. Stemmed goblets, bowls and tankards made of richly embossed but thin metal are typical. The designs were based on elaborate combinations of classical motifs. The best examples in Nuremberg style include panels of mythological scenes; more ordinary pieces have parts shaped to conform with classical architectural moldings, decorated with leaves and scrolls. Often a figure is used as a stem or top for a piece. A real shell or coconut may serve as the bowl of a vessel framed in hand-somely wrought silver, adding a surprising new texture. Rock-crystal or rhinoceros-horn bowls also turn up.

In the eighteenth century, English influence was important in the development of Continental silver design and one begins to see reflections of the English approach in teapots and other typical forms. The tradition of using the precious metals as a medium for decoration, however, also continued, with some amusing results from strange compromises in design.

Interest in the Renaissance tradition was very strong in the nineteenth century so that both reproductions and revival pieces were made. Craftsmen of the 1850's who worked in the stye of the 1600's produced work with noticeable inconsistencies. Too much effort was put into rendering leaves realistically and there was too great a concern for perspective. Often, the nineteenth-century craftsmen copied earlier pieces too hurriedly, using too large a scale to fit a whole subject into a specific panel. But keep in mind that many nineteenth-century craftsmen were very good and that their efforts are worth serious consideration as aspects of nineteenth-century craftsmanship. The mechanical reproductions show themselves through the dullness of the stamped details.

French silversmiths were closer to the English than to the German in their approach. They, too, admired the qualities of plain precious metal, although their characteristic work is a little fancier than that of the English. When French silver is discussed, we

Double salt, silver, by Pierre Balzac, Paris, 1766–68. Although Parisian silversmiths are best known for very elaborate efforts, they were capable of subtle, rich design. The fluted surface is a motif to suggest the shell, a logical container for salt.

tend to think of the monumental baroque efforts made for the court of Louis XIV or of the fabulous rococo designs of Louis XV. While these are historically important and show how French craftsmen emphasized fashion, they are not what is seen on the market today. One is far more likely to find simpler provincial pieces that echo fashion in functional examples.

Two common forms of French silver should be viewed with suspicion: the winetaster's bowl and the small beaker that was frequently a baptism gift. The bowls are shallow and small—a perfect ashtray size—and often plain with spiral twisted handles. The beakers have rounded bottoms and are commonly decorated with applied cut strips and engraving. Handsome examples from the beginning of the eighteenth century have been copied in the last seventy years, but there should be no problem in spotting them.

In the 1700's, Swedish, Danish, Dutch, Italian and Latvian silversmiths diverged from the German and English and developed national styles. The qualities of these styles are as important as those in English or American silver, but often collectors ignore anything that is unusual. It is worthwhile to remember that what may appear to be bad English design may be good Latvian. It is important to take the time to evaluate the unexpected.

Mass Production and Plated Silver

Although we think of mass production and its attendant ills as nineteenth-century phenomena,

it affected silver much earlier. In the 1760's silversmiths with large shops began to simplify the age-old hand techniques to reduce their prices. Often the quality went down with the price. Work in the neoclassical style lent itself particularly well to the new methods. Typical small shapes such as the oval or circular cylinder could be made by cutting, piecing together and soldering instead of raising. Crisp classical decoration was applied mechanically more easily than by hand. Because of their lesser skill, provincial craftsmen also simplified their methods, and their efforts have the charm that is found in country work in other fields. But the speed-up by city craftsmen brought no dispensing of ornament, and their frilly works are often of mediocre quality.

Early plated silver, or copper fused with silver, is a field that scares too many collectors. The term "plated silver" may make them wince as they think of the huge quantities of badly made pieces of recent vintage rather than of the fine products of eighteenth-century England. A practical method of plating silver was invented in 1743. By the 1770's it was used extensively for factory production, mostly in two centers, Sheffield and Birmingham. Sheffield is the name that is applied to much plated silver of this period. Designs tend to be conservative, so that simple tall rococo teapots were made long after neoclassicism had become fashionable. Neoclassical designs in plated silver are often more restrained than those in sterling, but the forms are well made and the decoration is suitable. Candlesticks, sugar bowls, salts and trays in plated silver tend to be in the hundreds while the better examples of sterling are in the upper thousands. One factor in price is that the silver surface is often worn and the copper shows through. Although many prefer to leave such pieces as they are, it is possible to have them replated, though care needs to be taken to avoid the overly bright look typical of contemporary plated pieces.

It is more important to pay attention to the sequence of styles in the late eighteenth and nineteenth centuries than to concentrate on the technological developments. Quality depends upon the attention given the production of an object, and mediocrity was not the exclusive domain of the large factory. The designer of the late 1700's, even if he worked for a factory, learned his history and was aware of the standards he was trying to meet. If what he produced sometimes seems funny to us, it is because he was a bit self-conscious in trying to use the correct elements of design; the result seems intellectual rather than inspired.

In 1840 electroplating—the chemical and electrical substitute for the Sheffield silver process—appeared on the scene. Finding enthusiasts for electroplated objects is almost as difficult as finding advocates of matricide. Even if a collector sees an example that looks good, he fears it will be a bad investment. Purists in design tend to think of electroplating as a kind of fraud that should be discouraged. Actually, electroplated silver is not fairly cast in its role as pariah. It was a rather wonderful expression of nineteenth-century taste, both in its design and in its embodiment of the fondness for inventions. Because it was a substitute for real silver, some manufacturers were carried away with the need to keep prices down and made things shabbily. But others did fine work.

Early examples of this process are somewhat hard to find. From the 1860's to the end of the century, however, an amazingly divergent number of examples exist. The larger manufacturers kept up with the latest fashions, and there are plated pieces that are contemporary with the sterling versions. Some are quite finely executed, and a number of the better pieces have careful hand engraving and hand embossing. In other cases the hand-embossed designs translated well into a stamped design. Many collectors will find enjoyment in this silver if they contemplate the examples one at a time, rather than condemning the entire shelf of electroplated objects without study. Prices for electroplated silver are below those for Sheffield, but they are unpredictable. The range should be $50 to $200 for a larger object or small tea set. Occasionally, outstanding examples will be in the upper hundreds.

Empire-Style Silver

At the end of the eighteenth century larger silver forms more specifically based on ancient models came into fashion. This appears to have been a reaction, as it was in other fields, to the delicacy of early neoclassicism. Squat heavy shapes were selected from the varied output of ancient Rome and given large-scale decoration in fairly high relief. The style was associated with Napoleon upon his accession to the imperial throne. The French and the Americans called it Empire. The English called it Regency, and in Austria-Hungary it was later dubbed Biedermeier. The eighteenth-century buff may find the Empire style gross and heavy. It is, indeed, almost monumental, but it is just beginning to be appreciated after a long period of neglect. The most important names or the highest fashion from each place is apt to be expensive. Frugal collectors, however, can still find fine ordinary pieces that are a lot less expensive than the works of the coveted 1700's.

Paris, London, Vienna, Copenhagen and just about any other city of any size had silversmiths producing work in the Empire style. Each city evolved a distinctive approach, but enumerating the particular elements is difficult. The most elaborate decorative efforts were produced in Paris and London. The French silversmiths Odiot and Biennais made silver for Napoleon with rich classical ornament of the highest quality. Silver and gilt silver were used for heavy forms with the richest details. Equivalent work from London bears the name of Paul Storr, who supplied a larger affluent group with the same kind of designs. Interest in heavy but accurate classical forms also showed in work of a more modest scale. Bold forms were used with minimal decoration or decoration that could be executed with relative ease. Mass-produced, stamped

Hot-water pot and coffeepot in silver, by Samuel Williamson, Philadelphia, about 1800. The urn shapes are designs that were increasingly important after 1800. The proportions were heavier in later examples. This is the beginning of a direction important for the Empire style.

borders were sold by the yard to silversmiths who needed them for inexpensive pieces.

Next to spoons, the objects most commonly found are tea sets, hot-water urns and beakers. Hollowware pieces such as tureens and bowls are often relatively plain with simple leaf borders in relief. Occasionally found, but much more rare, are elaborate pieces made to commemorate an important event. Ship captains who saved their cargoes in storms, generals (or even colonels) who performed heroic deeds and businessmen who executed an important piece of business were gratefully awarded large vases based on famous Roman models. Often the Greco-Roman decoration is relieved by plaques representing contemporary scenes in relief.

Victorian Silver

The Empire style held sway for a remarkably long time, 1800 to 1850, but by the 1830's and 1840's a number of styles were competing. Books on design and architecture from the period urged this style or that, based on some earlier historic period, but few of the suggestions took root. Gothic was used for decorative objects to some extent but rococo, which was revived as a conservative antidote to the neoclassical, became the important style from 1840 to 1860.

Although rococo revival silver was made all over, most examples in local antique shops will probably be American. Occasional pieces are based on eighteenth-century ro-

opposite
"Magnolia Vase," silver and enamel, by
Tiffany & Co., New York, 1892

*Silver hot-water kettle and stand, by J. C. Moore,
for Ball, Tompkins & Black, New York, about
1850. Rococo revival ornament is more
naturalistic than eighteenth-century rococo
work, as is evident in the grapes on this piece.*

coco models, but for the most part the designers adapted freely. The forms tend to be squat and are covered with embossed decoration. The usual tea sets, bowls and the like were made; water pitchers and stemmed goblets came into fashion as popular gifts. The best rococo revival examples are embellished with fine floral ornament; almost realistic roses and water lilies appear on more elaborate pieces. Engraving in the eighteenth-century spirit was also used, and is often cut deeper and less effectively than on earlier work. Rococo revival examples are at their best when the adaptation is free and are rather dull when more like a reproduction.

One reaction to the rococo revival set in at about the time of the American Civil War.

This was called the Renaissance revival. Typical examples are fairly flat and angular with classical ornamentation. In a few instances shapes or motifs can actually be traced to the Renaissance, but more frequently the designs mix elements from all past periods of classicism. The inspirations were models from the Paris of Louis XVI, the London of Adam, Roman motifs of the first century and sixteenth-century Renaissance decoration. The range in quality is just as broad. Some work continued the careful techniques of the preceding century, but other products were obviously destined for the cut-rate market. The names Gorham, Tiffany & Co. and Ball have been found on the better examples.

In the 1870's and 1880's new designs showed the influence of the Middle and Far East. After two-thirds of a century of continued use and reuse of Western models this oriental influence seemed a breath of fresh air. The first impulse toward Eastern design came from esthetes and reformers, but the taste caught on widely, with the public apparently magnetized by the patterns and romance of the mysterious Orient. Silver began to appear in new shapes inspired by Middle Eastern metalwork, glass and pottery. Globular forms like mosque lamps, elongated shapes reminiscent of Islamic ewers and squat pots adapted from pottery all turn up. Flat engraved floral and fish patterns were inspired by designs on Japanese screens and pottery. Rich repoussée ornament was embossed on the best pieces and stamped on the more popular-priced examples, which were also sometimes engraved in restrained patterns.

By the end of the century traditional Western styles were back in favor in the sorts of adaptations that are still made today. Following the lead of contemporary architects such as McKim, Mead & White, silver designers concentrated on distinctive variations of the styles prevalent before 1825. But the new technology and the new manners brought forth objects never heard of before. The Medici and Marie Antoinette herself never had so many silver forks, spoons, holders for cards, plates, hooks, trays and other doodads as any affluent 1890's lady in Indianapolis.

Those who abhorred the revivals that were so much a part of the 1800's attempted to find new directions: some went into a historic period that had been overlooked, the early Christian era; others really thought they were starting from scratch in developing what was to be called Art Nouveau. Those who looked backward found a special fascination in the geometric patterns used in various cultures after the fall of Rome, especially those of the Vikings and the Celts. Researchers enjoyed exploring the treasures of barbarians who were to be converted in the course of time. The designs were fresh, with rough textures that were a relief from the over-refinement of most nineteenth-century silver. The "barbarian" influence appears on work by the major companies such as Tiffany and on that of the artist-craftsmen who were beginning to work in silver at the end of the nineteenth century.

Enamel teapot by Theodore Rückert, Russia, 1895

A few of the innovators who worked in the Art Nouveau style were also indebted to the early Christian era. One group of designers—mainly in Germany and Central Europe—used geometric patterns inspired by the early work. More typically, Art Nouveau designs exploit naturalistic floral and leaf motifs or show elongated shapes dominated by long flowing lines in relief. One outstanding motif was the young girl with long flowing hair, either nude or in a gauzy dress. Art Nouveau was a stronger trend on the Continent than in the United States, but an amazing amount of American Art Nouveau silver is gradually turning up.

To pass off the nineteenth century as a period of uninspired efforts would be a serious error. Although much nineteenth-century design is less appealing than earlier work, in silver we find much work that is well done, showing that many nineteenth-century craftsmen carried on the traditions of fine silversmithing. Distinguishing the shabby examples made by companies without standards is no challenge; learning to love the more ambitious decorative efforts of the late 1800's is. Prices for a lot of very fine nineteenth-century silver are low, but it depends on where you look. Many people like the glitter of flamboyant design and seem to prefer the late revivals of the rococo to the real thing. A tea set of 1880 might go for $200 in an auction featuring eighteenth-century pieces, while the same tea set will bring thousands in a shop in a booming suburb. The nineteenth century's love of innovation and gadgetry means that there is a stunning

234

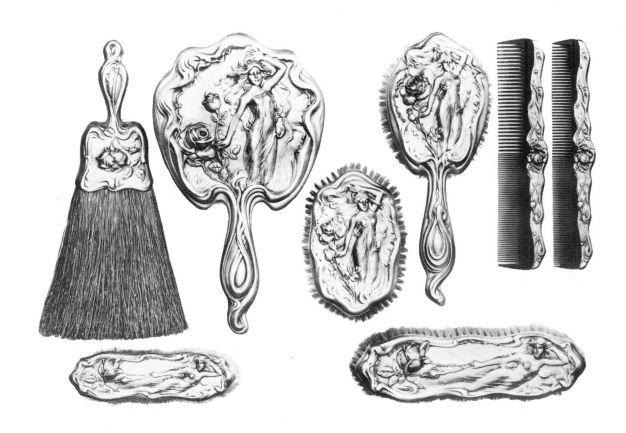

Bowl, silver and glass, by Jean Puiforcat, Paris, 1934. Simple lines were favored by the craftsmen working in the modern idiom in the 1920's and 1930's. In the style called Art Deco, this piece is the work of the most famous silversmith of the period. American manufacturers produced Art Deco silver too.

array of silver objects—both sterling and plated—from the period. There must have been many families that "had everything": ice-water pitchers mounted on frames that allowed them to swing for easy pouring, tobacco boxes, table scrapers, napkin rings, jewel boxes with patented closures, toilet sets, dresser sets and nobody knows what else. Some of the gadgets are so tricky that their purpose remains a mystery unless an illustrative picture turns up in a catalogue.

The silver story ends up on a rather doleful note. In the affluent 1920's, supposedly exact copies of English and American designs of the period before 1840 were reproduced. These can sometimes be confused with the real thing. Unless the price makes it worth a gamble, avoid buying anything you can't compare with a documented example. Whether she knows it or not, the dear little old lady who is preparing to part with the family treasure may be offering something little more than fifty years old. Often all she knows is that it has been in the family "as long as she can remember." It is not over-cynical to remember that most Mayflower descendants have inherited relatively little that was used by the family in 1640—or even 1840.

ENAMELS

Enamels, made by fusing glass powder to a metal base, are second only to the precious metals in their decorative qualities. Enamels have been known since ancient times, but practically speaking, collectors rarely meet anything made before the Renaissance. Typical early examples are known as painted enamels. These are enamel on both sides, with pictorial representation painted over the enamel. One early Renaissance center for enamel production was Limoges, and painted enamels of all origins are often referred to as Limoges. Grisailles—the decoration is black and white—based on engravings of the period were favored in the 1500's. The more important sources of enamel for collectors are Chelsea and Battersea, England, where eighteenth-century rococo pieces were produced. Candlesticks, boxes of every sort and occasionally a platter were made there in a style that was a little provincial. More sophisticated efforts were produced in France, where the techniques seem to have been more advanced. Boxes with enamel over machine turning have unusual textures that are much in keeping with the virtuosity one would expect from Parisian craftsmen.

The Chinese made enamels in the eighteenth and nineteenth centuries. Like the jade of the period, these suggest that the craftsmen had more capable hands than eyes. The forms are repetitions of early designs that were rendered in bronze and they seem a little eerie in color. Besides the painted enamel technique, the Chinese adapted the earlier cloisonné technique, in which the design was outlined by metal wires that kept colors separate during the firing. Chinese enamels are often flamboyant and they appeal very strongly to those who like to see clear evidence of craftsmanship. Consequently, despite the fact that most students of Chinese art ignore the enamels, prices tend to be relatively high—in the thousands —even for work that lacks inspiration.

Enameling was revived in the nineteenth century but was never produced in large quantity. Fine examples in a neo-Gothic style do occasionally turn up as fantastic examples of craftsmanship. Occasionally in the 1870's and later, enamel designs were added to silver and there are tea sets with colorful decoration. This work was probably inspired

Enamel vase and boxes by Louis Comfort Tiffany, American, about 1900

Carnet de Bal, a card case by Jean Nicolas Defer, gold and enamel, Paris, 1784–85. Pictures were popular on eighteenth-century enamels. The nineteenth-century copies are never executed as consistently because too much attention is given certain details. Paintings by Chardin were adapted for this case.

by late eighteenth-century models, but it also reflects the influence of Near Eastern enamel decoration on glass. Jewelers, or at least those who made jewelry, used enamel in the late nineteenth century to decorate pins and the like. With the advent of the Art Deco in the 1920's there was a revival of Limoges; a variety of loudly patterned designs that vaguely reflect cubism were produced. Remember that very fussy or overly schematic flowers on eighteenth-century forms generally indicate work of the twentieth century.

PEWTER

Pewter is the most collectable of base metals. There are ancient and medieval rarities, great examples of the sixteenth and seventeenth centuries, fine pieces made in the eighteenth and early nineteenth centuries and challenging revival examples of more recent origin. Pewter has been used as a poor man's silver, and it has also served as a material for purely utilitarian pieces. Pewter is a tin alloy that resembles silver when it is highly polished. Historically there have been periods when it was fashionable to keep pewter highly polished and others when a dark gray surface was preferred. The content of pewter has likewise varied through the centuries. In ancient Rome it was made of tin and lead, and that combination was used in later periods

Tankard, pewter, German, seventeenth century. Continental pewterers used this form for centuries. It is also close to a form that was popular in Scotland. Unmarked pewter is therefore hard to attribute.

opposite
Food pail by Jacques Dussanssois, Paris, about 1775

for plain pieces. Finer later examples have contained copper in combination with antimony and bismuth. A fifteenth-century English regulation called for pewter made of tin and brass. English pewter in the eighteenth century generally had no lead while Continental pieces tended to include it.

Although pewter was used for utilitarian tablewares as early as the fourteenth century, almost all of the work surviving from before the late eighteenth century is decorative. The early tablewares have disappeared because pewter is a soft metal; as the pieces wore out they were melted down and the metal was remolded. Then, in the eighteenth and early nineteenth centuries, in town after town, people stopped using pewter and began using cheaper ceramic products. These pewter pieces, discarded or stored away, are what remains of old utilitarian ware. On the basis of appearance alone, pewter makes a logical substitute for silver. However, it owed its prevalence to more than utility. Pewter church vessels have had religious sanction for use in the liturgy since the Middle Ages. A synod of 1074 in Rouen, for example, allowed pewter to be used in place of gold or silver for church vessels. Yet, for some reason, although copper and brass can be made to look like gold, they were never officially accepted as pewter was.

The simple functional shapes that pewter took in the thirteenth and fourteenth centuries, which we recognize from archeological research, were still being made in the sixteenth and seventeenth centuries. Dutch paintings show the same kinds of tankards and flagons that have been dug up. Some of the sixteenth- and seventeenth-century examples still turn up from time to time because they were used as decoration rather than for drinking, or for presentation, as shown by their inscriptions. In the nineteenth century these simple early pieces were prized. A number of reproductions were made by a spinning process rather than by casting, and this can be detected. In the late nineteenth century there was much faking, and the frauds are harder to detect. Reference to an authentic earlier work is a help. Some of the most elaborate sixteenth-century pewter came from the Continental shops of François Briot and Caspar Enderlein. Their work, elaborate relief in classical motifs, epitomizes the best of sixteenth-century

Typical pewter marks.

Renaissance design. But one can almost pledge that a true example of the work of either will not be found at large. So great was their reputation that collectors of the nineteenth century were content with reproductions when the real thing was impossible to locate. The twentieth-century buyer may be getting a nineteenth-century copy or an even more recent reproduction.

Many seventeenth- and eighteenth-century pieces were based on silver designs. Candlesticks are a prime case, but there are also tureens and pots for coffee and tea. In the eighteenth and nineteenth centuries pewterers on the Continent continued to follow the silver designs, particularly the rococo, more than their colleagues in England

opposite
Pewter tankard by William Will, American, about 1780

Pewter mug and two plates, by Jacob Whitmore, Connecticut, 1760–90. American pewterers used conservative designs. The plates look like porcelain examples of the 1720–50 period. The mug is a form that continued to be important for decades after 1800.

and America. A typical example is the tureen with spiral fluted sides topped by a pomegranate finial, produced by many German shops. Neoclassical designs familiar in silver were echoed in Continental pewter. There has been no great demand for Continental pewter in the United States, but it is nonetheless becoming hard to find. One advantage for the collector is that it is generally less expensive than the English and American, but bear in mind that it has been widely reproduced.

English and American pewter stand out because they represent a great combination of functional and decorative design as well as metal of high quality. English craftsmen were subject to regulations on the content of

their pewter and, to compete, the Americans followed suit. Both used a fine alloy of tin with copper and antimony. Although many collectors are strongly attracted to one or the other, the English and the American have more likenesses than differences. Both products reflect silver design but are not loaded with ornament. The pewterers favored stylish shapes but were restrained by a certain conservatism. Mugs and tankards are typical and workmen made the pear-shaped teapot from the 1730's into the 1800's. American work appeared in fewer forms than the English and its present-day rarity has made eighteenth-century examples almost as expensive as simple silver. In many instances only the mark makes the origin evident, but the

premium for the appropriate mark is high. Tankards are coveted most but plates are easiest to find. Inkstands and chamberpots are among the exotic items on the list. Going through a collection makes the enthusiasm of collectors clear: American pewter offers the grace of eighteenth-century forms in a metal that is an appealing subtle gray. Collectors who have insisted on buying the more expensive American examples have been rewarded by seeing their pieces appreciate in value faster than English or Continental objects. English manufacturers tried to prolong the popularity of pewter by improving the metal just as it was going out of style: at the end of the eighteenth century they introduced a refined version that they named Britannia. At about the same time, casting was replaced by spinning as the technique for creating hollowware. Thus, although pewter spoons and plates were no longer wanted, teapots and bowls, in fashionable shapes made possible by spinning, sold well. Decorative objects in Britannia metal graced many rural display cabinets in the first half of the 1800's.

In the 1850's and 1860's pewter was all but forgotten, but it was revived after that as a decorative medium. German and English manufacturers initiated the revival with reproductions of early designs and with efforts at innovation. As in silver, geometric patterns echoing Celtic and Viking art were used, along with Art Nouveau patterns.

TINWARE

Tinware is actually sheet iron painted or coated with tin. It is often called by its French name, tôle. All of the forms of tinware were dictated by the simple processes of their manufacture—cutting, bending and soldering. Most of the tinware found today is of nineteenth-century origin, and the most popular items for collecting are trays. When tinware is left plain gray, it is often decorated with a simple punchwork pattern. The plain gray was used for modified Empire-style pots that are straight or tapering cylinders or a mixture of both and for sconces and candleholders. The gray work is hard to date because peddlers sold these wares over a long period. It is probably wise to assume that whatever you find is from the nineteenth century and to pay accordingly. The painted examples range from fashionable work mass-produced in Continental centers to primitive folk pieces made in rural American workshops. The technique that is best known—japanning—imitates oriental lacquer with paint and varnish; this process was used at Pontypool, one of the early English tinware centers. This name is often applied to all sorts of English tinware, but most of the English examples were made in Birmingham several decades after the 1760's, when the industry began to flourish there.

Besides the prevalent trays, the English produced an extensive list of objects: urns, kettles, caddies, boxes of all sorts and such odd objects as chestnut servers, cruet frames and plate warmers. The backgrounds—green, red, brown, yellow or black—are ornamented with Chinese motifs, scenes and floral arrangements. As the nineteenth century moved along, the pieces were made more quickly, with an increasing number of stamped and cast parts. The decoration tended to become black and gold, and ornate floral motifs helped to cover the shoddiness of manufacture. Small trays from the beginning of the nineteenth century, the most popular of the painted tinware pieces available today, go for $50. Large trays with important scenes, however, are more likely to be $500 and up.

The prevalence of the word "tôle" for tinware arises from the attribution of a good deal of stylish nineteenth-century work to French workmen. This is not always accurate, although there was a French tinware industry at the time. The elaborate Empire decorations may well be French, but the style was popular all over the Western world. The tinware generally thought of as French is vermilion, decorated with classical motifs in gold. Hot-water urns, vases, flowerpots and teapots are most commonly found in this combination. Prices depend upon decoration, ranging from $30 for the ordinary work to $600 for something fine.

American pieces were made for a good part of the nineteenth century in plain shapes that seem to derive mainly from Empire models. Astute collectors of American painted tinware can distinguish regional variations in the bright, flat floral patterns, although these may be a more refined talent than most collectors want. The painted de-

Coffeepot or teapot, painted sheet iron known as tinware, Pennsylvania, about 1820. Black, yellow or red backgrounds were used to suggest lacquer on an extensive group of metal objects that are decorated in abstract floral designs borrowed from porcelain.

Wall sconce, tin-coated sheet iron, American, about 1820. Plain tooled tin objects have to be examined with care because reproductions are common. Early examples have turned-over ends on borders and other details to show they received lots of attention.

signs were repeated endlessly; many are rather close to those used on English pottery of the same period intended for export to America, which in turn derived from earlier oriental models. The difference between the American decorations and the oriental is so great that the painters of tin probably had no idea that they were continuing the tradition of japanning—making oriental—that started in the seventeenth century.

A series of patents that begins in 1804 and continues to the middle of the century shows the tinker as a craftsman who did a lot of handwork, utilizing small machines to simplify and speed his task. Coffeepots, sugar bowls, caddies, teapots, mugs, deed boxes and trays were fashioned in simple designs and painted black, red or yellow. The decoration on the ground is generally flowers that have been simplified into an almost abstract pattern, with leaves and blossoms that look like feathers the most popular. Exceptional examples, mainly attributed to Maine, have pansies that look more realistic. Price tags for the American ware begin low, but the best examples are $500 and over.

A great variety of goods sold in retail shops from about 1880 to 1930 were packaged in or dispensed from bright tin boxes. These come in all sizes and colors, some with pictures on the sides. Although the relatively plain examples are handsome, those with illustrations show the work of the most interesting artists of the time—the popular level of art from a period better known for Impressionism and Expressionism.

IRON

Wrought and cast iron come in many forms, from tiny trivets to large settees and fussily made mirror frames. Wrought iron, or metal hammered into shape, was the more common form before nineteenth-century innovations made cast iron more practical. Wrought iron, generally rougher, was used in large medieval structures, in farmhouses of almost every period and in interiors, like those of Tudor England, of stone or stucco. At the turn of the century, when the Tudor style was revived in large and small suburban houses on both sides of the Atlantic, wrought iron was revived, too. Andirons, stands, candlesticks, oil lamps, locks, keys and hinges were made of wrought iron over a considerable period of time. The early examples are

Knocker, cast iron, American, early nineteenth century. Patriotic motifs such as the eagle were popular following the Revolution.

Iron mantelpiece, by Jules Bouy, American, about 1930. The angular designs of the Art Deco style were used for every kind of object. Occasionally architectural elements are available when rooms are remodeled.

difficult to date exactly because they are rough and timeless in appearance. Early work is thick and imaginatively but subtly shaped. Later pieces are often thinner and have "accidental" hammer marks carefully arranged in rows.

In the casting of iron, a wooden model is pushed down into sand to create an indentation of the proper contour. The model is then pulled out and molten iron poured into the temporary sand mold. Cast iron was regularly used in the 1600's and 1700's to create stoves and firebacks, the rectangular plaques put in the backs of fireplaces to reflect the heat. American firebacks and stoves are often fascinating because they were used as vehicles for decoration in the folk manner. Pennsylvania ironmongers, for example, used symbolic floral motifs above biblical inscriptions. Parts of stoves and firebacks done in elaborate eighteenth-century fashion, in Europe as well as America, have been collected since the late 1800's. In some cases these pieces of ornamental iron were used as decorative elements on the walls of houses. These are now sometimes dug out of the walls and resold. Because these objects are so heavy they are inexpensive when found, but they are not easily come by. The demolition that is part of urban renewal the world over is bringing onto the market cast-iron architectural elements, particularly railings and window guards. The earliest of these, from the 1770's, are delicate examples of the neoclassical style. Heavier later neoclassical work is also found, as well as objects in the rococo, Gothic and Renaissance revival modes. These elements look best if left untouched, but even a fragment is a worthwhile collectable.

The manufacture of cast iron advanced greatly in the nineteenth century, and it became possible to make small decorative objects. Mirror frames in intricate rococo designs are typical; these are not very expensive. In recent years they have been copied in white metal. After 1850 many toys and small banks were made of iron. These are favored by a small group of collectors who see them as a charming, compact manifestation of popular art. During this period, cast-iron furniture became important, both indoors and outdoors. Most of what is available today was originally made for the garden, and these examples have been copied extensively. Rococo patterns are best known. From the 1870's on, Renaissance designs were used.

Learned histories of metalwork take up sixteenth-century steel objects, but there is little chance of finding these now. Armor and weapons that appear to be of sixteenth-century manufacture will more often turn out to be from the mid nineteenth century, when imitations were quite adept. The cut steel that is most likely to be found was made after the 1770's, when the enterprising entrepreneur Matthew Boulton began to use steel for small objects and jewelry. French and Russian manufacturers produced similar pieces and sometimes objects as large as tables and beds.

COPPER, BRONZE AND BRASS

The usual milk cans, pots and pans are far from the whole story of what can be collected in copper and its alloys, bronze and brass. The history of the use of all three goes back to ancient times. Copper, in fact, was one of the first metals to be mined. It most frequently appears, however, in one of its alloys. Bronze is a combination of copper and tin. Brass combines copper and zinc. The distinctions between these have not always been clear: zinc and tin were confused in ancient times, and Biblical references to brass really mean bronze.

For as little as $100 you can buy a small bronze animal that could be of truly ancient origin. The Amlash, Luristan and related ancient cultures of the Near East are coming to

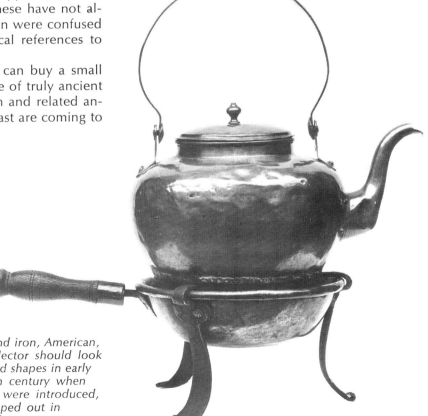

Kettle and brazier, copper and iron, American, eighteenth century. The collector should look for hammer marks and good shapes in early copper. In the nineteenth century when mass-production techniques were introduced, the pieces were stamped out in less appealing shapes.

Bronze jug, Egyptian, Roman period, possibly first century A.D. Ancient objects generally were made in forms that are simple. Ornament was frequently used on borders. Patina provides an attractive textured surface but it can be faked. When it is more regular than on this jug, it should be questioned.

Bronze laver, Flemish, fifteenth century. Bright gold-colored bronze, not very different from brass, turns up in rare early forms. It was also used for the thin wares made in the nineteenth century.

light now under the archeologist's pick, and objects from their prime period, 1000 to 700 B.C., do find their way onto the art market. Unfortunately, so do a vast number of fakes. The authentic objects are clearly based on observation and understanding of animal anatomy. The copyists, or more accurately, creative fakers who are adding to the supply, use straight geometric elements such as the cylinder to create forms that are simple and almost abstract. They also have to simulate patina and the green usually turns out to be paint. The fakes cost even less than $100, and if you suspect that you've been stung, probably the best thing to do is decide that you have a Picasso in the rough. The work of Roman times causes much confusion. Small sculptures are quite expensive, but pitchers, beakers and bowls of varied quality and detail can be bought for $50 to $1,000. The Roman culture covered a good stretch of Europe and Asia, and such pieces have been unearthed all over the area. When you are confronted with a simple bowl that might be Roman, look for consistency in execution. The green patina need not be all over a piece, since the golden bronze color often shows through where the piece has been handled.

Bronze continued to be used for utilitarian objects all through the middle ages and the Renaissance. Although the earlier works are rare, sixteenth-century pieces do turn up. These objects—pots, plaques, bells and mortars—can be either plain or decorated in the Renaissance manner, with intricate over-all classical designs. It is tempting to assume that such objects are Italian or French, but the Spanish, English and German examples are in just about the same style. There is less demand for plain sixteenth-century bronze mortars than for eighteenth-century brass examples, and the prices reflect this.

In the Renaissance, small sculptures and decorative but useful objects such as inkwells were popular. The sculptors took their inspiration from ancient Roman times; one artist whose work often passed for Roman was known as l'Antico. Mythological subjects, urns, crabs and weird little monsters were used as motifs for inkwells, candlesticks and similar objects. Some of the small bronzes are the work of the most talented sculptors of the period and are worth more than the others. Prices for works whose crea-

Sleeping cupid, bronze, Italian, possibly Venetian, about 1500. Renaissance figures small in scale were meant to recall ancient Roman examples. They were duplicated in the nineteenth century. Although some were by famous artists, many are by people who cannot be identified today.

Bronze bull, by Rosa Bonheur, French, 1846. Animals were a very popular subject for small sculpture of the nineteenth century. Bonheur is better known as a painter but more often the small sculpture was the work of specialists.

tors have not been identified are in the hundreds; pieces by known artists go for over $10,000.

Bronze was less important after the 1500's because brass came into use for practical objects. The finer furniture mounts of the eighteenth and early nineteenth centuries, however, were made of gilt bronze—ormolu —as well as brass. Large sculpture continued to be cast in bronze, too, although in the seventeenth and eighteenth centuries the small bronzes were eclipsed in fashion by pottery and porcelain figures. In the nineteenth century bronze was revived as a medium for small sculpture. One of the first to make small bronzes was the sculptor Antoine Louis Barye (1795–1875), a Frenchman who first made small lively animals as a quick way to earn money. Barye had been rejected by the Salon of 1837; he then started to sell miniatures of his works directly to the public. His animals achieved great popularity and inspired a large group of sculptors, les Animaliers, who confined themselves to making animals. The earliest creatures were romantically fierce; in the 1860's and toward the end of the century they became precise and scientific. There are also a number of renditions of dogs that appear sentimental if not downright cute. Besides Barye, the favored names, all French, are Pierre-Jules Mène (1810–79), Auguste-Nicholas Cain (1822–94) and Emanuel Fremiet (1824–1910). Many others followed the fashion and produced miniature animals of good quality. Examples of the 1840's, like the Delacroix

paintings of African lions, represented an aspect of the Romantic movement. The virtuosity of most of the pieces gave them an almost universal appeal. For a collector one chronic problem is the late imitations of the more important works. In the early 1900's the most valued examples were recast. Although made as honest reproductions, these are sometimes passed off as originals. The bronzes of the late 1800's include small human figures. Reproductions of the more famous French works of the eighteenth century were popular, as were sentimental scenes such as children waving good-by. European sculptors touched a broad range of subjects, all realized with meticulous attention to detail. These were widely bought by

opposite
Brass mortar and pestle, English, about 1740

Plate, brass, German, sixteenth century. Gothic letters surround an angel in the Renaissance style. The technique of hammering brass sheets into appropriate forms was used until the nineteenth century when a quicker process was developed to spin the metal into shape.

that large portion of the public that was unaware of the achievements of such experimental artists of the time as Rodin. Prices for nineteenth-century bronzes vary greatly. Good but unimportant subjects go for as little as $50; the most desirable of the Barye animals will be priced at $10,000. However, $200 to $500 should be enough for an example of the many more interesting animals.

Brass-manufacturing centers flourished in northern Europe as early as the fifteenth century. Dinanderie, one name for the brass work created through hammering, derives from the name of a center in the Meuse valley, Dinant. One of the most popular objects that has survived from the fifteenth and sixteenth centuries is the decorative platter. These platters often have inscriptions in a Gothic script and religious scenes in the center with floral decoration and modified classical patterns. Pitchers and small covered bowls that once had some liturgical use also turn up from time to time. Brasses from the period before the eighteenth century, however, are far harder to find than the eighteenth- and nineteenth-century objects that are cast rather than hammered.

Candlesticks of the eighteenth century make a good collection because they subtly reflect the course of fashion. At the beginning of the century, classicism was the inspiration for columnar designs that tended to be proportionately heavy. By the 1720's the forms were lighter, and in the middle of the century the whimsey of the rococo was suggested in the scalloped corners of the

bases and lips. When in the 1770's the neoclassical came into fashion, delicate designs returned and pure classical motifs were exploited with linear precision.

Brass was used so extensively in the eighteenth and nineteenth centuries that it is difficult to decide how to limit the discussion. The strength of the mixture and the appeal of the gold color made brass as important in the kitchen or stable as in the parlor and bedroom. Surprisingly, early brass is not easy to find, but fabulous examples have a way of being uncovered among junk. My favorite candlesticks are a pair of 1720–30 vintage that I found in a mass of 1890–1930 candlesticks in a peculiar shop in Cannes that seemed to have nothing else from before 1850. No dealer has the reputation of being a specialist in eighteenth-century brass fishing reels, but they do exist and, along with any number of other gadgets can be found occasionally by the patient collector.

Braziers, or workers in brass, created many small decorative objects such as inkstands, tea caddies and tobacco boxes, which were also made in silver. Buttons are another item that both the silversmith and brass founder produced before 1800 by casting, and later by stamping them out. Molds were also used for early door-knockers, knobs, hinges and furniture pulls. All of these useful gadgets follow the sequence of fashionable styles. The classicism of 1700–20 is followed first by the lighter rococo, then by an equally light but more precise neoclassicism and finally by a relatively heavy version of clas-

Brass tobacco box, Dutch, seventeenth century. Brass is an excellent material for engraving. The Dutch used a variety of popular prints as the inspiration for decorating boxes and bowls. Similar techniques were used for nineteenth-century Indian and Persian metalwork.

sicism. Later repetition can be distinguished because the pieces are lighter and are stamped rather than cast. Local taste inspired Continental braziers to be a little more elaborate than those working in England, and American craftsmen tended to be the most simple. Few examples are marked, but the most careful scrutiny will occasionally prove fruitful by uncovering the name or initials of the brazier. American collectors are fondest of documentary pieces stamped with makers' names.

Instruments such as compasses, quadrants, measures for the surveyor, steelyards and balances form a category of brass that offers many collectors a challenge. The instrument makers were able craftsmen intent on em-

bellishing their useful products with timely decoration. Engraved floral patterns and lettering, as well as molded details that are at once decorative and useful, reflect the style of the period in which the piece was made. The economy of detail on instruments made before 1850 gives them a special appeal. Brass was also a favorite material for objects to be used around the fireplace. Andirons and the shovels and tongs made to match were designed to complement the basic classical designs of the fireplace. Americans burned wood long after English and Continental householders had switched to coal, so American andirons of the early nineteenth century are better known than Old World examples. By the 1770's grates to hold coal

were a part of the fashionable interior in England. Kettles, pitchers, skillets and mortars are the forms in which brass appeared in the kitchen. Often the designs are hard to date; for example, three-legged skillets (known also as posnets and pans) vary little between 1600 and 1800. Braziers produced sturdy pieces in familiar functional designs, but toward the end of the eighteenth century the metal was thinner.

The hammering of brass was a technique that continued to be significant until it was replaced by mass-production stamping in the nineteenth century. The taste for relief ornamentation kept sheet-brass objects in production on the Continent much longer than in England or America. Sconces of Dutch origin, elaborately decorated with rich floral patterns accentuated by borders of inverted flutings are good examples of the persistence of the seventeenth-century styles into the eighteenth century. Small boxes for tobacco and snuff were cut from sheet brass and decorated with engraving, either simple scenes or just ornaments. These boxes come in a variety of shapes, but those made in the Netherlands, generally long and narrow (5 inches by 1½ inches would be average), are particularly plentiful. The Dutch boxes sometimes have sophisticated relief ornamentation and at other times are engraved very schematically.

Fashionable eighteenth-century brass is not inexpensive; prices in general are in the hundreds rather than the thousands. Exceptions occur in items such as American andirons, where the magic of the Revere name turns the base metal to gold. Revere set up a brass foundry that produced impressive bells and a host of other objects, including andirons. Marked Revere andirons are very much in demand and are priced in the thousands, while those marked with lesser names will often go for $500 or $600. Handling some early brass will give you an idea of its heaviness and color. The later examples are lighter and less carefully executed.

Generally the only copper that can be hunted down antiquing dates from the late eighteenth and early nineteenth centuries; the finely decorated earlier pieces have all but disappeared. Copper pots and pans in all sizes were available as early as the 1730's and remained popular through a good part of the nineteenth century. Early examples are

Brass candelabrum by Josef Hofmann, Austria, about 1905

generally shaped subtly while the nineteenth-century forms could be made quickly. Since copper was also the base for plated silver, a certain number of elaborate copper pieces are actually stripped-down plated silver. Teapots and hot-water urns, however, were sometimes made of unplated copper.

Copper was an important material for useful objects throughout the nineteenth century. It was stronger and less likely to wear out than tin or iron so that it gained in popularity. Containers in unusual shapes can often be identified as parts of eighteenth- or nineteenth-century stills used for white lightning or other homebrew. After reading recipes for homebrew one understands the origin of the term rotgut; the copper devices in which the brew was cooked wore out more slowly than the drinkers' throats. In the second half of the nineteenth century copper weathervanes, fairly sophisticated renditions of animals and figures, were mass-produced in factories. Although these are collected by folk-art enthusiasts, they were in fact made by manufacturers who sought to create figures in the highest style.

Almost no one has any concern for the decorative copper objects made by craftsmen involved in the Arts and Crafts Movement that began in England in the 1880's and spread all over Europe and the United States before 1900. Following the advice of theorists such as William Morris, the craftsmen turned to medieval design for inspiration. While the results are not exactly Romanesque, Byzantine or Gothic, they were

Brass andirons, English, eighteenth century. The English and Americans preferred brass fire equipment throughout the eighteenth century. Urn and columnar shapes are usual.

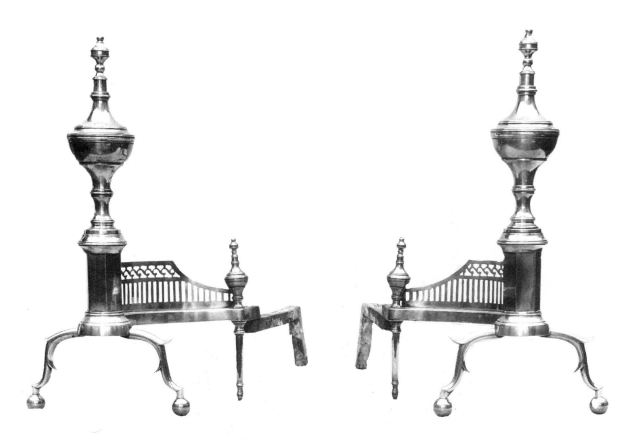

given an emphatic handmade look—an overall surface pattern of hammer marks. Pitchers, bowls, goblets, plaques and lighting fixtures are part of the long list of copper objects that were being put out at the turn of the century. Designs are distinctive and the efforts were serious, but they probably look too much like summer cottage cast-offs to be appreciated by most. American reformers of the early twentieth century, such as Gustave Stickley (whose Craftsman furniture is better known), produced copper reflecting the Arts and Crafts approach, but others are less familiar. It is a field worth investigating.

Glass

Ewer, latticino glass, Venetian style, German, sixteenth century

THE COMPELLING ESTHETIC

Glass-collecting may be the oddest field in antiques. Antique collectors in general are interested in objects of a certain age used originally in the home. But the appeal of glass seems to override the categories of age and function. Brand-new Steuben glass, for instance, pops into antique shops the moment its owner has tired of it. Kitchen tumblers of World War II vintage, electric-line insulators weathered to a pretty iridescence, bottles that yesterday held Jim Beam whisky or Avon cosmetics—all have their ardent collectors. The magic of the glass itself has much to do with this fascination. Its color and translucence or transparency are compelling. Call up the picture of the tiny child squatting on the beach studying a piece of glass, the edges worn smooth by the tides, and you see the power of the glass esthetic. In addition, unlike, say, furniture or silver, glass can often be found rather than bought, which is another factor having to do with its appeal. An aged bottle uncovered in the weeds or on a junk pile is sometimes the start of a collection.

The makers of glass also issue continual invitations to collect. "Get the complete set," the gasoline station or cottage-cheese maker cries, as he offers drinking glasses decorated with buildings from a world's fair or with emblems of football teams. Bottles shaped like men, women, birds, cannon and trains, used by enterprises to enhance the sales appeal—and prices—of their wares, are designed to be collected. It is a tradition that can be traced back to the 1800's, when nos-

trums and mineral waters were first offered in these unusual containers. That the makers' invitations are taken up ever more eagerly can be seen in the prices people are willing to pay for these new bottles, which sometimes cost more than bottles over sixty years old.

In fact, if there is any criticism of the glass collector to be offered, it is that he plays it too safe. Too many people collect glass that was mass-produced, trying for a selection in a single pattern or in a number of patterns made by one process within a relatively short span of time. Big spenders choose pressed glass of the 1830's, medium spenders pick pressed glass from later in the century and the budget-bound head for Depression glass, the inexpensive pressed ware of the 1920's to the 1940's. As in all fields, this kind of concentration educates the collector and enables him to avoid purchasing reproductions unwittingly. But these popular areas are rife with copies whose mere existence tends to diminish the collector's pleasure by making his triumphs seem less like rarities and, incidentally, also reduces the cash value of authentic items. If collectors would branch out, they might find the chase more fun and the owning more satisfying.

Glass may be opaque, simulating semiprecious stones, colorless like rock crystal or colored and transparent. Its universal characteristics are that it is brittle and impervious to liquids. Historically glass gives evidence of man's ability to make something out of the most simple materials, for glass consists of nothing more than sand and potash, or, in chemical terms, silica and alkalis. These are liquefied and fused by heat, then hardened by cooling. The glass is shaped while molten, and this liquid glass is called metal by the experts. Casting in a mold and blowing have been the chief ways of shaping glass since shortly before the time of Jesus.

Glass prices have little to do with age. For $10 you can get Depression glass or a strange little object of great age. Turn-of-the-century English cameo glass, the type carved by hand in elaborate designs, brings tens of thousands when the example is outstanding; a fine Venetian bowl of the 1400's may be had for considerably less. The demand for nineteenth-century pressed glass and art glass has pushed these prices up beyond those for a lot of quite interesting eighteenth-century work. There are a number of neglected types of glass, however. Those feeling their way into the field would do well to learn what they can about the development and qualities of the various kinds if they are to be adventuresome and concentrate outside the areas of heaviest trade.

An important factor to bear in mind in collecting glass is that it does not show its age as obviously as furniture, silver or even ceramics. In furniture and silver, one looks for signs of wear to reinforce the hints of age revealed by the design and material. But glass may be very old and show no signs of wear. To make matters more difficult, chemical differences that help in dating ceramics are less evident in glass. With experience and care, knowledge of the age of glass can be mastered to a large degree.

However, even the experts have problems. The late George McKearin, dean of American glass connoisseurs, told of buying a blue glass candlestick blown and hand-tooled in a way he was sure could be proven to be a technique used in New Jersey in the early 1800's. Package in hand, he stopped on his way home to visit Fred Leighton, who sells contemporary Mexican objects, and he found a mate to his new candlestick. McKearin was always big enough to take a chance and wise enough to know when he missed, qualities every collector should have.

ANCIENT GLASS

The possibilities are slight for making great finds in the field of ancient glass, although small, relatively insignificant but fascinating pieces from various centers of ancient glass-making do turn up. Ancient glass has been collected since the 1700's, when tourists began inspecting ruins, and the men on American ships who visited North Africa and western Asia in the early 1800's are known to have brought home samples of early glass as souvenirs.

The earliest glass was opaque and made to simulate semiprecious stones. It was used first by itself, rather than as an ornamental covering for stone or some other material, in Western Asia during the third millennium B.C. Vessels made of glass, however, do not

Vase, opaque glass in plum color, yellow and white, Egyptian, Eighteenth Dynasty. The pattern is regular but based on the graining found in stone. Originating early, opaque glass was also made in the Roman era, and inspired plain striped glass of nineteenth century.

Jug, blue mold-blown glass, Roman, first to fourth century A.D. Relief decoration on molded forms varies from simple fluting to full figures. Transparent colored Roman glass is often very thin. It can be confused with the later Near Eastern examples. Reproductions of the last century are another problem.

date from before 1600 B.C., the earliest Egyptian examples being just a little more recent than that. Examples were either a single color, often blue, or striated in a regular pattern inspired by marble. Pieces were built up around a core, or created by fusing sections of rods of glass, or ground and cut out of a solid block, or cast in a mold. Although there is a certain amount of variety, small vials, bowls and pots are much alike over the span of ten centuries. One finds varicolored bodies marbleized or in mosaic patterns, a colorless type and any number of useful forms.

The art of glassblowing was developed roughly fifty years before the start of the Christian era. Probably evolved in Phoenicia, the technique had spread all over the Roman Empire by the end of the first century. With glass in wide use during the Roman era, clear and colored glass, molded and blown, survives from this time. Nero is said to have paid the equivalent of a small fortune for a fine bowl, but inexpensive glass could readily be purchased by the average Roman. Virtuoso efforts by Roman craftsmen have been an inspiration to glassmakers of more recent times. Classical patterns introduced in molded pieces were the basis for several nineteenth-century developments. Elaborately cut designs and carving in glass in a cameo technique have more lately been revived.

Simple Roman glass bottles and bowls, probably used in ordinary households, are not prohibitively expensive when they can be found. A fine Roman pitcher in a greenish or smoky color will cost a few hundred dollars; a small vial should be much less. Generally the authentic pieces are unbelievably light, and they have an interesting pattern caused by bubbles in the glass. They may be iridescent, creating a beautiful surface, though not all have this quality by any means. In the 1880's a passion for ancient objects inspired a rash of reproductions, but these easily give themselves away. They tend to be a bit thick and the imperfections are fairly regular. Confronted with old and recent pieces, the collector rarely needs more than a moment to decide which is which.

LATER GLASS

There is little likelihood of finding medieval glass because it is much scarcer than Roman: it was made with less variety and in fewer forms. At first such glass was made of soda-lime substances. Later, potash became the major ingredient. Most glass in the Middle Ages was blown and just about the only decoration involved a technique called trailing—the application of thin strings of glass to the surface. The glass was generally tinged green, blue or amber because of imperfections in the metal. The shapes are functional in appearance.

Plain glass like that in the Middle Ages was produced from the middle of the eighteenth to the late nineteenth century, and glass in the familiar greens and ambers came from

Bottle, cut glass, Persian, ninth to tenth century. Cutting and engraving had been introduced in ancient Rome. Cutting done in the Persian glasshouses has patterns on a large scale and decoration appears a little rough. The long neck was favored in nineteenth century.

272

a

Mosque lamp, enameled glass, Syrian, 1300–50. Brown, blue and gold generally dominate the palette of decoration applied to such lamps. Flowers and vines in flat flowing patterns are motifs that were repeated on the nineteenth-century versions popular after the rediscovery of Near Eastern design in the 1870's.

b

Green glass beaker, German, fifteenth to sixteenth century. The green glass made in Germany as late as the eighteenth century was relatively rough in appearance. Prunts, the pointed gathers of glass applied as decoration, were typical of pieces made in northern Europe.

c

Goblet, colorless and blue clear glass with engraving, Venetian, sixteenth century. Fine clear glass in excitingly decorative forms is characteristic of the Venetian glasshouses. The early hand is a little heavy and the more recent, particularly the nineteenth-century efforts, are fussy and intricate. Wings projecting from the stem are a part of the Venetian style that was copied wherever it was influential.

a

b

c

small glasshouses in Europe and America during this period. At first the shapes were functional, like those known earlier, but after 1800 they relate more to current fashion. At the same time, a relatively similar ware, known as peasant glass, was being produced by French, German, Dutch and Scandinavian craftsmen. This almost clear glass is tinged with color from imperfections. If the items are thin, with an excess of bubbles that appear deliberate, they may well be modern Mexican or from another recent source.

In the Middle East, from the ninth to the fifteenth century, Islamic craftsmen carried on the art of fine glassmaking. Cut glass made in Baghdad and Basra in the ninth century shows the versatility of craftsmen continuing a tradition that began centuries before. Persian pieces were often cut in stylized abstract patterns. From the twelfth century on, these craftsmen developed a repertory of distinctive forms usually decorated in enamel and gold with inscriptions and special designs. Ewers with long narrow necks projecting from globular squat bodies, lamps, beakers and tall vases with waists are the forms best known. An authentic piece is not easily found, although surprising discoveries are made from time to time in small shops. At the height of popularity for things Moorish, in the late nineteenth century, Islamic glass was reproduced extensively, so copies crop up often. It is helpful to remember that early Islamic glass was generally colorless but tinged amber or yellow. In the seventeenth and eighteenth centuries blue was used.

Venice carried on the tradition of fine glassmaking in the West. The craft can be traced there to the tenth century, but it was not until the beginning of the Renaissance that a crystal-like product was made. By 1400 blue, green, purple, turquoise and white appeared along with the colorless item. The characteristic Venetian glass that collectors seek—thin, delicate, clear glass shapes with enamel decoration or engraving—is a product of the fifteenth to the eighteenth century.

Venetian craftsmen showed off their skill by making long-stemmed glasses with intricate winged decorative elements flaring out from the stem. These date from the seventeenth century and inspired copyists all over Europe. Venice was also famous for developing latticino, a ware in which rods of opaque

white glass were incorporated into the body of clear glass. Authentic examples range from very delicate to coarse, but thick rods often suggest that the piece was made outside of Venice. Façon de Venise is a term applied to all attempts at copying Venetian glass. The French, Spanish and German variations can be amusing. By 1800, latticino was produced in Europe and the United States, but the results are distinctly Victorian.

When Renaissance bowls of fine Venetian glass go up for sale, the price is generally in the low thousands. Winged goblets, at prices in the hundreds, are not to be overlooked: Victorian interpretations are often as expensive as the originals. Venice in the seventeenth century was famous for its delicately formed colorless goblets. Exported all over Europe, these are now the hardest to find. Their impact can be seen in German, Dutch and English developments of the seventeenth and eighteenth centuries.

Although Venetian glassmakers exercised a great deal of influence, some northern European craftsmen—mainly German—ignored their accomplishments. Instead of working as hard as the Venetians to make a colorless metal reminiscent of rock crystal, they continued to use glass tinged in the pale colors typical of the medieval product. Unlike the smaller producers of the eighteenth and nineteenth centuries, they made sophisticated shapes with fairly advanced kinds of decoration, such as gilding, delicate engraving and painting in enamel colors. Sophisticated green glass was made in Germany as early as the sixteenth century, when colorless Venetian glass was coming into its own, and was at its height of popularity in the seventeenth century. Tall green beakers decorated with enamel painting are typical and were prime subjects for reproduction in the 1800's. They had cylindrical stems and were frequently engraved around the bowl. The main decoration was formed by prunts—drops or globules of glass—applied to the surface.

Roemer—goblets with broad bowls on varied stems—are the grandfathers of the Rhine wine glasses of the late nineteenth century.

Although seventeenth- and eighteenth-century examples are getting very rare, $100 or $200 is about all the simpler glasses bring. The finest work, of course, gets considerably more expensive.

Toward the end of the seventeenth century the Venetian influence inspired efforts that veered away from the originals. German and Central European (particularly Bohemian) glasshouses produced a fine colorless metal that was shaped into thick baroque forms that could be lavishly cut and engraved. The metal was the result of a formula that included potash instead of soda, but no lead, and this turned out a metal hard enough to be handled like rock crystal. Relief decoration was popular on the finest examples. Samples of this crystal-like glass are sometimes available at prices under $300. Those who are not familiar with authentic work sometimes confuse late nineteenth-century pieces for the real thing. The quality of the decoration, however, will guide anyone who is willing to take the time.

Tumbler, or humpen, enameled glass, German, 1648–1708. Oversize beakers with elaborate decoration were made of clear greenish glass typical of the German glasshouses. Frequently reproduced in the nineteenth century, with more detailed decoration.

ENGLISH GLASS

English glass is an important field for collectors. Although seasoned hunters are in despair about the rapid rise in prices during the last few years, the material is still available and the cost is a lot less than for contemporary rarities in silver. Not long ago a decent English wineglass cost $15 or $20; now the price is more apt to be $100. Considering values generally, this development is not unexpected. The term English glass generally makes one think of work from the eighteenth and early nineteenth centuries: lead glass, the distinctive metal first introduced in England, blown in the fashionable shapes of the day and sometimes embellished with cut decoration. The word "crystal" is also sometimes applied to such glass, but it is a term

Covered goblet, clear colorless glass, English, about 1680. Fine English glass developed in the seventeenth century was thicker than the earlier Venetian. The tooling of the molten metal into a decorative border shows a cross between the north European and Italian tradition. This work was repeated on fine early nineteenth-century American glass.

that connotes quality rather than a specific glass formula; its use by a dealer is sometimes capricious.

The origins of fine English glass are found in the late seventeenth century at about the same time that the new colorless glass was being introduced on the Continent. English and Continental glassmakers alike were inspired by Venice, but each produced a distinctive style seeking to answer the particular needs of his own locality. George Ravenscroft was the Englishman who finally succeeded in making colorless glass after a series of earlier attempts had failed. About 1675 he developed a formula that included lead oxides. The result, lead or flint glass, is softer and more malleable and has greater refractive power than earlier glass. It is also heavier and darker. Typical English designs of the eighteenth and early nineteenth centuries make full use of these characteristics.

The earliest examples of lead glass, dating from 1680 to 1720, are now all but impossible to find. They tend to be large forms, such as covered chalices, pitchers and man-sized goblets to which are applied gathers: small clumps of glass tooled in gadroons, chains or loose designs hard to describe. The forms seem more casual than those made on the Continent with an equivalent formula.

The variety in wineglasses produced between 1710 and 1800 has attracted many collectors. Bowls, stems and feet were all subject to the exuberance of the designer's imagination. One finds simple conical bowls along with others formed like bells or buckets. The stems may be molded in baluster shapes or blown in any of several ways. The feet may be completely flat or with rims of glass folded under; or they may be dome-shaped or raised in a pyramidal design. Sizes vary, too. There is no contemporary description to explain any of these variations. The more desirable types have stems in a baluster shape, with a small teardrop inside. Also interesting are the straight stems into which twisted tubes of air have been blown or opaque rods set in patterns reminiscent of latticino. Stems were also cut in small facets in the late eighteenth century, when highly reflective surfaces were considered particularly attractive.

A relatively small number of glasses was decorated with engraving on the bowls. Simple floral designs were popular, but the more

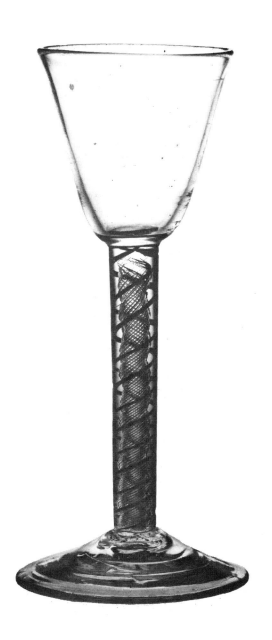

Wineglass, colorless glass, English, 1760–90. English glass, called flint or lead glass because it contained lead, was at its height in the eighteenth century. The stem has an opaque rod and a spiral of imprisoned air as decoration, so that it is known as an air-twist stem. It is distinctively English. On the Continent opaque rods were introduced into stems alone. The domical foot was flattened in later work.

important examples have special symbols or inscriptions. Mid-century glasses sometimes bore emblems associated with the Stuart Pretender, Bonnie Prince Charlie—the fleur-de-lis, thistle and rose of the Stuart partisans who tried to place him on the throne in 1715 and 1745. Inscriptions included toasts to monarchs, slogans for causes and more personal messages.

Pitchers, bowls, candlesticks and stemmed pieces designed to hold sweetmeats are more significant expressions of eighteenth-century styles, but these are much harder to find.

In reviewing the glass made between 1720 and 1800, one quickly notes a sharp change in style and taste that sets in at about 1750.

Where earlier examples are characterized by generous use of a heavy lead metal, the later pieces are fashioned of lighter glass in smaller proportions. The decoration also shifts, from applied gathers of glass to engraving and cutting. Although 1750 marked the moment when rococo was becoming a highly influential style in England, the change to lighter glass may have been more than just a matter of taste. A 1745-46 excise duty on glass was based on weight, which probably inspired the craftsmen to use as little glass as possible in making any specific object.

The shift in the manner of decoration is harder to account for with any conviction. It may have been a practical means of further reducing the weight of the glass or an esthetic effort to create a more reflective surface. Cutting had been well known in Germany, Bohemia and the Netherlands before 1700, but English glasshouses rarely employed it. Then in 1750 it was picked up rather quickly, apparently through the hiring away of German craftsmen. Another reason for the popularity of the cut glass may have been the formula for lead glass in the eighteenth century, which made it a better vehicle for cutting. But whatever the reason for the late start in England, English cut glass was in great demand between 1760 and 1830. The output was of prime quality, compared with European work of the same period.

English cut glass of the eighteenth and early nineteenth centuries has not attracted the attention of collectors as much as earlier

Candlestick, cut glass, English, 1760–70. Glass-cutting involved making facets to reflect light from the fine hard metal. Eighteenth-century patterns are basically more subtle than those of nineteenth century.

opposite
Tankard, opaque white glass with enamel decoration and silver cover, Danish, about 1750

blown and later art glass, so there are frequently bargains to be found in this area. Although knowing dealers will charge a few hundred dollars for a good bowl, a cut-glass decanter from about 1770 may go for as little as $40. Turn-of-the-century cut glass, which was inscribed with deeper and flashier patterns, is a lot more expensive. It takes a little study to distinguish fine early cut glass from the more routine work made to simulate it in the last forty years.

The neoclassical vogue that began in the 1760's spurred the popularity of cut glass. The delicacy of the motifs was neoclassical in spirit, and the patterns did relate in some slight way to those on ancient Roman cut glass. There is a good chance that the idea of using cutting as a means of embellishing glass was inspired by discoveries of ancient cut glass. Patterns followed the general trends of fashion, with earlier examples having the delicacy of the Adam style and later ones from about 1790 to 1830 cut deeper, in the spirit of later neoclassical design. Lead glass was constantly improved in the eighteenth century and this made deeper cut designs possible.

The glass cutter employed a limited number of basic motifs for a fairly broad range of designs. For the low relief patterns favored before 1790, he would make triangular, four-sided and crescent-shaped slices in the metal to form pyramids or diamonds. He might also hollow out oval or circular grooves in bands or over-all designs. The shallow cutting emphasized shadows and the play of light without sacrificing the transparency of the glass. Deeper ridges and grooves were used later to create patterns such as the raised diamond and to make a surface that was all glitter and impossible to see through.

English colored glass is usually attributed to glasshouses outside of London; nearby Bristol and Nailsea are towns whose names have become generic for types of colored glass. Bristol is credited with an opaque glass that was made as a substitute for porcelain and with a brilliantly colored transparent glass used for fashionable neoclassical designs as well as for forms of no particular style. The opaque white, which was called enamel glass in advertisements of the 1760's, is an intensely white, brittle material produced in shapes inspired by Chinese porcelain. Frequently examples are decorated with

Flask, deep blue and opaque white striated glass, probably Nailsea, about 1800. Nailsea is one of a number of centers of glassmaking that produced colored glass that looks primitive but was based on ancient Roman models. The stripes resemble one type made first in Egypt and later in Rome.

polychrome floral designs or black transfer prints. A tax of 1777 made it impractical to continue producing enamel glass as such, but payment was avoided by making a variation in the formula—to one of soda-lime-potash, producing a cream color rather than a strong white. Opaque white was also altered into the opalescent, an iridescent white that became popular in the early nineteenth century under the name of opaline. Although it was made in many centers, a number of collectors associate all opaline glass with Bristol. The name Bristol remained pre-eminent, with catalogues of American silver companies in the 1880's offering "Bristol glass fittings" for novelties they were making.

Transparent Bristol glass was most popular in blue, ruby and green. These colors were used for simple blown pieces, some with relief patterns formed in a part-sized mold. This kind of mold was important in much of the history of glass: the glass was blown into it, then removed and expanded to the desired size and shape through blowing. Empire-style decanters and brilliantly colored plates decorated with bold gold patterns were produced in huge quantity. The signature "Jacobs, Bristol" sometimes appears on fashionable examples, but this kind of glass was made elsewhere, too.

Nailsea is considered the production center for a cruder product. A dark green ground irregularly embellished with white, red, black and blue opaque splotches is characteristic. The results look rough and accidental, but similar glass of ancient Roman origin suggests that the texture was intentional. Rolling pins with souvenir inscriptions, bottles of all sizes and colors, walking sticks and giant tobacco pipes head a complex list of forms produced at Nailsea and other centers working in the same spirit. Thick trails of opaque glass, a variation of the latticino technique, make the Nailsea product reminiscent of certain contemporary American efforts.

It is hard to be sure that colored glass is from either Bristol or Nailsea, since other centers were duplicating the work. For pieces of the period, prices are about the same for Bristol and Nailsea wares as for those made elsewhere. These range from $50 for a small unmarked piece to $1,000 for a large documented example.

Cruet set, opaque white glass, Bristol, about 1760. The opaque white glass was a substitute for porcelain, although it rarely confused anyone. Eighteenth-century product was relatively thin.

IRISH, BOHEMIAN AND FRENCH GLASS

Few serious collectors of cut glass can·remain dispassionate about Irish glass. Either they are sworn devotees or they scorn it with a vengeance. Enthusiasts consider it the best kind of flint glass produced between 1780 and 1830. Others insist it is obviously derivative, with little merit in either decoration or metal. The controversy is further confused by disputes as to what is and what isn't Irish glass. One early study discusses the handsome blue tint; another tries to prove that the best work never had a trace of this color. The long-standing mystique of Irish glass now makes it very difficult to be sure just what it was made of. Very little glass of any sort is marked and its attribution has been based on feeling rather than documentation; thus many pieces designated as Irish may have been made elsewhere.

When taxes became prohibitively high in the 1780's, Ireland was a refuge for English glassmakers. Waterford, the most famous name in Irish glass, had a glasshouse operated by men from Stourbridge, England, but there were Irish craftsmen producing glass in Dublin, Cork and Belfast. In looking over documented pieces, one sees clearly that most Irish glass was distinctive, because the pieces have a consistency of approach. The metal of prime examples is frequently a little darker than the English. The cutting tends to be bolder and less subtle than in the finest English work. Irish designers appear to have favored less complex patterns than their English counterparts, and areas of cutting are often framed by plain sections.

At the turn of the century, blue-tinted Irish glass was sometimes faked. If you are considering a piece and the blue comes through too clearly, study the cutting carefully; an imitation will have flatter cutting, a result of the later machine work.

To the eighteenth-century buff, Bohemian glass means the sometimes clear and the sometimes brilliantly colored product of the 1700's. It was handsomely engraved and cut in delicate low relief giving an over-all impression that is frequently closer to the baroque of the 1600's than to the rococo of the 1700's. Most people, however, think of Bohemian glass as nineteenth-century ware made in France, England and the United States as well as in Bohemia. It has a layer or two of colored glass over clear glass, the outer layers cut and engraved away to create designs in two or three colors. Objects most easily come by have a layer of ruby red, but on the finest examples, it is a pale opaque blue. The shapes are generally the same as the conservative ones of the eighteenth century, but the decoration is simpler and bolder over-all, sometimes with fussier details that show on examination.

Early examples are hard to find, but later repetitions are abundant—including examples from the present day. The decoration of mid nineteenth-century work was cut away with conviction; later efforts have vine borders and the like casually scratched on. One variation in Bohemian glass involves brushing stain on the piece rather than using layers of glass. First used in Bohemia in 1804, this

Bowl, cut glass, possibly Irish, about 1800. Faceting was executed in larger-scaled patterns at the end of the eighteenth century. The upper border must have been inspired by ancient Roman metalwork or molded glass. Irish work and English work of the period are not always easily differentiated.

opposite
Goblet, overlay blue and clear glass, Bohemian
style, Viennese, about 1830

French paperweight from period between 1850 and 1880 is typical of revival of virtuoso glassblowing. Millefiore ends are used here, but latticino and small insects were also used as embellishments.

shortcut is not necessarily an indication that the work is of recent origin.

Great Bohemian glass is in short supply because it has been prized from its first appearance. Covered chalices and decanters are good examples that appear most frequently, but on hasty examination these can be confused with routine recent copies. If a large decanter is less than $50 you can probably arrange to meet the man who made it; adequate bona fide examples can be found for less than $100.

The French, who gave the world the glorious stained-glass windows of the Gothic cathedrals, made no important contribution to glassmaking in the period from 1300 to 1800. During those five centuries all that the French apparently did was to try to keep up with developments in Venice, Germany, Bohemia and England. They did, however, make a green glass, called verre de fougère, which was produced from the fall of Rome to the 1800's.

French glassmakers then started to make up for their centuries of quiet by becoming innovators in design. The first to achieve renown was an artist named Desprez who, about 1800, created portrait profiles in opaque white glass, which were encased in mugs, decanters and paperweights. The key French manufacturers began their distinctive and important work early in the nineteenth century, although the houses had been founded a century earlier. Baccarat, established in 1765, did not have any major impact until 1820, when its complete sets of

matching glasses caught on and started a new fashion. The Crystalleries St.-Louis uses 1765 as its founding date, but it, too, did not make a mark until it began producing paperweights in the 1840's.

The paperweight, a finely made dome-shaped casing for a fantasy of glass rods, is a French innovation, even though there is a tendency to emphasize its Venetian antecedents. The techniques are Venetian, but the concept did not catch on until the French glassmakers began their work. St.-Louis, Clichy and a host of other houses made their most delicate and intricate paperweights between about 1845 and 1870. At the same time, France established her reputation as a manufacturer of fine glass, setting the fash-

ion with work that showed her artisans to be careful students of history.

Collectors will have a lot less trouble finding opalescent glass made in France between 1825 and 1850 than the paperweights. The French opalescent, often called opaline or agathe, is a variation on the ware made in Bristol, but it is generally framed in a more ornate way. Vases, bowls and boxes range in price from about $50 to $400, while paperweights of the finest quality go for $20,000 and more. Cut glass by Baccarat and its competitors has appeal as a distinctive interpretation of classical design of the nineteenth century. Prices are on a par with those for slightly earlier English cut glass: $200 to $500 will buy a good small decanter and glasses.

AMERICAN GLASS

Americans like to collect American glass, which puts a premium on the price. But as much as any other field, early American glass is fraught with confusion. No early examples go begging, but the period makes many collectors nervous about what the early Americans actually made and about later forgeries and reproductions. The greatest interest thus focuses on American art glass of the late nineteenth century, where price tags of $10,000 and $15,000 are not as shocking as they might seem. If your interest in American glass is esthetic rather than patriotic, you can economize by finding European equivalents of the eighteenth and nineteenth centuries. Simple blown wares are much less expensive when their nationality cannot be identified

Bottle, enameled glass, attributed to W. H. Stiegel, American, about 1770. This bottle was found in the area of the Stiegel glasshouse. Its decoration is more restrained than most examples of European origin, but the difference is subtle.

with authority. Although the American product has distinctive elements, it is also representative of its period.

Documents of the 1600's and 1700's reveal that Americans have made glass since the first settlement of Virginia in 1607. But to prove that a piece is from the first glasshouse, which was in Jamestown, or from any of the others of the seventeenth century, is virtually impossible. Records disclose that glassblowers at Jamestown did some work before the massacre there, and the output in New Amsterdam is well recorded and was probably considerable, but there are no key pieces from either place to serve as touchstones for authenticity. Nor is it easier to find comparable European work of this date. Ordinary drinking vessels of about 1600 are in the main out of reach for private collectors and to be found mostly in museums.

American glass from the early eighteenth century is almost as rare. Caspar Wistar founded a glasshouse in southern New Jersey in 1739, but most of the glass once attributed to it is of later manufacture. A few authenticated examples, however, do exist. Wistar made blown-glass objects for the table from window and bottle glass—that is, green or brown—that was ornamented with tooled molten glass gathers. This type of object was also popular in the nineteenth century, and later glassmakers carried on the older technique of blowing individual pieces by hand. European examples of blown green glass, in forms more or less related to Wistar, turn up from time to time. Eighteenth-century examples are delicate and neoclassical or rococo; nineteenth-century forms tend to be more massive.

Less is known of the surviving output of eighteenth-century New York glasshouses, although they advertised a variety of tablewares and bottles of all sizes. The Glass House Company, which in the 1750's operated one plant in Manhattan and another in New Windsor, New York, must have made a respectable amount of glass—but no documented pieces are known.

STIEGEL AND HIS IMITATORS

The best-known American glassmaker of the eighteenth century is William Henry Stiegel, who founded a glasshouse, the American Flint Glass Manufactory, in Manheim, Pennsylvania, in 1763. His biography is colorful. He came to America from Germany with no funds, married well and started a glass business that was at first very successful. But he overextended himself and went bankrupt in 1774, ending his days as a poor school-master.

Stiegel visited Bristol to see what was being produced and asserted that his glass had the same composition as the English—flint with a high lead content. But analysis of the better authenticated examples has shown inconsistency in the glass content; it could

Tumbler, engraved molded glass, attributed to W. H. Stiegel, American, about 1770. Also from the neighborhood of the Stiegel glasshouse. The form is one that was made extensively on both sides of the Atlantic. Simple engraving in geometric patterns varies only slightly on American, German and Spanish pieces.

never be called lead glass and certainly would never be mistaken for the better English glass. Some of Stiegel's efforts in colored glass can be compared to those of Bristol, however; others resemble the output of middle-sized factories all over the Continent. In any case, most of his workmen were Continental and his work reflected a combination of English and German influences.

Diamond-patterned molded glass in blue, green, red and yellow is characteristic. Typical of his work are small bottles, sugar bowls, salt cellars and other small objects. Stiegel used part-sized molds to create relief decoration: patterns were impressed in the gather of glass and these expanded as the piece was blown. The best examples are lightly but clearly patterned.

In collecting Stiegel, one must be cautious because there are many twentieth-century reproductions. Close inspection will give these away, however, because the later molding is more precise. Stiegel was most popular with collectors in the 1920's, when a number of reproductions were made in Czechoslovakia. When considering a putative Stiegel, take time to examine an authenticated piece, too. Verified Stiegel bottles cost $500 to $1,000 and the sugar bowls are even more, so beware the extraordinary bargain. Glass from Bristol comes in similar small molded forms of a colored metal, with prices considerably lower, but the pieces are generally not as handsomely shaped as those by Stiegel.

The American Midwest—meaning Pittsburgh and westward—is another source of glass like Stiegel's. Colors are more varied—amethyst and yellow as well as blue, green and colorless—and the sugar bowls are differently shaped. Eighteenth-century examples are based on Chinese porcelains; they have pear-shaped sides and shallow saucer-like tops. Later pieces have straighter sides and a high, domed cover similar to those on Empire silver or porcelain.

The Continental technique of applying painted enamel decoration to colorless or blue glass was also popular at the Stiegel glasshouse. Stiegel's workmen are thought to have restricted the enamel palette to six opaque colors: nile green, brick red, black, a special shade of blue, white and yellow. Lovebirds were just about a Stiegel signature, and inscriptions in English bolster the con-

Sugar bowl, molded glass, American, attributed to W. H. Stiegel, about 1770

fidence of Stiegel connoisseurs. The expected forms for enameled Stiegel are bottles and tumblers, but Spanish, Portuguese, German and Central European glasshouses made them, too.

Stiegel produced large tumblers of colorless glass that were often paneled and engraved with a simple pattern, particularly primitive florals, engraved in broad strokes. Similar work was done all over Europe and German and Spanish examples abound. Stiegel mugs and covered forms in engraved glass are strongly under the Continental influence; again German examples turn up often. It is thus unwise to pay more than $30 to $50—the price usually asked for a Continental tumbler—for something that is being offered as Stiegel.

The second most famous American glasshouse of the eighteenth century was founded in 1784 by John Frederick Amelung near Frederick-town, Maryland. Called the New Bremen Glass Manufactory, it was an ambitious project captalized by German and American backers. In its period of operation, until 1795, it made tumblers, wineglasses, decanters, mugs and "every other sort of Table Glass," to quote an early advertisement. Finding authenticated samples is quite difficult. Like Stiegel, Amelung said that he made flint glass, but tests on documented examples do not disclose the proper lead content and the glasses are not as colorless as they should be. Among the examples are some pieces similar to Stiegel works, and others with more elaborately tooled

decorations in a technique also used by New Jersey glasshouses.

Gamblers should remember one form, the wineglass. Although records show that the early American glass houses made stemmed wineglasses, it is difficult to be sure what they look like. Examples that have turned up near the sites of the Stiegel and Amelung factories are fairly plain and most often a little smoky. It is not possible to prove they were made locally, but when research into the content of American glass becomes more refined, it may be easy to distinguish the American from the mediocre Continental examples. At that point some of the glasses will become a lot more valuable, so if you like taking risks, wineglasses are a likely field.

Stiegel and Amelung appeal to specialized tastes that are somewhat difficult to indulge. For most collectors early American glass means molded or pressed glass made in the nineteenth century, and in this context 1820 is considered early indeed.

AMERICAN MOLDED AND PRESSED GLASS

Two key nineteenth-century developments in glass were molding and pressing—processes that speeded production. The old part-sized mold used in glassblowing was replaced by a full-sized mold. This mold was made of two to five hinged parts that could be opened up for removal of the glass object. Although all of the seams are visible, this kind of glass is popularly known as blown-three-mold glass. The mold patterns were related to designs then being cut into glass by the English and Irish houses, but they were simplified and flattened. When English craftsmen molded glass the effect was close to that of cut glass, although inspection shows the edges to be a little smoother. When the Americans adapted cut patterns, they used a lower relief and the product appears more distinctively molded.

Most blown-three-mold glass dates from about 1820 to 1840. It seems to have been produced mainly in New England, although there are examples from Kent, Ohio, and New York State. Tracing particular patterns to particular houses is not yet possible, although the problem has been researched by a great glass connoisseur, Helen McKearin. The first results of her research have been published in a book, *American Glass*, which she wrote with her late father, George Mc-Kearin.

Blown-three-mold glass gives perfect expression to the American neoclassical taste, and it is contemporary with Greek revival architecture. The glass looks American because it combines surface roughness with

Sugar bowl, amethyst glass, by Bakewell, Page & Bakewell, Pittsburgh, about 1820. The fluted sides and dome top with the emphatic lip on the cover are details that were adapted from Empire-style silver models.

opposite
Sugar and salt shakers, opaque white glass with enamel decoration, Mount Washington Glass Company, Massachusetts, about 1890

Pitcher, blown three-mold glass, American, about 1820. The glass blown in full-size mold is generally in regular relatively high-relief patterns. The modified sunburst, the diamond and the fluting can all be traced to ancient Roman models.

patterns that are knowingly conceived in a way that seems to have particularly suited Americans of the early 1800's. The smoothness, irregularities and seams create a texture that feels distinctive when handled and is a far cry from the more mechanical later reproductions. A collector of glass should not find it difficult to learn to distinguish the nineteenth century from the twentieth century, even though the challenge of recognizing in which state an example was made should be left to the superexpert.

Pressed glass was a further development in mass production. Instead of being blown into a mold, the molten glass was poured in. The craftsman needed less skill and the process was much faster. Design became the responsibility of the mold maker.

Pressed glass probably originated in the United States, but Deming Jarves of Massachusetts, the man credited with the first major manufacture, said it had first been made in England. On the other hand, an Englishman of the same period declared pressed glass to be American, so everyone seems embarrassed to claim the honor. The process was developed in the 1820's, but unfortunately the patent records of the period are gone. By 1830, in a form called lacy glass, in which the mold is cut into intricate lace-like patterns, pressed glass had come into its own. Some believe that lacy glass was developed to conceal impurities in the glass metal. Many of the most elaborate examples were made at Deming Jarves's Boston and Sandwich Glass Company and at the New

England Glass Company in Cambridge, Massachusetts, but these were just two of the sixteen or more recorded American makers.

From 1830 to 1850, when lacy glass was at its height, it was used for a wide variety of tablewares. Favored by collectors is the cup plate. This was intended as a resting place for the cup while the saucer was being drunk from, a necessity that indicates great delicacy of approach to a habit now considered merely gross. Cup plates were only about three inches in diameter, but they were made in at least a thousand different designs. The more interesting have historical subjects and commemorate heroes, great ships, monuments or notable events. Less interesting but more prevalent are those with conventional designs of the period—the scroll and rosette. The most common cup plates are of clear glass; rare examples are colored or opalescent. They range in cost from a few hundred dollars to $10 or $20, according to rarity.

European examples have interesting variations. One must keep in mind, however, that some European cup plates were made close to 1900; these should not be included in collections showing pressed glass in its prime. French pressed glass of the 1830's does look different from American but has the same fussy detail. Later French work is of a finer, less decorated metal.

Small salts, rectangular or curved but sometimes boat-shaped, represent another field worth studying in detail. Some bear the company mark but most do not. The earliest

Compote, pressed lacy glass, American, 1830–50. Pressed glass has metal forced manually rather than blown into the mold. Early patterns were probably intricate, or "lacy," to conceal the bubbles formed in the manufacturing process.

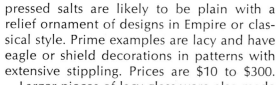

Candlestick in the form of a dolphin, yellow and iridescent glass, American, 1875–1900. The dolphin was first used on pressed-glass candlesticks in the 1840's but the late examples have dome-shaped bases and flatter, more complex ornamentation.

pressed salts are likely to be plain with a relief ornament of designs in Empire or classical style. Prime examples are lacy and have eagle or shield decorations in patterns with extensive stippling. Prices are $10 to $300.

Larger pieces of lacy glass were also made for the table. Celery vases, compotes, bowls, butter dishes and the like were often found on the tables of the middle class in the 1830's. Colored examples are now quite rare and it is not surprising to discover that a fine compote will cost $2,000 to $3,000. Such work was turned out at the Boston and Sandwich Glass Company and the New England Glass Company, as well as at factories in the Pittsburgh area.

In the 1840's pressed glass became plainer, largely because of a change in popular taste but also because the cost of lacy molds had become prohibitive. Bolder, plainer classical forms in the Empire style appear as a reaction to the earlier work. Bowls, compotes, celery vases and oil lamps are particularly appealing in deep reds, blues, greens and purples.

The 1840's also marked the introduction of the dolphin as a motif for supports or stems on candlesticks and compotes. Although distinctly in the Empire style (it was employed on furniture), the dolphin was to remain popular in pressed glass for the rest of the century. Vaseline glass—yellow-green in color—was used for plain bold dolphins on square pedestals in the 1840's and for fussier, more detailed dolphins on dome-shaped feet in the 1880's and later.

Compote in the diamond thumbprint pattern, pressed glass, American, late nineteenth century. The combination of the oval depression and the diamond are an obvious translation of cut-glass design to the requirements of the mold.

Tureen of pressed milk glass made by McKee Brothers, Pittsburgh, about 1870. Post-Civil War pressed glass was made in a variety of shapes, with quaint animals and birds particularly popular. By the turn of the century, ships with a bust of Admiral Dewey were being made to commemorate the Spanish-American War.

The pressed glass most familiar to us today dates from after 1860. The typical designs are plainer than lacy glass but more intricate than the work of the 1840's and 1850's. This late pressed glass—known as pattern glass—was produced in great variety by glasshouses all over the United States as well as in France and England. Some rare examples are thought to have been made before 1850, although most were products of the period 1860 to 1900. There has been little interest shown in European examples, but American pattern glass has had its devotees since the 1920's, when it first went out of style.

Originally most pattern glass was clear glass, but some was in opaque white—or milk glass; exceptional colored pieces do turn up. A few designs, clearly based on cut-glass models, have sharply faceted surfaces and resemble glass of the 1830's. Flattened undulations or a series of large oval or round indentations seem to have suited the molding process better; these patterns became popular under the names Thumbprint, Argus, Ashburton and Excelsoir. Ribbed surfaces serve as a background for vines of various kinds in a number of popular patterns. The cable became a popular motif after the transatlantic cable was laid. Drapery, suggesting the festoons used in mourning, was introduced on glass memorials to Lincoln and, later, Garfield. Hundreds of patterns were made, few of them the exclusive domain of a single company. The New England Glass Company, Bakewell, Pears & Co., McKee of Pittsburgh and Hobbs, Brockunier & Co. of Wheeling, West Virginia, were among the important names of the period, but since the glass was not marked and designs were widely copied, one should not pay a premium just because a piece of pattern glass is ascribed to a big name.

Collecting glass from this period is a little like collecting stamps—rarity dictates the price rather than esthetics. Common patterns can be bought for $10 a goblet; rarer items go for $50 to $200. Modern reproductions are being made of some of the favorites, so "bargains" are likely to be new pieces.

ART GLASS

Art glass first became popular about 1850. As its name implies, it is purely decorative and its appeal derives from the ingenuity and skill involved in its manufacture rather than from any practical virtue the item might have for holding salt or milk. Art glass is a mass-produced product that was conceived as a luxury. Major glasshouses all over Europe and the United States produced it throughout the second half of the nineteenth century.

At its inception it was a reaction to the various forms of cut glass that had held such an important place in the glass market. To replace the classical designs of both the clear colorless and the colorful Bohemian cut glass, manufacturers turned to opaque glass,

Vase, cameo decoration on colored glass, by George Woodall of Thomas Webb & Sons, Stourbridge, England, about 1905. Virtuoso carving in designs best described as late Victorian are associated with a small group of English glassmakers. Woodall was one of the finest craftsmen making cameo glass. Webb & Sons also produced simpler work.

which they decorated like porcelain. The influence of Venice and ancient Rome was felt again with the reappearance of latticino and cameo glass. The French and Venetian glasshouses are generally considered to have drawn upon traditional techniques, while the English were more adventuresome.

After the 1870's pale, opaque renditions of Near Eastern and oriental forms were produced by the major English art glass manufacturers. Matte or glossy finishes were used on surfaces that were sometimes plain and sometimes textured appropriately. The shapes were occasionally direct steals from earlier porcelain models, but others were typical inventions of the time and show all the scalloping fashionable in that period. These exotic shapes seem contorted and difficult, the pale colors hard to create, so that these prestigious objects of art glass have become fairly expensive.

If exotica appeals to you, bear in mind that there are imitations currently being made in Italy. Several giftware importers keep many small dealers constantly supplied with brand-new antiques. Do not spend $500 for a pretty pink bowl unless you can compare it with another example that has been proved authentic. In England Thomas Webb, Richardson and Stevens & Williams were among the most prominent manufacturers including art glass in their lines. Besides the exotic, they also produced designs reviving classical themes.

Nineteenth-century cameo glass comes in patterns that combine the neoclassical revival with exoticism. A few examples are reminiscent of works by the nineteenth-century painters Gerome and Alma-Tadema, both of whom liked erotic representations of Turkish bazaars and harems. White reliefs were cut with precision into a ground of rich yellow, offbeat red or pale blue. Looking at English cameo glass through a magnifying glass is great fun. This awesome detailing attracts many collectors, so prices are relatively high for vases, pitchers and small flasks in cameo glass: $400 to $1,500 buys a fine but modest example. At the turn of the century there were some truly virtuoso renditions, such as a reproduction of the Portland Vase. When one of these is offered, it will bring $20,000 or more.

The period of art glass in the United States ran from the 1880's to 1920. This dec-

Cameo glass vase by Thomas Webb & Sons, England, about 1900

orative ware was made originally to sell at a relatively high price, as befits what has become known as the Gilded Age. Generally art glass looks as though it really challenged the technical abilities of the maker, but it nonetheless represented a commercial venture and arty is a more accurate term for the product than art. Most art glass is still popular and still expensive, although some types have been reproduced widely.

Art glass responded to the demand for decoration that would go with Near Eastern and oriental motifs. Multicolored glass, opaque or transparent, was worked plain or was decorated to seem hard to make. Extra smooth or rough textures in an unusual range of colors are typical.

Although the English and French made art glass first, the most important American examples achieved international renown. Most art glass formulas were patented, and rights to a number of American patents were acquired by English manufacturers. One of the first American patents for art glass was granted in 1881 to William Dean and Alphonse Peltier for an opaque matte-finished product called satin glass that was made in plain pale or in gradated colors. This work was occasionally decorated with enamel paint or gold, and the surfaces were sometimes ornamented with quilting in relief. One variation, called Mother of Pearl, was generally in gradated colors and patterned in relief. English and American versions are hard to tell apart. Another type, Burmese, patented in 1885 by the Mount Washington Glass

Amberina glass bowl in inverted thumbprint patterns by the New England Glass Company, American, about 1885. Rich patented colors and unusual exotic shapes were typical of art glass.

Company of New Bedford, Massachusetts, is similar. This varicolored opaque glass ranges from yellow at the base to a brownish pink at the top. An English manufacturer, Thomas Webb & Sons, was licensed to produce the pattern in 1886. Queen Victoria owned a set of Burmese with a floral enamel decoration that came to be known as Queen's Design. About 1885 the New England Glass Company made a variation that deepened from white to a rich strawberry. When this was offered as Wild Rose it did not sell well, but it was a huge hit when renamed Peach Blow, after a pair of oriental porcelain vases that had broken auction records in 1886. Hobbs, Brockunier & Co. also made a Peach Blow, but the colors were different—orange to red. Additional opaque designs were added to the repertory in the 1890's. The Mount Washington Glass Company made Crown Milano in shades of tan, and Royal Flemish in terra cotta and tans.

The opaque types, in matte or glossy finishes, are very expensive. Because surface decoration adds considerably to the prices, some present-day decorators busily add embellishments. One group of contemporary decorators has tried to better the artisans of the 1890's by adding Arabic scenes with men on camels. Italian glassmakers create acceptable satin glass that is offered by several giftware wholesalers. Unfortunately, a number of pieces sold wholesale as giftware become antiques on the retail circuit.

Transparent colored glass was made in special combinations of color. The best known, Amberina, was patented in 1883 by the New England Glass Company. Gradating from yellow at the bottom to a dark red at the top, Amberina appeared in a variety of pressed and blown models. In 1886 the Mount Washington Glass Company brought out a subtle variation called Rose Amber; the same year Hobbs, Brockunier obtained a license to make Amberina.

In 1885 the New England Glass Company patented a process of acid-staining to create a frosted surface and simplified it a few years later. The company called the resulting glass Pomona.

Overlay glass, still another type of art glass, has relief decoration applied to pieces that are either glossy or have textured surfaces that look sandy. Ornament consists of flowers and vines rendered with some attention to detail. Examples signed by Stevens & Williams, an English company, are known, but no documented American examples have been discovered.

Art glass is perfect for those who like flamboyance. Strong colors and carefully executed details are the main attractions, but occasionally the glitter is so glaring it makes it hard to notice the inconsistency of detail marking later imitations.

Prices for the rarest art glass can range into the thousands for a fine bowl and up to $200 for a tumbler. Amberina, for example, will be very high when it is of pre-1900 origin. Twentieth-century pieces sell for considerably less and are collected with gusto. A toothpick holder will cost $50; pitchers are $100 to $300.

TIFFANY AND HIS IMITATORS

When Tiffany glass appeared at the turn of the century, it became internationally popular; as much was sold in Europe as in the United States. When one encounters a great example in an Edwardian London townhouse, a refined German home or a Parisian apartment furnished in the 1890's, it is evidence that Tiffany glass was a great favorite of the stylish long before its recent era of chic, which began about twenty years ago.

The glassmaker Louis Comfort Tiffany was the scion of the New York jewelry family. Born in 1848, he studied painting with George Inness before being drawn into the decorative arts. He first founded a decorating firm and then went into glass. He began experimenting with blown glass in 1892, and by 1896 was selling his products at the Parisian shop of S. Bing, La Maison de l'Art Nouveau. The work began as an expression of artistic craftsmanship on the finest plane, but by the time production ceased in the 1930's it was dull. Authentic Tiffany, therefore, can be great and it can be terrible.

The glass for which Tiffany is best known is iridescent and richly colored. The vases, pitchers and bowls often look almost accidental or appear to be the result of natural growth. The early work may have uneven textures, to make it appear as if the surfaces had been weathered. Elongated shapes, sometimes naturalistic and at other times inspired by Near Eastern forms, express the taste of Art Nouveau. Tiffany called this glass Favrile. In two publications (around 1896) he offered two explanations for the name: it came from the Old English "fabrile," meaning a craft product, and from the German "farbe," meaning color. Both stories are convincing. His first products created such a stir in Paris that before 1900 several European glasshouses were making imitations. Loetz, an Austrian glasshouse, was a notable imitator, and a string of others soon followed suit. The key difference between great early Tiffany and later work is that with time the decoration became standardized—more predictable and less exciting.

Tiffany is marked by paper labels affixed to the bases and a signature and code number that are scratched on. Since either one raises the value of a piece tremendously, fake paper labels and kits for scratching on

Vase, Favrile glass by Louis Comfort Tiffany, American, about 1890

the signatures have been available. The appearance of the object, however, should be the only identification required. Mediocre signed genuine Tiffany is a lot less appealing —and much more costly—than the better imitations such as the efforts of Quezal Art Glass and the Kew Blas line of the Union Glass Company. Great early Tiffany is priced in the $2,000-to-$30,000 range; more routine compotes and bowls are available at $200 to $500.

Tiffany stained glass was used in public and domestic structures at the turn of the century. Iridescent and plain-colored transparent glass were artfully combined to create landscape scenes. Prices for the best of these windows are $10,000 to $50,000; lesser work, although it captures the spirit, lacks the touch of genius and should go for much less.

Stained-glass shades for lamps and chandeliers are another turn-of-the-century phenomenon associated with Tiffany. Here too, the Tiffany colors and the Tiffany spirit— turning floral or leaf patterns into a shade for an early electric or oil fixture—achieve a result that is distinctive. Whereas the Wisteria lamp, a design of about 1902, has the essence of late Monet, cheap commercial efforts of the same date are as delightful as a Lillian Russell poster and just as dated.

LATER CUT GLASS

Cut glass made between 1880 and 1920—the so-called Brilliant Period—is attracting growing interest. Advances in chemistry had brought about a glass metal that was purer, clearer and harder than any before, and this lent itself particularly well to cutting. At the same time, new sources of energy—gas and electricity—were harnessed for the power equipment used in cutting, and the cutting or grinding could be made deeper and more varied. These advances coincided with a new taste for a really sparkling, reflective surface. The new work had its major impact in the years when Art Nouveau flourished, and the contrast is marked. The subtle dark colors of Art Nouveau were far removed from the bright sparkle of cut glass. Where Art Nouveau was an attempt at innovation, the cut glass of the Brilliant Period was strongly rooted in tradition .

It is amazing how many variations there can be in patterns based on the single idea of cutting or grinding away glass at angles that will catch the light. The basic diamond and fan motifs were revived, but they also appeared in new juxtapositions. The classical rectangles and circles of the 1700's re-emerge at the turn of the century as complex hexagons and stars. The small diamonds of early patterns are transfigured into diamonds of many sizes, with the emphasis on glitter. An innovation was the placement of flowers, cut relatively shallow, on flat areas to serve as foils for the glitter.

Cut glass suggests the opulence of its time in every way. The staggering diversity of forms—vases, bowls, plates, jars, decanters, pitchers, lamps, salt cellars and sconces—gives one the idea that opulence was extended to every corner of the late nineteenth-century home.

The cut-glass designs were patented, so that design and maker were documented to a certain degree. As in the automotive era, promoters of names seem to have kept their imaginations well exercised. Sometimes the names were to the point—Diamond Daisy, for example. Sometimes their intent seems to stir the imagination—Victoria, Amore, Lorraine and Stratford. One of the great designs of the period got stuck with the wrong name because the company acted too hastily. In 1882 Philip McDonald of T. G. Hawkes & Company of Corning, New York, patented a variation of the star-and-hobnail design. In a burst of pleasure after the Russian Embassy in Washington ordered a complete banquet service, the pattern was named Russian. If the Hawkes company had waited, it would have done even better. In 1885, in the Administration of Grover Cleveland, the pattern was selected for the White House. It remained in use there until the Administration of Franklin D. Roosevelt, but it was never renamed Presidential. By any name, however, Russian is one of the most highly valued of the characteristic designs of the Brilliant Period.

The Harvard pattern, which was listed in a number of catalogues, was also called Chair Bottom. It vaguely resembles chair caning, with the basic motifs symmetrically placed

Bowl, cut glass, American, about 1900. Brilliant cut glass made after 1880 is characterized by deep-cut decoration in complex patterns. Each motif was used in the late eighteenth century, but never in the intricate designs of the late period.

and smaller in scale than many of the flamboyant Brilliant patterns.

Manufacturers of cut glass abounded in 1900. Eighty were mentioned in a speech by William Dorflinger, a manufacturer of the time, but it is almost impossible to attribute work to any but a few of them. Most glass was not marked, although a few names were getting to be well known. The successor to the New England Glass Company, Libbey (which is still flourishing in Toledo), made and marked some of the greatest cut glass of the Brilliant Period. Hawkes, now a part of the Corning Glass Works, played a prominent role in cut-glass manufacture and marked some of its output. Lesser names also turn up, but they still account for only a very

small percentage of the manufacturers listed in directories of the day. It is best for the collector to avoid the "name game" and to concentrate on the designs. Despite all recent efforts to research patent records, many patterns yet remain to be identified. The enthusiast should seek work done in the proper spirit—work suggesting the sumptious elegance of the turn of the century through its glitter.

The best examples are of high-quality blown glass, but many manufacturers took shortcuts to grandeur by using molded glass. At first glance these versions sometimes look right, but further inspection uncovers mold marks or poor imitations of cutting. By the early 1900's these imitations were usually too bad to cause confusion, yet once in a while a hasty decision will lead to mistakes. An amazing range in prices exists. Representative examples at $5 and $10 may still be had, although $50 is more frequently the bottom figure in shops that specialize in cut glass. Rarities such as candlesticks or punch bowls in the Russian or Harvard patterns cost thousands.

RECENT GLASS, DEPRESSION AND CARNIVAL

Glass collectors show only a casual concern for the age of the objects they treasure. Almost as soon as a major manufacturer discontinues a line of glassware, people begin to collect it. Steuben, Fenton, Bryce Brothers, Imperial Glass and Libbey works from the 1920's, 1930's and more recent times are all found in collections, principally of those who consider earlier glass too hard to find. The most appealing of recent works are the decorative pieces. Some were designed with Tiffany or a competitor in mind; other pieces are more original.

Carnival glass has stirred lots of interest. It thrills many but horrifies traditional collectors. Those who favor it consider this iridescent pressed glass a suitable popularization

Covered vase, by Maurice Marinot, French, about 1930. Marinot was an outstanding artist-craftsman who exploited glass as a textured material in forms in the simple Art Deco style.

of Tiffany's Favrile. Those opposed see it as a bad imitation, noting how poor the metal is rather than finding charm in stubby little renderings of fruit, flowers and other classical objects under a layer of iridescence. Carnival glass may have been introduced at the turn of the century but is best known in examples of the 1930's, when it was given away at movie houses and offered as prizes at the carnivals from which it gets its name. Prices for the rarest carnival glass are in the hundreds—about as high as for reasonable Tiffany glass. Not surprisingly, this has inspired the original producers to go back into production. The result is confusion for those who seek pre-1940 examples.

Another recent type of glass now being collected is Depression glass, which got its name before anyone stopped to think if it was appropriate. Depression glass is the inexpensive pressed ware made into whole table services from the 1920's to the 1950's. Cheaper than pottery, it served as a substitute for families that could not afford china, or could not afford a "company" set. The first collectors viewed Depression glass nostalgically as something they knew when times were hard; there have probably been almost as many family fights over who gets the glass dishes as over who gets something that was originally of great price. This pressed glass was turned out at factories all over the country. Some efforts have been made at identifying the sources of the patterns, but the area is still green. The designs are consistently conservative; although there are a great many, not a single pattern in the Art Deco style has shown up.

More than most fields in antiques, glass is peppered with names. Names for types of glass, designs, makers and quantities of subdivisions are bandied about, sometimes with accuracy, sometimes in a wholly inventive spirit. Collectors and dealers have developed a whole lexicon for types of glass that went nameless for decades. Cranberry (a color), Mary Gregory (a decorator), hobnail (a pattern) and Heisey (a manufacturer) are all part of a vocabulary that can be picked up quickly when needed.

In glass, as in other fields, it is important not to be bullied by an apparent expert. If you see something you like, pursue it, find good examples and study their characteristics. You will then be able to buy with confidence in authenticity and price, whatever name and cachet the seller may use to embellish his wares.

Collecting Bargains

*Fan, parchment and wood, Italian, eighteenth
century*

SOME OFFBEAT OBJECTS AND A NEGLECTED PERIOD

Collecting small objects is the best way for the budget-bound to become connoisseurs. The objects can be primarily utilitarian or they can be decorative, but the main thing is that they be in styles now unappreciated. Little boxes, buttons, spoons, fans and a number of other small pieces fall into this category. Worthwhile collections can be built of pieces that are generally from the period between 1880 and 1920, although a few older examples will improve the display. The challenge is in picking an area that is not too restricted, because 125 napkin rings, even if all are different, make a stupefying collection. I also have difficulty understanding why some people want to collect such materials as barbed wire. Although there is a bit of variety in the forms of the barbs, and there is an amazing amount that is marked, it takes special refinement to be able to discern esthetic differences. Collectors who admire barbed wire see it as a symbol of the conquest of the West; they can hear shots fired by the cowmen guarding their land from the sheep men. Imaginative collectors have assembled their prizes in attractive frames, but there still is not very much to knowing the characteristics of each brand of wire.

Some other primarily functional objects present a similar problem to me. The expertise boils down to names and numbers marked on examples; electric insulators, for instance. These glass holders for power lines, which have fallen into fields as the wires have been repaired, generally have a wonderful patina. As bits of glitter, they are handsome; collected seriously by name and number, they seem preposterous. Nonetheless there is a lot of interest, and prices keep going up as people research the field and start hunting for rarities.

Bottles lie between the functional and the stylish, and bottle collectors are a large, avid and diverse group. Some collectors concentrate on particular kinds of bottles, others on those of particular periods. Too many, unfortunately, are perfectly delighted with modern bottles created for collectors: the Jim Beam, Avon and other bottles that win no museum award for good design. These bottles sell well and appreciate steadily in value, but my complaint is that the designs reflect little of current taste and rely heavily on ersatz nostalgia for their appeal. Much more worthwhile are bottles that are true reflections of past periods, plain or elaborately ornamented. Old milk and soda bottles have an appeal because their shapes are simple and their only ornament—the lettering—has a bygone charm. They are hard to date because they were made in pressing machines that went unchanged for close to half of the nineteenth century and continued on into the twentieth century. Collectors who have stopped at the milk-bottle stage and are prepared to pay dearly for a milk bottle with a misspelled name should realize that for the same amount—under $100— they could get a Roman bottle from the second or third century that would give their collection diversity and interest.

opposite
*Spice boxes, wood bound in metal, Shaker
style, American, about 1850*

*Bottle with portrait of Louis Kossuth, American,
about 1850. For bottle collectors 1850
is quite old. This shape has been reproduced, but
copies more often portray Jenny Lind.*

Bottles in the shape of figures are a great favorite with collectors. These examples, in a sense the forefathers of the Avon bottles, were at their height about 1900. Americans tend to prefer American-made examples, but these were made all over Europe in a variety of shapes. Some are really figures; others are locomotives, houses or whatever inspired the manufacturer. Rare examples date from before 1850, but most figural bottles are Edwardian and Victorian.

American flasks of the 1820–50 period are the most coveted of collectable bottles and the most dangerous. When bottles began to be mass-produced in the 1820's, relief decoration was applied and there was great interest in patriotic motifs. Washington, Polk, and Jenny Lind are among the personalities represented. Campaign slogans were used on flasks that were given away at election time in the Harrison campaign and later. These bottles are easy to fake; there are huge numbers of reproductions around, some selling for $1 in the supermarket. The molding process used in the originals was not so refined; details are sometimes fuzzy, but the character of the details may indicate authenticity. Recent imitations have elements picked out as an afterthought and the lip of the bottle will be less elaborately formed. The prices on flasks are dictated by subject matter, so a rare example will cost $300 and a common one may be $75. Constant caution against fakes is necessary.

Plain early bottles of the 1700's are dark green or amber and very attractive. Simple curves produce handsome lines, and occasional seals show the date of the bottles. Forms were fairly standard for any particular decade, and prices should be $50 to $100 but they keep going up.

The limited editions of commemorative bottles have become unbelievably popular these days. Bottle collectors swarmed into Las Vegas recently when one bottle commemorating something there went on sale. The whisky was poured out by single-minded collectors and within a few days the prices had doubled. I suspect that in a few years there will be little interest in these pieces because they are so easy to duplicate and they have minimal significance. The simple, square-based bottles of the early 1800's that now sell for $20 or less are getting scarce and will probably be much more important in thirty years.

Serious collecting should involve some tussle with esthetics and authenticity. Bottles involve these matters somewhat, but they are tame stuff; objects wholly connected with the cycles of fashion—buttons or fans, for instance—are more difficult to evaluate and more fun to investigate.

Buttons, for those who get beyond the obvious recently marked examples, are a worthy challenge. Although there is great interest in brass buttons of the last century, that field is narrow. Buttons were used in the 1400's, and with some effort it is possible to find such examples. There are many examples of the 1700's that can also be turned up with hard work. Buttons have been made of many materials; brass, iron, gold, silver, ivory, horn, pearl and ceramic should be part of any serious collection. The manufacturers at Birmingham, England, in the 1700's and 1800's supplied a large number of buttons to a good part of the world. Their early designs are an interesting reflection of the taste of the time. Belated rococo designs were made, along with any number of neoclassical variations. Birmingham manufacturers were among the first to make a composite button of two materials, and Wedgwood jasperware plaques were incorporated into buttons early as well as later.

The Victorian examples are easier to track down than the eighteenth-century ones, and there is variety to be found in them. While it is tempting to concentrate on the rococo and neoclassical revival designs, a lot of interesting eclectic work of the 1880's and later is worth considering. The important goal is a collection of highlights that suggests the diversity of approaches to design.

Bells, like buttons, are small objects that reflect fashion. Most bell collectors find themselves concentrating on late examples. The functional bells that come in small sizes tend to be from the late 1880's, although patience occasionally rewards one with a rarity from the 1700's. Bells small enough to be used on the table were made at least as early as 1700, but they seldom turn up. Sometimes they are set in inkstands. Silver bells in the form of a woman with a wide skirt must have been introduced early, but it is the 1905 version that is found with the novelties at most antique shops. Aside from cow and sleigh bells, there are other curiosities. Glass examples in handsome colors were produced in England and the United States in the 1820's and later. All the large silver manufacturers from the 1880's on produced small bells, sterling and plated, that were called tea bells. Exotic Indian bells with enamel decoration come in forms that relate to sleigh bells and these must have been an important souvenir at the turn of the century, since most examples date from after 1890. An interesting collection of bells could be assembled, with care, consisting of examples with an average cost of under $25 each.

Fans are a field that allows for variety, and a collection can be started inexpensively. Every flea market has amusing fans for a few dollars. These are mostly souvenirs of dances or even drugstores; the designs tend to concentrate on the inscription rather than ornament, but they can be interesting documents. The decorative examples of ivory and lace tend to be expensive—somewhat so if modern and much more so if they have some age.

Fans with advertising on them date from the 1500's in Italy and this fact might stimulate some careful hunting. By the 1700's there were examples with political connotations, as satirical prints were adapted to fans. Hogarth's *Harlot's Progress* was a popular subject for fans in the 1740's; before the end of the century there were examples that demonstrated the user's abolitionist sentiments. Prints were an easy way of introducing varied subjects, and scenes were also

Bells, glass, English, about 1800. Although metal
is the more usual, ceramic and glass bells may
be found. Colored glass was used for
bells in the area of Bristol, England, as well as in
Pittsburgh region in the United States.

popular. The landmarks of major capitals can be found on fans made in the early 1800's.

The most expensive fans are those with painted decoration. The work of popular artists of the 1700's such as Boucher and Reynolds inspired any number of contemporary fan decorators. Although artists of the 1800's occasionally did fans, more often the fans from this period were skilled adaptations of works of the previous century. Thus, if a premium is asked for a fan because the picture is a Boucher, there ought to be some very concrete proof that it is not a later adaptation. Alarm bells should ring if much is made of the signature. Look at the picture: figures, and particularly female figures, were

unconsciously updated by the fan painter of the late 1800's. Facial features are more emphatically picked out in color and the coiffures are more like those in nineteenth-century fashion plates. Since the finest early examples cost $1,000 or $2,000, collectors have to decide if they want to settle for the imitations. Probably a wiser course would be to hold out for nineteenth-century examples that are typical of their own time. Toward the end of the century many highly popular painters tried their hands at decorating fans and their work is sometimes unnoticed at shops that are preoccupied with later renditions of 1700's design.

Boxes are an ideal objective for the collector seeking wide variety. With patience and an astute eye, it is possible to assemble a group that spans a few thousand years. Boxes come in many materials: metal, ceramic, glass, stone, wood and even basketry. Small, plain boxes made in ancient Rome sometimes cost less than $200. Recent examples that are representative of their period can be found for under $10.

The most decorative examples are small boxes of enamel or gold that were created in the 1700's to store the patches women wore on their faces as beauty marks. These are among the finest expressions of the style of the era and they are quite expensive; outstanding work will be $20,000 to $30,000, and even imitations from the 1800's are sometimes high. Even if price were no factor, the novice collector should avoid such rarities and concentrate on little-known examples in distinctive styles of the nineteenth and twentieth centuries. Rococo revival work can be distinctive, but too often small enamel boxes of the 1800's are bad imitations of the 1700's, and these are of less interest.

Miniature furniture forms were a popular design for jewel boxes of the 1700's and 1800's. These are amusing and can be quite well made.

Simple wooden boxes were mass-produced by the Shakers and handmade by American Indians and European peasants. Oval and circular boxes that were made for utility can be the basis of an interesting collection. Sometimes bold primitive patterns that almost look like abstract flowers and figures were painted on boxes.

Tobacco and snuff boxes come in a variety of shapes. The brass and copper examples have become scarce but there are nineteenth-century boxes in pewter, silver and papier-mâché available. Later examples with advertising can be even more interesting since the decoration is a variation of poster art and a significant reflection of taste.

Another field of bargains tends to evaporate as soon as ink hits paper: objects of repellent aspect. As soon as some object is pointed out as stunningly ugly, collectors rush forward and it ceases to be a bargain. It is true that yesterday's "camp" has been re-evalued and some of it is now unveiled as Art Deco, but I am talking about the amazing uglies that I doubt will ever look very different to us. In the 1890's, when eclecticism reached the mass market, manu-

Cup and saucer, porcelain and silver, by Lenox and Reed & Barton, early twentieth century

facturers began combining motifs to attract as much of the market as they could. The results sometimes defy description. I recently saw what I considered the ultimate lamp, a mixture of owls and imitation Tiffany glass, and I wanted to buy it as a joke for a friend. But sure enough, someone was willing to pay a few thousand dollars for it.

An intelligent haven for the collector on a budget is the one serious style that has yet to be rediscovered. This dates from the turn of the century. While interest in the Art Nouveau of this period has flourished, and the popular design of the era has been discussed at length, there still remain the efforts of eclectic traditionalists. Their basic inspiration was the periods of past elegance; seventeenth-, eighteenth-, and nineteenth-century sources were often combined. Probably the most correct name for this style is Beaux Arts, because it was best expressed by the architects who studied at the Ecole des Beaux Arts in Paris and provided the affluent with elaborate homes that have left their mark all over the world. Santiago, Lisbon, New York and Singapore can all boast town houses in the Beaux Arts style. And the architects who built these palaces often designed objects to go into them. They also stocked the houses with antiques and never made it terribly clear to their customers which was which. Now close examination discloses more originality than would be expected; there are designs that come out of no book. Often the work was executed by the most able craftsmen of the period and what may

at first look like ugly 1600's is really handsome 1910. Since the furniture was frequently monstrous in size, it turns up in white elephant sales at relatively low prices. It is usually thrown in with the mass-produced efforts of the same period.

The bargain hunter has an advantage: his restrictions of budget often drive him onto the ground floor of an undiscovered field. He is likely to become more expert than dealers who have their eyes on more popular objects. But in truth, becoming an expert in any field of antiques takes only the development and education of the five senses, care and time.

Flagler mansion, Palm Beach, Fla., interior by Carriere & Hastings, about 1900. The typical elaborate house of the turn of the century was furnished with a combination of antiques and reproductions that were often designed for the house by the architect's staff.

Tea caddy, wood veneer, Baltimore, about 1800. Fine cabinetmaking techniques are evident in the box, but tea caddies can be collected more for their amusement than esthetic value.

Further Studies

The bibliography that follows is a selection of books published in the past twenty years. These books might be available in small libraries and at specialized booksellers. If you have access to a large library, you would do better to begin your search for books in the card catalogue. The books listed are not necessarily the final word on the subject, but they do have information and they can lead you to deeper studies. Keep in mind, however, that reading is less important than looking and examining objects. Because photographs in books tend to distort, it is easy to be misled if you try to determine the origin of an object by comparing it with book illustrations. Spend the time tracking down other objects; restrict your research to learning the basic facts that can be helpful in developing an understanding of general fields.

Furniture

Aronson, Joseph, *Encyclopedia of Furniture* (Crown Publishers, New York, 1966)

Boger, Louise Ade, *Furniture Past and Present* (Doubleday, Garden City, N.Y., 1966)

Hayward, Helena, editor, *World Furniture* (McGraw-Hill, New York, 1965)

AMERICAN FURNITURE

Comstock, Helen, *American Furniture: Seventeenth, Eighteenth, and Nineteenth Century Styles* (Viking Press, New York, 1962)

Comstock, Helen, editor, *Concise Encyclopedia of American Antiques* (Hawthorn Books, New York, 1958)

ENGLISH FURNITURE

Coleridge, Anthony, *Chippendale Furniture, circa 1745–1765: The Work of Thomas Chippendale and His Contemporaries in the Rococo Taste* (Faber & Faber, London, 1968; Potter, New York, 1968)

Dean, Margery, *English Antique Furniture, 1450–1850* (Universe Books, New York, 1969; The Merlin Press Ltd., London, 1969)

Edwards, Ralph, *The Shorter Dictionary of English Furniture* (Tudor, New York, 1965; Country Life, London, 1964)

Fastnedge, R. W., *English Furniture Styles from 1500–1830* (Penguin Books, Baltimore, 1964)

Fastnedge, R. W., *Sheraton Furniture* (Faber & Faber, London, 1968)

Musgrave, Clifford, *Adam and Hepplewhite and Other Neo-Classical Furniture* (Taplinger, New York, 1966)

Ramsey, L. G., editor, *The Connoisseur's New Guide to Antique English Furniture* (Connoisseur, London, 1961)

FRENCH FURNITURE

Constantino, Ruth T., *How to Know French Antiques* (New American Library, New York, 1961)

Frégnac, Claude (completed under the general direction of), foreword by Pierre Verlet, *French Cabinetmakers of the 18th Century* (French & European Pubns., New York, 1965; Hachette, Paris, 1965)

Ledoux-Lebard, Denise, *Les Ebénistes Parisiens du XIXe Siècle (1795–1870) Leurs Oeuvres et Leurs Marques* (De Nobele, Paris, 1965)

Textiles

COVERLETS

Colby, Averil, *Patchwork* (Batsford, London, 1958; Charles T. Branford Co., Newton Centre, Mass., 1965)

Robertson, Elizabeth Wells, *American Quilts* (Studio Publications, New York, 1948)

SAMPLERS

Colby, Averil, *Samplers* (Batsford, London, 1964; Charles T. Branford Co., Newton Centre, Mass., 1965)

BAROQUE AND ROCOCO SILKS

Hunton, W. Gordon, *English Decorative Textiles* (tapestry and chintz, their design and development from the earliest times to the nineteenth century) (Alec Tiranti Ltd., London, 1930)

Thornton, Peter, *Baroque and Rococo Silks* (Faber & Faber, London, 1965)

RUGS

HOOKED

Kent, William Winthrop, *The Hooked Rug* (a record of its ancient origin, modern development, methods of making, sources of design, value as a handicraft, the growth of collections, probable future in America, and other data) (Dodd, Mead, New York, 1930)

Ries, Estelle H., *American Rugs* (World Publishing Co., New York, 1950)

ORIENTAL

Dilley, Arthur Urbane, revised by Maurice S. Dimand, *Oriental Rugs and Carpets* (Lippincott, Philadelphia, 1959)

Erdmann, Kurt, edited by Hanna Erdmann, translated by May H. Beattie and Hildegard Herzog, *Seven Hundred Years of Oriental Carpets* (University of California Press, Berkeley, Calif., 1970)

NEEDLEPOINT

Kendrick, Albert Frank, *English Needlework*, 2nd edition revised by Patricia Wardle (Barnes & Noble, New York, 1967; Black, London, 1967)

TAPESTRIES

FRENCH

Weigert, Roger-Armand, translated by Donald and Monique King, *French Tapestry* (Charles T. Branford Co., Newton, Mass., 1962)

FLEMISH

Göbel, Heinrich, translated by Robert West, *Tapestries of the Lowlands* (Brentano, New York, 1947)

D. Hulst, Roger Adolf, translated from the Dutch by Frances J. Stillman, *Flemish Tapestries* (Universe Books, New York, 1967)

The Metropolitan Museum of Art, *Medieval Tapestries, a Picture Book* (The Metropolitan Museum of Art, New York, 1947)

ENGLISH

Hunton, W. Gordon, *English Decorative Textiles* (tapestry and chintz, their design and development from the earliest times to the nineteenth century) (Alec Tiranti Ltd., London, 1930)

Ceramics

Chaffers, William, *Marks and Monograms on European and Oriental Pottery and Porcelain,* 15th revised edition (W. Reeves, London, 1965; Dover, New York, 1965)

Savage, George, *Porcelain Through the Ages* (Penguin Books, Baltimore, 1954)

Savage, George, *Pottery Through the Ages* (Penguin Books, Baltimore, 1959)

AMERICAN

Altman, Seymour and Violet, *Book of Buffalo Pottery* (Crown Publishers, New York, 1969)

Barret, Richard C., *Bennington Pottery and Porcelain* (Crown Publishers, New York, 1958)

Peck, Herbert, *Book of Rookwood Pottery* (Crown Publishers, New York, 1968)

Schwartz, Marvin D., *Collector's Guide to Antique American Ceramics* (Doubleday, Garden City, N.Y., 1969)

ENGLISH

Charleston, Robert J., *English Porcelain, 1745–1850* (University of Toronto Press, Toronto, 1965; E. Benn, London, 1965)

Cushion, J. P., *English China Collecting for Amateurs* (Frederick Muller, London, 1967)

Hughes, G. B., *English Pottery and Porcelain Figures* (Luttersworth, London, 1964; Praeger, New York, 1968)

Lewis, Griselda, *Collector's History of English Pottery* (Studio Vista, London, 1969; Viking Press, New York, 1969)

Wakefield, Hugh, *Victorian Pottery* (Universe Books, New York, 1970)

EUROPEAN

Cushion, J. P. *Continental China Collecting for Amateurs* (Frederick Muller, London, 1970)

Ducret, Siegfried, *German Porcelain and Faience* (Universe Books, New York, 1962)

Savage, George, *17th and 18th Century French Porcelain* (Spring Books, London, 1969)

Stazzi, Francesco, *Italian Porcelain of the Eighteenth Century* (Putnam, New York, 1967)

Pictures

Biggs, John R., *Wood–Engravings, Linocuts, and Prints by Related Methods of Relief Print Making* (Blandford Press, London, 1958)

Man, Felix H., *150 Years of Artists' Lithographs, 1803–1953* (Heinemann, London, 1953)

Mayer, A. Hyatt, *Prints and People: A Social History of Printed Pictures* (The Metropolitan Museum of Art, New York, 1971)

Metals

GOLD AND SILVER

Douglas, Jane, *How to Collect: Silver, Furniture, Glass, China, Things* (Newnes, London, 1966)

Rosenberg, Marc, *Der Goldschmiede Merkzeichen* (Frankfurter, Frankfurt, 1961)

Taylor, Gerald, *Art in Silver and Gold* (Studio Vista, London, 1964; Dutton, New York, 1964)

ENGLISH

Hughes, G. B, *Three Centuries of English Domestic Silver* (Praeger, New York, 1968)

Jackson, Charles J., *English Goldsmiths and Their Marks* (Dover, New York, 1964)

AMERICAN

Hood, Graham, *American Silver: A History of Style, 1650–1900* (Praeger, New York, 1970)

Rainwater, Dorothy T., *American Silver Manufacturers* (Everybodys Press, Hanover, Pa., 1966)

PEWTER

Laughlin, Ledlie, *Pewter in America: Its Makers & Their Marks* (Barre Publishers, Barre, Mass., 1969)

Masse, H. J., *Chats on Old Pewter*, revised edition (Dover, New York, 1971)

IRON, COPPER, ETC.

Kauffman, Henry J., *American Copper and Brass* (Thomas Nelson, Camden, N.J., 1968)

Lindsay, J. Seymour, *Iron and Brass Implements of the English and American House* (C. Jacobs, Bass River, Mass., 1964)

Wills, Geoffrey, *The Book of Copper and Brass* (Country Life, London, 1968)

Glass

HISTORY

Haynes, Edward Barrington, *Glass Through the Ages,* revised edition (Penguin Books, Baltimore, 1964)

Robertson, R. A., *Chats on Old Glass,* revised with new chapter on American Glass by Kenneth M. Wilson (Dover, New York, 1969)

AMERICAN

McKearin, George S. and Helen, *American Glass* (Crown Publishers, New York, 1941)

Schwartz, Marvin D., *Collector's Guide to Antique American Glass* (Doubleday, Garden City, N. Y., 1969)

ENGLISH

Hughes, George Bernard, *English Glass for the Collector, 1660–1860* (Luttersworth, London, 1958; Praeger, New York, 1968)

Victoria and Albert Museum, South Kensington, *English Glass,* Exhibition July 4-August 31, 1968 (Victoria and Albert Museum, London, 1968)

Wakefield, Hugh, *19th Century British Glass* (Faber & Faber, London, 1961)

GERMAN

Von Saldern, Axel, *German Enamelled Glass; The Edwin J. Beinecke Collection and Related Pieces* (The Corning Museum of Glass, Corning, N. Y., 1965)

NINETEENTH CENTURY

Revi, Albert Christian, *American Art Nouveau Glass* (Thomas Nelson, Camden, N.J., 1968)

Revi, Albert Christian, *19th Century Glass: Its Genesis and Development* (Thomas Nelson, Camden, N. J., 1959)

ROMAN

Mariacher, Giovanni, translated by Michael Bullock and Johanna Capra, *Italian Blown Glass, from Ancient Rome to Venice* (McGraw-Hill, New York, 1961)

SPANISH

Frothingham, A. W., *Spanish Glass* (Faber & Faber, London, 1963; Hispanic Society, New York, 1964)

TIFFANY

Koch, Robert, *Louis C. Tiffany: Rebel in Glass* (Crown Publishers, New York, 1966)

Photo Credits

52: MMA, Kennedy Fund, 1918

53: Helga photo for John S. Walton, Inc., New York, N.Y.

54: MMA, purchase 1958, Mrs. Russell Sage gift

55: From Ginsburg & Levy, photo by Bill Aller, The New York Times Studio

56: Brooklyn Museum, purchase 1964

57: Connecticut Historical Society

60: top and below-MMA, gift of Samuel H. Kress Foundation, 1958

61: MMA, gift of Samuel H. Kress Foundation, 1958

62: MMA, gift of Morris Loeb, 1955

63: Helga photo for Gene Tyson, Inc., New York, N.Y.

65: MMA, gift of Mrs. J. Insley Blair, 1947

66: MMA, Rogers Fund, 1913

67: top-MMA, Fletcher Fund, 1929; below-MMA, gift of the family of Mr. and Mrs. Andrew Varick Stout in their memory, 1965

68: Ginsburg & Levy

69: MMA, Rogers Fund, 1923

71: MMA, the Edgar J. Kaufmann Charitable Foundation Fund, 1968

74: MMA, the Edgar J. Kaufmann Charitable Foundation Fund, 1968

75: MMA, gift of Mary E. Steers, 1961

76: Brooklyn Museum, gift of the estate of Elsie Patchen Halstead, 1960

78: Lillian Nassau, New York, N.Y.

79: MMA, gift of Charles Tisch, 1889

80: MMA, Edward C. Moore, Jr. Gift Fund, 1926

81: MMA, Edward C. Moore, Jr. Gift Fund, 1925

83: MMA, bequest of Carolyn L. Griggs, 1950

85: Cooper-Hewitt Museum of the Smithsonian Institution

86: MMA, Rogers Fund, 1938

87: top-Cooper-Hewitt Museum; middle-MMA, Rogers Fund, 1938; bottom-MMA, anonymous gift, 1955

88: Cooper-Hewitt Museum

89: MMA, Rogers Fund, 1962

90: MMA, bequest of Charles Allen Munn, 1924

91: MMA, Rogers Fund, 1939

92: MMA, gift of Mary Stillman Harkness, 1944

94: Detroit Institute of Art

95: MMA, gift of Harriet Barnes Pratt, 1945, in memory of her husband, Irving Pratt

96: MMA, gift of Thomas Emery, 1954

97: MMA, gift of Ann Payne Robertson, 1964

99: MMA, Rogers Fund, 1922

100: MMA, gift of Mrs. L. H. Robertson, 1956

101: From Ginsburg & Levy, photo by Bill Aller

102: MMA, Fletcher Fund, 1927

103: Ginsburg & Levy

104: MMA, gift of Mrs. Thomas J. Watson, 1939

105: top-MMA, bequest of Mrs. Lathrop Colgate Harper, 1957; below-Ginsburg & Levy

106: MMA, gift of Mrs. Robert W. de Forest, 1933

107: MMA, gift of Mr. and Mrs. William A. Moore, 1923

108: MMA, gift of Mrs. Russell Sage, 1909

109: From Ginsburg & Levy, photo by Bill Aller

110: Brooklyn Museum, Dick S. Ramsay Fund, 1949

111: MMA, Sansbury-Mills Fund, 1961

112: MMA, gift of Mrs. Robert Armstrong, 1958

112-13: MMA, gift of Katherine Keyes, 1938, in memory of her father, Homer Eton Keyes

114: top-Private Collection; below-Private Collection

117: Tupperware Collection

119: MMA, Rogers Fund, 1920

120: MMA, purchase 1896

122: Tupperware Collection

123: MMA, gift of H. O. Havemeyer, 1929

125: John Gordon, New York, N.Y.

126: top-MMA, Rogers Fund, 1924; below-MMA, gift of Robert W. de Forest, 1933

127: MMA, gift of Edward S. Harkness, 1926

128: MMA, Fletcher Fund, 1964

129: MMA, bequest of Benjamin Altman, 1913

130: MMA, Rogers Fund, 1940

131: MMA, gift of George Blumenthal, 1941

132: MMA, gift of Mrs. Alexandria Sinsheimer, 1959

133: MMA, gift of J. Pierpont Morgan, 1965

134: MMA, gift of Julia A. Berwind, 1953

135: MMA, gift of R. Thornton Wilson, 1954, in memory of Florence Ellsworth Wilson

137: MMA, gift of R. Thornton Wilson, 1950, in memory of Florence Ellsworth Wilson

138: MMA, gift of Henry G. Marquand, 1894

139: Helga photo for Ginsburg & Levy

140: top and below-MMA, gift of Henry G. Marquand, 1894

141: MMA, gift of Henry G. Marquand, 1894

142: MMA, gift of Henry G. Marquand, 1894

143: top and below-MMA, gift of Mrs. Russell S. Carter, 1945

144: MMA, gift of J. Pierpont Morgan, 1917

145: MMA, gift of R. Thornton Wilson, 1950, in memory of Florence Ellsworth Wilson

147: MMA, gift of R. Thornton Wilson, 1950, in memory of Florence Ellsworth Wilson

148: MMA, gift of Mrs. Russell S. Carter, 1945

149: top-MMA, gift of Mrs. Russell S. Carter, 1945; below-Brooklyn Museum, gift of Emily Winthrop Miles, 1964

150: MMA, gift of Mrs. Heyward Cutting, 1942

151: MMA, gift of R. Thornton Wilson, 1943, in memory of Florence Ellsworth Wilson

152: MMA, gift of Mrs. May Leask, 1916

153: From Lillian Nassau, photo by Bill Aller

154: top and below-Brooklyn Museum, gift of Arthur W. Clement, 1943

155: MMA, Rogers Fund, 1913

156: MMA, gift of R. Thornton Wilson, 1954, in memory of Florence Ellsworth Wilson

157: Tupperware Collection

158: MMA, Rogers Fund, 1917

159: MMA, gift of Mrs. Russell S. Carter, 1945

160: Brooklyn Museum, gift of Arthur W. Clement, 1943

161: Brooklyn Museum, gift of Emily Winthrop Miles, 1960

163: MMA, gift of George F. Baker, 1931

165: MMA, gift of Charles Davis, 1948

167: Helga photo for J. Rochelle Thomas, Inc., New York, N.Y.

168: MMA, gift of R. Thornton Wilson, 1943, in memory of Florence Ellsworth Wilson

169: Brooklyn Museum, gift of the Rev. Alfred Duane Pell, 1904

170: MMA, gift of the estate of James Hazen Hyde, 1959

171: Collection of Mr. and Mrs. Charles B. Wrightsman

172: MMA, gift of R. Thornton Wilson, 1950, in memory of Florence Ellsworth Wilson

173: MMA, Harris Brisbane Dick Fund, 1938

174: MMA, gift of George B. McClellan, 1941

174 and 5: MMA, gift of R. Thornton Wilson, 1950, 54, in memory of Florence Ellsworth Wilson

176: top-Brooklyn Museum, gift of the Rev. Alfred Duane Pell, 1903; below-MMA, gift of Mr. and Mrs. Luke Vincent Lockwood, 1939

177: From Lillian Nassau, photo by Bill Aller

178: top-Brooklyn Museum, gift of the Rev. Alfred Duane Pell, 1903; below-Brooklyn Museum, Dick S. Ramsay Fund, 1945

179: Brooklyn Museum, gift of Carll and Franklin Chace, 1943, in memory of their mother, Pastora Forest Smith Chace, daughter of Thomas Carll Smith

180: MMA, bequest of Mrs. Maria P. James, 1911

181: top-Brooklyn Museum, gift of Arthur W. Clement, 1943; below-MMA, gift of Charles W. Green, 1947

183: From Lillian Nassau, photo by Bill Aller

185: From Lillian Nassau, photo by Bill Aller

187: MMA, gift of the estate of Marie L. Russell, 1941

191: John Gordon

192: MMA, Rogers Fund, 1939

194: Hancock Shaker Village, Pittsfield, Mass.

195: Collection of Col. Edgar William and Bernice Chrysler Garbisch

196: MMA, Mary Martin Fund, 1958

198: top-MMA, Library Fund, 1921; below-MMA, gift of Mrs. William H. Osborn, 1967, in memory of L. Redmond Johnston

199: top-MMA, Rogers Fund, 1922; below-MMA, Harris Brisbane Dick Fund, 1932

200: MMA, Harris Brisbane Dick Fund, 1937

201: MMA, gift of Mrs. Russell Sage, 1910

202: a-MMA, the Sylmaris Collection, gift of George Coe Graves, 1920; b-MMA, gift of Miss Georgiana W. Sargent, 1924, in memory of John Osborne Sargent; c-MMA, bequest of Charles Allen Munn, 1924

203: MMA, bequest of Mrs. H. O. Havemeyer, 1929

204: top-MMA, Harris Brisbane Dick Fund, 1917; below-MMA, Harris Brisbane Dick Fund, 1932

205: MMA, gift of A. S. Colgate, 1951

206: MMA, Harris Brisbane Dick Fund, 1929

207: MMA, gift of Mrs. Bessie Potter Vonnoh, 1946

208: MMA, bequest of Edward W. C. Arnold, 1954

209: MMA, purchase 1933, Joseph Pulitzer bequest

211: MMA, Cloisters Collection, purchase 1947

217: top-David Stockwell, Wilmington, Del.; below-Yale University Art Gallery, Mabel Brady Garvan Collection, 1934

218: MMA, bequest of A. T. Clearwater, 1933

219: MMA, bequest of A. T. Clearwater, 1933

220-21: Tupperware Collection

222: a-MMA, gift of George D. Widener and Eleanor W. Dixon, 1958; b-MMA, gift of Vivian W. Lehman, 1965; c-MMA, Rogers Fund, 1913

223: MMA, bequest of Rupert L. Joseph, 1959

224: MMA, gift of Miss Frances Arnold, 1969

225: MMA, bequest of A. T. Clearwater, 1933

226: MMA, gift of Mrs. L. Hoe Sterling, 1964, in memory of her father, Robert Hoe, Jr., a founder of the museum

227: MMA, bequest of Catherine D. Wentworth, 1948

229: Smithsonian Institution, gift of Miss Harriet Keen

230: MMA, gift of Mrs. F. R. Lefferts, 1969

231: MMA, gift of Mrs. Winthrop Atwell, 1899

233: From Lillian Nassau, photo by Bill Aller

234: top-International Silver Historical Library, Meriden, Conn.; below-MMA, Edward C. Moore, Jr. Gift Fund, 1934

237: From Lillian Nassau, photo by Bill Aller

238: MMA, gift of J. Pierpont Morgan, 1917

240: Harry Hirsch, New York, N.Y.

241: Tupperware Collection

243: Helga photo for Thomas D. Williams, Litchfield, Conn.

244: Helga photo for Thomas D. Williams

245: MMA, gift of Mrs. J. Insley Blair, 1949

247: MMA, gift of Mrs. Robert W. de Forest, 1933

248: MMA, Rogers Fund, 1933

249: Tupperware Collection

250: MMA, Rogers Fund, 1924

251: MMA, gift of Juliette B. Castle and Mrs. Paul Dahlstrom, 1968

253: MMA, gift of Mrs. Robert W. de Forest, 1931

254: top-MMA, bequest of Theodore M. Davis, 1930; MMA, the Cloisters Collection, gift of John D. Rockefeller, Jr., 1947

255: MMA, Chapman Fund, 1951

256: MMA, gift of the estate of Mrs. Edward Robinson, 1952

257: Tupperware Collection

258: Private Collection

259: Tupperware Collection

260: Brooklyn Museum, gift of C. G. Mourraile, 1957

261: Tupperware Collection

263: From Lillian Nassau, photo by Bill Aller

264: MMA, gift of George Coe Graves, 1930

265: MMA, gift of Julia A. Berwind, 1953

269: MMA, gift of Miss Lily Place, 1923

270: MMA, gift of George D. Pratt, 1935

271: MMA, Harris Brisbane Dick Fund, 1963

272: a-MMA, gift of Edward C. Moore, 1891; b-MMA, purchase 1927; c-MMA, gift of James Jackson Jarves, 1881

274: MMA, gift of William B. Osgood Field, 1902

276: Brooklyn Museum, purchase 1913

277: Brooklyn Museum, purchase 1913

278: MMA, gift of George Coe Graves, 1930

279: Tupperware Collection

280: MMA, gift of Mrs. Edward Holbrook and John S. Holbrook, 1921

281: MMA, gift of Mrs. J. Insley Blair, 1931

283: MMA, gift of George Coe Graves, 1930

284: Private Collection

285: Tupperware Collection

287: MMA, gift of F. W. Hunter, 1913

289: MMA, gift of F. W. Hunter, 1913

291: MMA, gift of Mrs. Charles W. Green, 1951, in memory of Dr. Charles W. Green

293: Detroit Institute of Art

294: MMA, Rogers Fund, 1910

295: Tupperware Collection

296: a-MMA, gift of Mrs. Charles W. Green, 1951, in memory of Dr. Charles W. Green; b-MMA, gift of Emily Winthrop Miles, 1946

297: top and bottom-MMA, gift of Emily Winthrop Miles, 1946

299: MMA, gift of Ethel Lyman Mackey and Ruth Watrous Hellow, 1960

301: From Lillian Nassau, photo by Bill Aller

302: MMA, gift of Emily Winthrop Miles, 1946

303: MMA, Edgar J. Kaufmann Charitable Foundation Fund, 1969

305: MMA, gift of H. O. Havemeyer, 1896

308: MMA, gift of John C. Cattus, 1968

310: MMA, Rogers Fund, 1970

311: From Lillian Nassau, photo by Bill Aller

313: MMA, gift of Mrs. William Randolph Hearst, 1963

316: Brooklyn Museum

317: Tupperware Collection

319: James Robinson, Inc., New York, N.Y.

321: Tupperware Collection

322: Ginsburg & Levy

322-3: The Flagler Mansion, Palm Beach, Fla.

Index